DEPUTY:

ONCE UPON A TIME IN MISSISSIPPI

A Novel

by

Merle Temple

Southern Literature Publishing
www.southernliteraturepublishing.com

Deputy: Once Upon a Time in Mississippi

Copyright ©2016 Southern Literature Publishing

ISBN: 978-0-9911475-9-5

Printed in the United States of America

Unless otherwise noted, all scripture references are taken from the Holy Bible, New International Version. Copyright 1973, 1978, 1984 International Bible Society. Used by permission. All rights reserved.

Where noted, scripture references taken from the Holy Bible, King James Version, kingjamesbibleonline.org. Used by permission. All rights reserved.

Also where noted, scripture references taken from the Holy Bible, English Standard Version. Copyright 2001. All rights reserved.

All characters appearing in this work are fictitious. Any resemblance to real persons, living or deceased, is purely coincidental.

Southern Literature Publishing
www.southernliteraturepublishing.com

www.merletemple.com

Reviews for *Deputy: Once Upon a Time in Mississippi*

"*Deputy* is Southern Gothic literature—a complex tale of flawed but fascinating characters, mystery, and the supernatural. Paints images that burrow into your soul, captures the grand stage and social order of 1970, explores race relations and narrows divides. Twists and turns keep you guessing and gasping. Graveyards, mobsters, murder, seduction, and irony...a story that won't let you go."—Jim Clemente, *Criminal Minds*

"A roller coaster ride gasping for air...a thought-provoking, nail-biting, intriguing masterpiece that stimulates your mind and stirs your soul. Stereotypes and racial boundaries are displayed in such a creative way that you're challenged to revisit the 70's to take inventory of your own life. A must read!"—Tammie Tubbs, Christian Television Network

"A great read about what a sheriff was faced with in those days. Today is not much different. It is my faith in Jesus that keeps me in step each day. I hope you enjoy the tales in this book, but most of all, I pray that your walk with Christ is strengthened."—Sheriff Jim H. Johnson, Lee County, MS

"North Mississippi, Southern-style drama of a deputy lawman who must work between the shadows cast by the lost and the redeemed, yet strive to keep his own integrity intact. Draws you in like the smell of fried chicken and pecan pie on a sultry afternoon." —Richie L., Christian Talk That Rocks

"A brilliant writer...masterful use of words allows the reader to 'see' the terrain, villains, heroes and action...portrays the true South, evil versus good, and proves redemption cleanses the soul... from start to finish."—Brenda Lee Daher, *Baldwyn News*

"Merle Temple is to writing what Rembrandt was to art. He creates written masterpieces."—Lisa Love, *Southern Reader Magazine*

"Welcome to the very heart of Dixie...Amidst murder and mayhem, the Light burns bright in the darkness, where we learn that every saint has a past...every sinner a future."—Pat Sabiston, The Write Place

"Corruption fueled by moonshine, money, and malevolence…
Merle Temple has created a following with his (books)…"—Errol
Castens, *Tupelo Daily Journal*

"Southern Gothic writing at its raw and uncompromised best. What
a ride! What characters! What a story!"—KB Schaller, *Indian Life
Newspaper*, Award-Winning Author

"Captivating…a keen understanding of humanity and its limitations."—Will Stauff, WMCG-FM Macon, Georgia

"Temple writes fiction that reveals the mettle of heroes."—*The
Daily Corinthian*

"His books whisper Jesus louder than most scream Him."—Rev.
Danny Bell, Gray's Creek Church, Hernando, Mississippi

To Dr. Chester Quarles,
who first warned me that the shadows
are populated by dragons.

To Sheriff Bill Mitchell,
who let me fight them.

To Deputy L.W. Warden,
who tutored me on "dragon-slaying 101."

To "Mary Allison"
…the reason we fight the dragons.

—Merle Temple

PREFACE

We might as well start at the beginning…

The sun was setting on the America that Michael Parker thought he knew. The echo of the republic's yesteryear lingered on the horizon and then fell away, leaving a gaping hole in the nation's self-image. Darkness crept over the land.

The Vietnam War lingered on, a massacre took place in a village called My Lai, the Weathermen were exploding bombs in the name of peace, and the Chicago Seven were acquitted of inciting riots. Richard Nixon declared war on drugs, and national wounds that had been opened after the assassinations of Martin Luther King, Jr. and Bobby Kennedy were still bleeding.

National Guardsmen killed four Kent State students; police fired into a crowd at Jackson State, killing two and injuring twelve; and nearly a half million gathered at Woodstock—a moment that captured youth in revolt against the old order.

The Beatles broke up, Jimi Hendrix died, and Charles Manson was convicted of murdering Sharon Tate. After Timothy Leary's speech to 30,000 hippies in San Francisco, some of them turned on to drugs, tuned in to the beat of their own drummers, and dropped out of the culture in search of a new way. Nixon's "Silent Majority" found respite in their new escape, Monday Night Football, and even though people couldn't get along on earth, most watched one of their own walk on the moon.

But gangsters were still gangsters, and politicians were still roaming the South, pitching the same subliminal message: "Buy me, I'm for sale!"

Into this world ventured Deputy Sheriff Michael Parker, spit and polished, quixotic and certain, looking for damsels in distress to rescue and dragons to slay.

But deep down, he knew it was all wrong—as wrong as Christmas in August.

"Fairy tales are more than true: not because they tell us that dragons exist, but because they tell us that dragons can be beaten."—G.K. Chesterton

"Like some angel's haloed brow, you reek of purity...with sword held high...(but) a vulture sits upon your silver shield."
—Procol Harum, "Conquistador"

CHAPTER ONE

"Beneath the smiles and southern
hospitality and politeness were a lot
of guns and liquor and secrets."
—*James McBride,* The Color of Water

"Hey Mr. Landlord, lock up all the doors.
When the police comes around, just tell 'em
that the joint is closed."—*Levine-Johnson,*
"Let the Good Times Roll."

The hour was late.

A cloud of dust followed Lee County, Mississippi, sheriff's patrol unit 18 as it snaked down county backroads beneath a blue-black sky peppered with a million winking-blinking stars sprinkled over a fallen world.

Distant flickering flashes of lightning showed in approaching thunderheads, highlighting the haloed moon; glints of light reflected from ice crystals in lofty cirrus clouds preceding the advancing storm. A hard rain was coming soon.

The whipping wind yanked dry cones from the boughs in the pine forests, and the dry grasses were rustling and whispering secrets to the nocturnal inhabitants of the woodlands.

The man-in-the-moon was puckering up to give a big kiss to the morning sun just a few hours below the horizon as a shooting star streaked over the canopy of dense forests and troubled terrain somewhere between Saltillo and Guntown.

Unit 18 rattled along its way to no-man's-land—hard ground shrouded by mystery and hidden in a lawless wilderness where shadowed desires knew no shame and "Good-time Charlies and Charlenes" kicked against the nudges of their Creator, sinking beneath the weight of moral quicksand.

On Michael Parker's first honky-tonk patrol as a deputy-intern out of Ole Miss, he and Sergeant Bob "Sarge" Holcomb made the rounds of the county's nightclubs—Shannon's Gold Room, Palmetto's Cotton Patch, Tupelo's Shangri-la Club, and Mutt's Place (a county joint that no one deputy ever dared to enter alone). But around midnight, the deputies headed toward the Rendezvous Club, a lawless hole-in-the-wall outpost that made the others pale by comparison.

"I'm gonna show you things that your professors in the ivory towers of Oxford know nothing about," Michael's penguin-bellied mentor said as he smacked a wad of Doublemint gum to mask a severe case of tobacco breath.

Lee County Sheriff Gill Simpson, a well-known fiddle player before his election, had left his young deputy-intern from Ole Miss to be tutored by Sarge, his senior deputy.

"Fiddling Gill" had a glint of shrewdness in his dark eyes, and he found Michael to be naïve but likeable and an asset to the department. Parker had worked for the FBI as a fingerprint tech, and he mentored local kids in his Junior Law Enforcement Association. The sheriff thought that might be just the sort of wholesome stuff to highlight in his reelection campaign.

When Sarge was assigned to mentor Michael, he asked Gill what he thought of the intern. The sheriff wrinkled his furrowed brow and said, "Well, he's a romantic, a goody-two-shoes who *sirs* and *ma'ams* everyone he meets, and he probably shouldn't be in law enforcement. He's so trusting that he'd pet a Tombigbee River gator if it swam up to him. He's like a cat, and his endless curiosity will one day be his undoing, though I suspect he may have nine lives!

"He's always poking his nose where it doesn't belong and asking too many questions. He pushes and stretches so far sometimes that he forgets that it's a long walk back. The big words he uses in incident reports get on my last nerve and make my head hurt. I tell him, 'Son, just give me the basics, not *War and*

Peace.' But he is a truepenny…I would trust him with the lives of my family."

So…off they went to the Rendezvous Club.

With Michael riding shotgun, Sarge roared up the Natchez Trace and then traversed a *bumpety-bump* state highway until it ran out. He wheeled down a freshly paved blacktop road, slinging sticky black tar under the wheel well of the county cruiser, and fishtailed down a gravel road to a dead end overlooking a hidden valley nestled in thick Tombigbee forests.

Sarge brought the white police Ambassador to rest at the crest of the overlook. He sat there a bit for emphasis, chomping on his signature, smelly cigar and racing the special 360-cubic-inch engine in a steady *rum-rum-rum* cadence.

Beneath them was a perfect bowl cut out of the forest, an artificial amphitheater for night owls, where gangsters and the crème de la crème of Southern high society rubbed elbows, tossing back the stiff bottled liquor and hot moonshine served up in the dry county.

Bearded men in overalls danced the two-step with pink-faced darlings in baby-blue jeans, next to men in tuxedos and women in evening gowns trying to resurrect Chubby Checker's "Twist." The bands blended George Jones with The Doors and an occasional Doug Kershaw Cajun fiddle. It made for a raucous symphony composed in the bottoms of bottles and clouds of marijuana-fueled dreams, consumed with gusto by the regulars at the notorious honky-tonk.

Sarge picked up his binoculars and zeroed in on the parking lot. The remote nightspot was teeming with vehicles and the usual suspects from the tri-state area. The sudden brightness of the neon sign above the entrance to the club stung Sarge's eyes, and he winced, squinted, and looked again.

He thought the compound looked like the Lee Drive-In Theater in Tupelo…all those cars in rows pointing toward the screen—the club in this case—and this could be a gathering of fans of those all-night Elvis or Audie Murphy movies that Frank Hurd often ran there. He lowered his field glasses and thought again.

Maybe it's like a graveyard, rows and rows of tombs, and the club is a giant, flashing headstone. There's a reason that a colony of expectant buzzards perches on the tree line above the club each morning.

Such maudlin introspection made his head hurt and was better left to the college boy beside him.

Besides, this is prime Dixie Mafia turf. Buford Pusser is no longer sheriff in McNairy County, Tennessee; Towhead White, the vice-president of the Dixie Mafia, died in a hail of bullets at the El-Jay Motel south of Corinth; and Louise Hathcock, the outlaw queen, was shot dead by Pusser...but the Dixie Mafia lives on. The State Line crowd is well represented here tonight at the Rendezvous Club, where deals are struck so no high-stakes poker games will be robbed by any affiliate members. It's a safe house of sorts, neutral ground where anything goes.

The deputies sat silently staring down into the basin beneath them.

Pickups, some bearing giant replicas of the Stars and Bars, were in the club's lot. They were driven by chop-shop mechanics who serviced the infamous Tupelo-to-Corinth auto-theft corridor. The trucks were parked next to hot Cadillacs, quick-titled to members of Ace Connelly's gang from Memphis. Eighteen-wheeler cabs, belonging to outlaw truckers, dotted the landscape. They brought in the little white pills that wired players in the all-night card and dice games running nonstop in the backrooms of Lee County's network of clubs.

A long, black hearse, housing a shiny new casket with a false bottom for narcotics, sat alongside souped-up Mustangs owned by local bootleggers. The Corvettes of bored rich kids from Tupelo rounded out the eclectic car collection fronting the club. All the vehicles encircled a garishly lighted lean-to structure that seemed to stand without visible support—neon lights, fiberglass walls, and sawdust floors.

Sarge handed the field glasses to Michael and said, "See over there? The one with the swagger and the strut of petty authority is Constable Robbie Hawkins. He stands lookout for the local burglary ring between here and Pontotoc. He's a worthless, motherless excuse for a police officer...a former quarterback who was hit in the helmet once too often. Don't turn your back on him. He warns certain bootleggers when we're coming with our search warrants. That's why we never find anything."

Michael looked at Sarge as if he'd experienced a sudden epiphany.

"That shocks your sense of order, of right and wrong...you know, good guys and bad guys, white hats, black hats, and all of that storybook stuff, doesn't it?" he asked.

Michael just shook his head, evading the question, and peered through the binoculars.

Sarge sat in silence for a long while, drawing on the stub of his cigar. He finally turned to his young, baby-faced partner, who was trying to absorb all that the glasses revealed, and said, "They never taught you about this nasty reality in those criminal justice classes at Ole Miss, did they?"

Sarge sighed deeply, shook his head, and spit pieces of his cigar out the driver's window.

He hitched up his gun belt and asked, "You ready to ride down into perdition, son? Got your slapjack, Mr. Slyboots? Got your bullet, Barney?"

He laughed so hard that his belly jiggled like a tub of Jell-O. He turned the car radio wide open. WTUP was playing Jerry Reed, and Sarge belted out, "When you're hot, you're hot, Michael. When you're not, you're not! Let's go get 'em! They can tell it all down at city hall!"

He bumped the car into low gear, and they coasted silently down the slope and eased into the midst of the fray. As they exited the car, couples were dancing in the lot, swaying to the beat of the music inside—serenades to countless low-rent rendezvous. What

Yankees called "fireflies" (and Southerners knew were lightning bugs) sparkled, danced in the night air, and competed with the neon.

To their left, a man relieved himself from too much beer, and to their right, two frowzy men were wrestling in the mud, fighting over a blonde who watched them like a bored hen watches two roosters in the barnyard. She was wearing a white cowgirl hat adorned by blue feathers; the pink rhinestones covering her shirt twinkled in the light from the backwoods nightspot. Bored by her suitors and the spectacle, she gave Michael a long, appraising stare as he walked up. Then she offered him her best seductive, come-hither smile.

"My, you're a young one, aren't you? I'd loved to rock your cradle, baby boy!" the long-in-the-tooth vixen cooed as sparks flew from the batting of fake eyelashes.

"Dolly's got lots of love. Save the last dance for me, cowboy!" the laughing lady challenged, hands on her hips.

Michael suspected that Dolly wasn't offering real love but something else—a cheap imitation of the real thing—and the price of admission would be too steep to bear. He also thought that if practice made perfect, she might be an expert—not at real love, but at frictional games. He also suspected that the illusion of beauty she proffered would melt away in the harsh light of the morning sun.

He'd listened to a radio pastor that very day. The preacher had sounded as if he was speaking directly to him when he'd said, "If you dance with the daughter of the devil, you got to know that her father will want to cut in."

So he just smiled and reminded himself that it was not his charm or good looks...but the badge. She was just one of many broken birds he would encounter in the clubs—women from the local factories and diners who were harmless in intent but deadly by design. They hurt no one more than they hurt themselves as they looked for love in all the wrong places and shouted to the world, "I want to be happy...so bad."

Michael kept moving. Robbie Hawkins, working a tooth-pick round and round in the right corner of his mouth, had joined them. Hawkins shot a look at him, one that suggested he thought Michael might be less than a real, red-blooded American male for not accepting Dolly's offer or at least giving her the customary slap on her behind. He thought it ungentlemanly and wondered if Michael would snitch on him. Robbie occasionally succumbed to the lure of the libertine's dream and bellied up to the world's buffet table to take a big bite out of Eve's apple.

During the department's orientation on the county nightspots and the department's policy of fraternizing with bar queens, Robbie was the one who had winked and whispered to Michael, "Yeah, but a man's gotta do what a man's gotta do, don't you know?"

As the officers passed a Lincoln with Lowndes County plates that spelled BARRISTER, a slender, intoxicated dandy fell out of the driver's side door, disheveled, with a cigarette affixed to the back of his right ear. He swept his long, blond hair from his eyes, looked wide-eyed at Michael, and said, "'Scuse me. My daddy tole me that I was going to drive him to drinking if I didn't stop driving my hot...rod...Lincoln."

He put out his hand to Michael and said, "My name is Reggie...Reggie Morris! Pleased to meet you, De-pu-ty!"

Michael nodded at the man and continued walking toward the club with Sarge. As they waited to be buzzed in by a burly bouncer with a crooked sneer, the band struck up a blues-driven ode to Janis Joplin, who had just been found dead in her Hollywood apartment.

A slurred, alcohol-tainted harmony rose from the inebriated partygoers inside: "Freedom's just another word for nothing left to lose." The hair of the dog that bit them all mangled "Me and Bobby McGee" beyond recognition.

The lightning bugs disappeared, the moon hid its face behind the clouds, and the first drizzle of rain swept in from the west, covering Michael's shiny new gold star on his chest with a fine mist. His grandmother, Pearl, had polished it until it gleamed for his first day on the job.

Michael squinted into the silver rain, suddenly glittering with blues and pinks from the reflection of the neon, and he remembered the dancing lights of the discos when he worked in Washington. His mind turned to the on-again, off-again relationship with a girl he'd met when he had worked in Washington—a girl with burnished blonde hair, mischievous charm, and a vitality that oozed from her pores.

"Sarge, I can't wait to tell my girlfriend in Memphis about this place. Dixie Lee will never believe it!"

His thoughts drifted from his girlfriend to the weekly reports he was required to submit to his Ole Miss professor, Tim Charles.

This one will be a doozy.

The door to the dark side flung open with a rattlesnake buzz. A rushing tsunami of guitars and saxophones and a chorus of hyena cackles washed over the deputies. A thousand eyes glared at the lawmen, stares from rebels who self-destructed in their rage against conformity and thought that meant they were free.

A palpable sense of evil seemed to hiss from every corner of the juke joint's makeshift walls and from beneath every layer of a sawdust floor soaked in beer and trampled by countless pairs of cowboy boots.

The door closed behind Michael, enveloping him in the murky belly of the beast just as the full brunt of the storm arrived outside with violent claps of thunder.

It was the first step into darkness and uncertainty for a naïve but heroic heart seeking a yardstick by which to measure the good and true...a rock on which to anchor himself. He had a sudden sense that nothing would ever be the same, and he remembered the radio pastor who had posed the question, "Will your life be chaotic and without purpose or a fine-tuned novel written in heaven?"

His eyes adjusted to the dark, and there on the wall of the Rendezvous Club was a sign that said, "If you have an itch, keep scratching. If you don't like the song that life is playing, unplug the jukebox."

CHAPTER TWO

"Southern Man, better keep your head.
Don't forget what your good book said."
—Neil Young, "Southern Man"

"I forget where all my love belongs…
sometimes it lasts all night long."
—Shafer-Owens, "Honky Tonk Amnesia"

"Fight!"

Someone shouted the news as Michael stepped onto the edge of the dance floor. The warning was too late. He didn't see the big clenched fist, knuckles all red and white, coming out of the dark like a missile.

In that split second, one thought registered in his mind… *This is going to hurt.*

He reflexively turned his head to the left just before the big paw ricocheted off the dense bone of his right forehead.

Stars exploded around him on a sick sea of numbness, and he rode a wave of nausea right to the shore of a place where his bruised mind wanted to stay and sleep the endless sleep. But the *whump, whop* of his assailant's blows brought him back to the Rendezvous.

Survival instincts and training took over. Michael ducked under the wild, mindless flailing, and then he came up with his chin tucked, shoulders and forearms high around his face. All arms and elbows, he was bobbing and weaving to dodge the flurry of fists, catching most on his shoulders and forearms as his mind raced.

Where's the referee? Someone should ring the bell and let us go back to our corners.

The band didn't stop playing. They just increased the tempo of a new release by Credence. Somewhere above the din of the club chatter and clatter, Michael heard, "The devil's on the loose. Better run through the jungle."

Whoever his assailant was, he would grunt with each swing as his cowboy boots kicked up the sawdust, and the crowd urged him on with calls of "Get him, Bart!" But there was no snap in the blows after the first few attempts. The man was breathing hard and pushing his punches as he banged away at Michael's shoulders and ribs.

Michael's arms were growing numb. He took a chance and reached for the slapjack in his hip pocket, but he felt someone behind him snatch it away. No help there, and he couldn't see Sarge anywhere.

The man moved in closer, huffing and puffing. He was sweating, and his breath was foul. He leaned on Michael, measuring him with his right hand, trying to find an open shot to his face to set him up for the finishing blow.

But Michael wanted that.

Closer, come closer.

As the big mitt clamped onto his shoulder to straighten him for the big left uppercut to the chin, he heard the man's voice for the first time: "I told you not to mess with Betty Ann!"

As the man reared back for the coup de grâce, Michael suddenly came out of his semi-squat and defensive curl. He pushed up with his legs for momentum like he once did as a discus thrower, aiming his right fist at the soft tissue just below the man's diaphragm. He thought he felt something crack and snap beneath his opponent's blubber when his clenched mitt drove through the mass for the man's spine.

With a big whoosh of air, the club fighter went down like a sack of potatoes and rolled over onto his hands and knees, holding his gut. He lay there moaning and cursing.

Michael pulled his cuffs from his belt and knelt quickly to pry the man's hands away from his belly, wrench his arms behind his back, and snap the bracelets on his wrists.

"I think you broke something in me," the big-bellied loud-mouth moaned.

He then looked at Michael like he'd seen him for the first time and said, "Who are you?"

"Deputy Michael Parker," Michael replied. "Who are you?"

"I'm Bart...Bart Whitlock. Why're you arresting me?" Bart asked.

"Because you attacked me," Michael answered.

"I did? I thought you was Sammy. He was messing with Betty Ann. I woke up in our motel room, and she had took all my money and ran off to go clubbing with Sammy," Bart said.

The handcuffed man shook his head and said, "I go a little crazy when I fight, especially when I drink. I ain't what you'd call real bright. No hard feelings, huh? Ouch! That cuff is a little tight there! Say, you ain't mad at me, are you?"

Michael looked over his shoulder and saw Sarge cuffing a drunk man Michael assumed was Sammy. A distraught woman with a heavy body, blank face, and thin, squeaky voice was hanging on Sarge's back. The dull-eyed honky-tonk angel named Betty Ann was begging Sarge to let one of her men go so she could catch a ride home with someone who could buy her beer and breakfast.

"That's the woman who inspired you to try to kill me?" Michael asked.

"Yeah," Bart said as he gulped in awe and anguish. "Ain't she beautiful? She melted my cold, cold heart," he said.

As the woman gave up on Bart and Sammy and walked out of the club with another port in the storm, Bart yelled, "Betty Ann! Dang it! Man, she never says goodbye when she leaves, day or night. I think I must be missing some marbles. It's a hex, I tell you...a Rendezvous spell. But she could kiss the ground in December and make the roses bloom."

Michael turned to see a sheepish Dolly holding his slapjack.

"I was a-trying to help you. I thought I'd grab it and toss it to you or something. Oh, I don't know what I was a-thanking," the country girl said.

Michael took his slapjack from her as Sarge approached.

"That's some black eye he gave you. It's shining like new money and will be so pretty by tomorrow!" Sarge said, pointing to Michael's right eye and laughing.

Sarge snickered. "You're lucky that the first sucker punch hit you on your big, ole hard head!"

Michael noticed a sudden odor. He took a long, deep breath and shivered. "What's that awful smell?"

"That's death, son. The Grim Reaper just walked over your grave," Sarge answered matter-of-factly.

"But never mind that now, unit 14 has arrived, and they have Sammy behind the car cage. Unit 16 is on the way in case we have more trouble. I'll walk ole Bart out to them now. They'll transport these boys to the holding tank in Tupelo. We'll let them sleep it off and sweat it out in the county's sauna," Sarge said.

As Sarge wrestled a moaning Bart to the front door, a waitress came up to Michael with a big draft of beer and said, "Jeanie, the lady over there, has bought you a drink, Deputy."

Michael looked at where she had pointed and saw a woman in a long, white evening dress. She was smiling provocatively as she raised her glass to him. Her eyes were like saucers, but her pupils were constricted. She appeared to be three sheets to the wind.

Sarge returned just as her mustached suitor-boyfriend jumped up from their table, tripped over his pointy-toed cowboy boots, and shouted, "Sarge, who's this junior deputy you got with you, and why's he flirting with my girl, Jeanie?"

Sarge looked at Michael and said, "You can't let these challenges go unanswered, or they'll know they can bluff you. The word will get around the county, and you'll put both of us in danger in all the clubs."

So Michael walked to the table and stared at the man, who had a grayish tint to his skin and was bubbling over with barroom bluster.

"Sir, you are drunk and disorderly and disturbing the peace of this establishment. You have a choice—you can voluntarily leave now, or you will be arrested and taken to the Lee County Jail," Michael said.

The woman watched one man and then the other, feeding off the moment and stirring the pot.

Michael whispered to him, "Don't make me do it!"

As Michael reached for his cuffs, the man jumped up, slipping and lurching as he stormed out of the club to howls of laughter and a chorus of hisses and boos.

Jeanie was a striking woman with fire-engine-red hair. She had milk-blue skin and glazed eyes like eclipsed suns. The party girl sprang up from her table, put her hands over her head, and said, "I think I'd give up my cigarettes, my happy pills, and even my tattoos for you! Search me, Deputy! Pat me down good! I might be hiding something dangerous!"

"Ma'am, I would, but I don't think I could control myself," Michael said with a winsome smile. He put his hands up, palms out, in a sign of mock surrender to the woman who, even in the dim club light, showed the abrasions of a hard life.

As he turned away from her, he almost tripped over a woman unconscious on the floor.

Her "friends" were stepping over and around her, two-stepping to the beat of the music.

"What's wrong with her?" Michael asked one of them.

A young woman with beaver teeth and a narrow forehead said, "Nothing, Deputy! Sue just can't hold her liquor."

Michael knelt beside the thirtyish woman and found her unresponsive. He took her pulse. She was clammy and reeked of alcohol. He saw a chain around her neck and pulled the American Diabetes Association medallion from beneath her blouse. She was a type 1 diabetic and insulin dependent.

"Call an ambulance, Sarge. I think she may be going into a diabetic coma!" he said.

"Lee unit 16 is coming down the hill now. They'll take her," Sarge answered.

A diabetic drinking! Madness! Michael sighed and shook his head.

Billy Payne, the owner of the club, was a hard-looking man who barked orders like he was the drill instructor and everyone else mere buck privates. He swaggered up to Michael and said, "You handled yourself well in that little fracas. You protected the club's interests, and we won't forget it. We can use young deputies like you."

With that, he stuffed a hundred-dollar bill in Michael's shirt pocket.

"This is a little token of our esteem. We'll call on you now and then and throw a little more your way," he said.

Michael pulled the bill from his pocket and looked at it with amazement.

A hundred dollars! Big money for a starving student-deputy!

He handed the crumpled bill back to Billy and said, "I'm sorry, but I'm not allowed to accept gratuities."

A hush fell over the club, and the patrons all stopped and gawked at Michael like he had just beamed down from the Starship Enterprise.

Payne was furious. The nostrils of his beaked nose flared, and his hard jaw jutted out, challenging Michael.

"Who are you to refuse my money? Not taking money? That's a sin and a shame to the buzzards. You're going to be trouble, aren't you, Little Lord Fauntleroy? We like to support our local police, but you've just spit in my face in front of everyone. I'm going to talk to the sheriff about you!" he shouted, wagging his finger at Michael as he turned and walked away.

Sarge watched Payne stomp off and said, "Billy was a rising star once, a real talent on the guitar and a voice like velvet. So much hope, so many stops and starts, but it all went wrong. Now life has passed him by, and all those fake friends who were just along for the ride—well, they found another shooting star. All the girls, the gold, and the glitter are gone, and it haunts him.

"Some of his new thug associates found him one night when he tried to check out of this world, just before the pills and booze did their intended job. Now he just marks time in the honky-tonk prison he built, and his creation is trying to eat him. You made him lose face by publicly refusing his money. You've made an enemy, Michael, and make no mistake—he's a dangerous man, one of the top criminals in the county."

Sarge paused and said, "You got to remember that we ain't Adam-12. I ain't Pete Malloy, and you're not Jim Reed, rookie. You need to loosen up a bit and practice some subtlety and discretion."

"I might just do that, Sarge," Michael said.

"Really? When?" Sarge asked with a puzzled look.

"Oh, the day that you give up cigars!" Michael replied with a grin.

"Son, you ain't right," Sarge said with a chuckle.

He put his hand on an aching sore shoulder Michael was nursing from the fight.

"But just remember, this is not a game. You can't teach these old mad dogs new tricks. They live in dark cages, and the zookeepers hung out the 'Do Not Feed the Animals' sign a long time ago. The world has been bleeding since time began. The best we can hope to do, Deputy, is to place a tourniquet on it. For us to think that we are anything more than traffic cops and battlefield medics is just vanity," he said.

Sarge left shortly thereafter with three intoxicated patrons. He suggested that Michael stay on for a while and catch a ride to the station with Robbie.

The rest of the night passed uneventfully as Michael nursed his sore body and pondered Sarge's words.

Then, at the witching hour, Robbie approached him with a woman in her early thirties hanging on his arm. She had a fresh mop of Clairol's best blonde hair and wide gaps between her front teeth when she smiled. Hiding behind them was a girl too young to be anywhere near clubs like the Rendezvous.

"Michael, me and Sally are going to the No-tell Motel. Ain't she pretty? You take her daughter home—or anyplace you want to take her. She thinks you're cute and wants to go with you. Her mama is breaking her in. This is the final lesson of the night for you...one more dose of reality to burst that little bubble you live in, college boy.

"Have fun!" he said.

Robbie and Sally walked away giggling conspiratorially, like it was the most normal thing in the world. Michael called after them, but they melted into the sea of bodies, leaving Michael with the dark-haired child, not yet five feet tall, who was gazing up at him adoringly.

"I thought you were so brave when that man attacked you. You were just like one of the heroes in the movies at the Lyric Theater," the diminutive, button-nosed girl said shyly.

"How old are you, honey?" Michael asked.

"I'm sixteen, almost seventeen," she said.

Michael knew that was a lie—closer to thirteen more likely.

"What's your name?" he asked the child with the orange butterfly pin in her black, wavy hair.

"Mary Allison," she answered.

"Well, Mary, Mary, quite contrary, I'm going to take you home!" he said.

"You don't like me? I'm not pretty enough for you? I wore my best dress, and Mama did my hair and makeup. Mama told me that I must be pleasing to men if I wanted to party with her," she pleaded. Her blue eyes began to float on salty seas beneath pintail curls that made circles within circles across her forehead.

She struck a pose that Michael imagined she had practiced before a mirror with her mother...a sad, grotesque imitation of life and love. His mind was churning.

I could strangle Robbie. It's criminal what her mother is doing.

"Mary, you're a beautiful girl, and one day some man will be proud to court you and ask you to marry him. But you need to go back to school, find a boy your own age, and take your time growing up. You need to stay out of bars. If I see you back here with your mother, I'm going to report her to child services!" Michael scolded. "Now sit here and wait until I can take you home!" he snapped.

As the club flashed the lights and sounded last call, the reluctant revelers began to leave, and Michael wondered why he had pursued this career. The band struck up one more tune to end the night, Procol Harum's Bach-derived mournful ode in C major—a song that resonated with Michael and stuck on the turntable of his mind...a haunting tune that he hummed for days afterward and never forgot.

"The crowd called out for more, the room was humming harder...Her face, at first just ghostly, turned a whiter shade of pale."

Michael motioned to Mary to come with him as he opened the door to the club. The sky was lightening prematurely. Already the club seemed diminished, smaller, fragile, and plain...just like the players who came there to find that elusive something they'd chased all of their lives—a love potion to deaden the incessant pain as they lost themselves in moments of frantic, mind-numbing parodies of joy.

But daylight was coming, and the vampires were waking from the burlesque, wincing at the harsh morning light that revealed too much. They were sobering up to find that the girl who had looked like Raquel Welch in the dim light of the club, and the haze of booze and pills, was long gone. The dashing charmer who had been a twin for Robert Redford now looked like the Pillsbury Doughboy with a case of advanced beer belly. The prizes of the night were just reflections of the images in their mirrors—the faces that forlorn fugitives, ravenous for romance and a cure for their aching loneliness, had come to the Rendezvous to escape.

The Rendezvous was like a corpse flower...pretty from a distance but up close, the stench was like ripe roadkill. The club was little more than a mirage on a desert of broken dreams, a hiccup of grunts and pants in a long nightmare. There was no beneficial social contract between peddler-pirates and wistful consumers, and no scruples—just a merciless, mercenary willingness to exploit their patrons' weaknesses…"Dangle the carrot before them, then…cash in, cash out, move on."

Just as the door of the Rendezvous was wheezing shut behind him, Michael heard one broken clubber sobbing into the shoulder of a companion. "I came here to hide from God, but the devil found me. They don't care. No one cares. Stop this train. It's run out of track, and I want off."

He raised his head, looked straight at Michael through haunted, wet eyes, and said, "I ain't going to hell for nobody! God's roaring louder than the demons in me!"

As Michael loaded the young girl into the squad car to take her home, she was crying softly. His forearms and shoulders ached from the barroom attack, his black eye was almost closed, and his ribs felt bruised and battered. When he breathed, he had a sudden catch of pain that made him wince. He felt like he'd been dragged up and down the old gravel road that ran through Parker Grove.

He was ready to leave this smoky, sweaty place, where dirty glasses clinked in mock sacrifices and salutes to the gods of barroom happiness, and the aroma of stale beer and the stench of burning marijuana tried to overcome the stink of cheap intimacy. The Rendezvous was a boiling cauldron, a grubby place hostile to claustrophobics and germ freaks like Michael. Underneath the gaudy glitter, the magic melted under sudden nearness. The noise became amplified in the tight confines, bringing the scents and sounds of everyone and every soiled thing too close.

He knew that he had been too harsh to the girl. He looked at her, smiled, and said, "It's going to be all right, princess. Someday, a boy will come along who's never believed in magic…until he sees you."

The girl managed a shy, crooked smile and an interruption of her sniffles.

"That's better," Michael said. "The air here is foul and dirty. So run far away from here, catch the fair winds, and never come back. And always remember to keep your chin up in life, or your crown will fall off," he said.

That made him laugh, and her, too.

Michael suddenly wanted to see Dixie Lee. He wanted to know more about her—things he'd never asked the irrepressible force of nature who had lit the flame of love in his heart.

Where'd you get all of those blonde curls and those sky-blue eyes so full of mischief? Were you named after the old South, or was Dixie a derivative of Dick, your father? Were you a happy child? Did you fall down and skin your knee? Have you sat under the apple tree with anyone else but me? Who was your first love? Was it me? Will our love survive this separation? Am I enough for your restless heart?

He wanted more—something of substance to starve the hungry images that wanted to feed on his mind. He wanted something to wash away the stench from the night—a tonic to erase the memories of man's cruelty to man, of mothers who barter away innocence in grown-up games, and of people who don't want any more from life than the mind-benders and heart-numbers that Billy Payne was selling at the Rendezvous Club.

But maybe it was all just as simple as Sarge said: "In a world inhabited by the hopeless with nothing to lose...being deputy ain't for sissies!"

CHAPTER THREE

"I seed them hoodoo women...makin' up
their low-down plans...told my fortune...
I'll go downtown...jump overboard and drown."
—Johnny Temple, "Hoodoo Women"

"I've seen a lot of people walkin' 'round
with tombstones in their eyes. But the pusher
don't care...if you live or if you die."
—Hoyt Axton, "The Pusher"

The bright constellations had dimmed, and the lingering thunder-boomers yielded reluctantly to the bright-yellow sun of morning as the storm's fading drumrolls of protest echoed over Tupelo.

The sun, which had peeked at Michael Parker through the upper terraces of the forests surrounding the Rendezvous Club, now illuminated James Streeter's office as he sat behind his desk after another all-nighter at the Pink Playhouse.

Streeter was big and hard, a man with fine wrinkles around his dark eyes and a sprinkling of gray in a crown of thick, black hair. The flattened cartilage of a nose broken many times gave him a look of brutality. Something in his eyes was reminiscent of the beaten and tormented pit bulls that ripped open the throats of other dogs for the illegal dogfights held just north of Baldwyn.

Streeter sat in his office on Green Street, reading *Ebony* magazine, sipping amber whiskey in a ceramic cup bearing the initials *JS* and eating a boiled cackleberry. He stopped and stared out the window at the new day and squeezed the cup handle until his knuckles cracked. He muttered to himself, his broad nostrils opening and closing, his jaw muscles protruding and jumping as he ground his teeth.

He listened to some dogs in the distance…the incessant baying and howling of the hounds when they've picked up the scent. It unsettled him. It was etched into his mind from the two years he'd spent at Parchman State Prison when he was young… back before he had learned how to play the game.

They'd always set the bloodhounds loose on the boys who ran. Some of the runners rubbed their feet with a mixture of creosote and pepper to confuse the dogs. They slogged through the bogs and the shallows of the Sunflower River to lose the hounds— but it always ended the same.

After running for their lives—through the knee-deep mud of a quaggy terrain filled with moccasins and waist-deep water rife with gators—they'd be dragged back in the morning hours… half-dead from the run, the hounds, and the beatings from the guards. Streeter always told folks that you can't outsmart the hounds. He swore that the day would come when he'd never have to listen to the dogs chasing his friends. He would never again be forced to drink the prison farm's harsh black coffee and eat that blackstrap molasses.

He had kept those promises and never looked back, but he was weary. He hadn't slept, and he was moody and gloomy. He squinted into the glare of bright light that flooded his office. A patchwork of tiny scars adorned his face, badges of honor and history for the man most in the black community called "The Pusher." The deeper scars on his forearms had come from knife fights, but they were partially obscured by voodoo and hoodoo tattoos—a tribute to his Creole great-aunt from New Orleans…a woman he called GAL, short for "Great-Aunt-Lizzie."

Above the door to his office was a bag of black-eyed peas for luck and wealth—more influence from GAL. When he was a kid in Louisiana, Streeter's mother, Vera, would wash his mouth out with soap for just mentioning the occult. GAL would tell her, "Leave the boy alone! It's just a light tap into the supernatural, mixed with a dash of Dixie Love Perfume, Dragon's Blood Sticks, and three tablespoons of Gnosticism. It ain't devil worship. It's just religion for us folks on the low end of the pecking order in the French Quarter."

Vera tried to get him away from that ole black magic by moving with her son and daughter to Tupelo in 1936 to help family recover from a massive tornado that had killed hundreds. The official number of dead was lowballed due to the poor records kept on the black population, and many bodies, black and white alike, were deposited by the tornado into the murky waters of Gum Pond at the edge of what locals called tornado alley.

Vera and her children moved into a shanty with her cousin, Charlene Littlesugar, who lived in Shake Rag, where the blues blared from cafés and festive house parties on wicked Saturday nights. Some shook their rags to flag down Tupelo's midnight trains to flee poker-game assassins or angry husbands, while others forsook the blues for gospel music and Sunday-morning hope in church, a refuge for the survivors of long nights of sin.

Vera took her son to a holiness church every Sunday. She arranged for him to be baptized at one revival meeting. He kicked and screamed, and the pastor had to hold him beneath the water. His flopping and thrashing displaced most of the water in the big metal tub and soaked many church members on the front pews. No one in the congregation believed that the immersion worked on Vera's bad seed. That was confirmed the following year when he was caught selling "autographed" pictures of Jesus to the devout.

Little Jim Streeter was determined to make his way. He took to the streets of Tupelo and crossed the boundaries of color. He met one of the survivors of the tornado of '36, a poor white boy named Elvis, who lived near Shake Rag. Streeter took him to the black clubs through the back doors, where blues guitarists like Willie Jones and Lonnie Williams played their riffs and breaks, and the trumpet-men played notes that just melted out of their horns.

Streeter also took him to the churches through the front doors to watch the flocks sway and wave fans in the Mississippi heat, and to listen to the Pentecostal hymns that played until the preachers gave out or the flocks fainted.

Streeter hung around the churches when the long funeral services were being preached. He would linger at the grave sites long after everyone else had left, until the evening sun pinked up the sky and the silvery moonlight came to accentuate the night shadows that crept over the fresh graves in eerie caresses.

He felt at home in the graveyards, and sometimes he would lie down on the final resting places of forgotten souls to learn the secrets of the dead. He pressed his ears to the soil that sealed their graves and talked to them while playing a mournful harmonica composition that he called "The Graveyard Blues."

In a ceremony learned from his aunt, he often sat on the mounds of dirt and sipped a concoction of spider webs, jimsonweed, honey, and sulphur while he clutched an old gris-gris of brimstone that GAL had given him when they left New Orleans.

He told his friends that one day he would be laid out in one of the lonesome pits and that they should make sure to lean his harmonica against his tombstone in case he got lonely and needed to wail the blues.

He lost touch with his friend Elvis when the Presleys moved to Memphis in 1948. Then, after his brief stint in Parchman, Streeter left for Chicago's south side to work for the white gangsters there in the bootlegging, numbers, and prostitution rackets in a part of the city called the Black Belt. He was part of a wave of black folks—as many as three thousand a week—arriving in Chicago from the South by the trainload.

He settled in near 35th and State Streets and went to Chicago Teachers College to polish his speech and grind off the rough edges of prison, all the while learning the trade of the hustler and honing his skills as an enforcer for the mob and an organizer for City Hall. He met Buford Pusser in Chicago at a small-time wrestling match. The big man had been discharged from the Marines due to asthma and was studying to be a mortician. Pusser was working in a box factory by day and trying his hand at wrestling by night.

But it was in the clubs of Chicago where Streeter later met Towhead White and adopted White's philosophy and tag line for crime. Streeter later used it for all of his Mississippi bootlegging and brothel operations—"Walk on your tiptoes or be drug to the grave by your heels."

Streeter used stories from his new life of crime in Chicago and from the old days in Mississippi when he presented his term papers in his classes on Urban Mores and Southern Studies. He often regaled them with stories of his midnight visits to the graveyard in Tupelo and how he tried to figure out life by communing with the dead and the walking dead. He got good grades, but his social life on campus suffered from his tales of the macabre.

Streeter also met Charles Evers there, but Evers gave up the gangster life and got religion after his brother, Medgar, was murdered. Charlie left Chicago, took over the NAACP, and got elected mayor in Fayette, Mississippi, just about the time that Streeter came home to Tupelo. The Pusher watched Evers from afar. He always smiled when he thought of ole Charlie riding around knocking on doors and saying, "The hands that picked cotton can now pick the mayor."

Now Charlie's running for governor—governor of Mississippi. Ain't that something? It all seemed simpler back then. Now the wolf's always at the door, and he's always hungry. Problems are everywhere now, and the man is always coming round wanting more, a bigger piece of the pie. I provide all the goodies that are hard to get and illegal, all the vices that men crave and other men make illegal so they, or their partners like me, can hustle them on the street and grow rich.

It's all a game. The real criminals wear suits and ties in the legislature...black robes in court. Some of them wear white robes by night. I wonder how Charlie will get along with all them crackers.

But that ain't my worry or my world. We got fields of that old devil weed to cultivate along the Tishomingo Creek near Belmont, shipments coming from McAllen, Texas, girls coming out of Ace Connelly's operations in Memphis, and the mushrooms and

LSD mindbenders that the white hippies like coming in from labs in California and Mexico.

Cissy Carter, the top female hustler in Mississippi, handles that orange sunshine for me out of her trading post near Shannon, and Frank Harland and his boys got things sewed up down in Chickasaw County when we need to party down there.

I move some of the rotgut whiskey and some of the prime shine that boys like Billy Payne at the Rendezvous and Cal Mattox at the Snake Pit run out of their clubs. I just steer clear of ole Cal when I can. The women like him with all that black hair, pompadour, and silver-tongued charm, but the Snake Pit is a good name for his club, 'cause that man is mean as a snake.

But he's got that burglary-hijacking ring with lots of boys stealing for him, killing for him, too. That feud he has with the fiddling sheriff makes him dangerous, someone to stay away from, but I promised Ace to get along with him. The boys in Memphis like his moonshine and fence the hot goods he runs into Memphis and Corinth.

Streeter's musings were interrupted by the wail of a siren as a Tupelo P.D. blue-and-white screamed by his office in pursuit of a speeder.

Yep, got to keep Ace happy and grease the palms of our little lap dogs inside the police department, those bow-wows on the force who tap the phones of our enemies, watch for undercover FBI, and run troublemakers out of town. I got to keep a little cut for them…and for the politicos and their girlies, who like that white powder. But Ace has got to control Freddie. That albino almost cost us a big load of whiskey and drugs coming out of Nashville.

Two in the morning, and he's speeding through Bucksnort, Tennessee. Some dumb constable can't sleep and pulls Freddie over. He could've slipped him a little money or just talked his way out of it with some bowing and scraping, but when the cop asked why the rear end of his car was riding so low, Freddie just smiled and said, "I don't know. Let's take a look in the trunk."

That boy riding with him said Fredrick unlocked the trunk, stepped back, and said, "It sure is dark. You got a flashlight?"

When the fat constable stepped up to look in and bent over the trunk with his light, Freddie pulled out that knife he carries and just opened him up from ear-to-ear. The boy said the lone streetlight captured a look on Freddie's face at that moment, as cold and heartless as anything he'd ever seen.

The boy reported it all to Ace before he left the gangster life for good. He said that Freddie rolled the cop's body into the trunk and made him drive the police car to an overhang in the forests along the Tennessee River.

They rifled through the cop's wallet, got his name and particulars, and then put the body behind the wheel and pushed the car over the edge, where it made a big splash under the moonlight and slowly sank to the depths of the river. The boy said that Fredrick was muttering some kind of incantation to the devil the whole time, and Fredrick forced him to write a letter to the county and the constable's family, supposedly from the constable, George Smith, saying he had run off with a waitress to find himself, and nobody should try to look for him.

The boy told Ace that he meant no offense, but he was leaving, getting as far away as he could from Freddie...from all of us.

I told Ace to keep that freak away from my brothels because he was rough with the girls. He's Ace's problem now. It's the live bodies that make money, not the dead ones.

I push drugs and other narcotics of the fleshly desires, and many peddle and hustle for me. I got peddlers and snitches in every barber shop, liquor store, and gambling game in town and down at Palmetto's black club, the Cotton Patch. Lots of poor busboys, shoe shiners, and floor sweepers are referring business to us...some churches, too, the ones seeking first the kingdom of the world. I just put a little extra in their collection plates...got people to deal with, no time for psychos like Freddie Hammel.

Streeter smiled and fingered a gospel tract one of the churches had left for him.

I profit in a world where there are two kinds of law—one for the black kids and one for the rich, white kids. The white ones make the bail and skate. I do what I can. I'm a fixer when I can and when it don't interfere with business, but I'm here to make money. Sometimes people come to me to get a sentence fixed or wanting someone punished. Sometimes the people they want me to punish…work for me. They're not dumb; they know it. But it's a game, and I give them satisfaction and respect when I can.

Lots of withdrawals from my heart's bank account and very few deposits, so the heart don't slow me down none. But you reap what you sow, or so they say. The preachers come around with their golden rule. Forget that. No mercy, no scruples…I do unto others before they do it unto me.

I just offer pain erasers…a little escape from the hard times and from the cross burners who want to put knots on black skulls. I see the knots on the heads that come to my clubs, and some of them knots…I put there.

A church bell chimed in the distance, turning his thoughts to his problem pastors, the ones who hid behind the shield of the cloth where he couldn't deal with them.

These churches are doing the same thing, taking money from folks who don't have it, churching up their racket, preaching some kind of cartoon Christianity—a pay-to-play salvation for suckers. They're knotting heads on the inside—preaching about Jesus. I ain't got nothing against Jesus. Jesus is all right with me. I guess we'll settle our accounts one day.

My sister, Tamara, prays for me. I need it, too. The pastors come around—not to save me—but to condemn me. They say that I care more about money than I do tomorrow, and that I'm gonna reap the bitter harvest. I tell 'em that all them little sins of theirs are the fastest road to hell. So maybe, just maybe…they'll beat me there.

Some say I'm a kind of Judas goat to my own community, and they gonna revoke my baptism! They jump all around, wagging their fingers at me, telling me that we gangsters are gonna turn on each other like the Moabites and the Ammonites and destroy each other. But the preachers are the real 'ites'…the parasites, feeding off the people and driving away business, and the termites, rotting away the foundations of my rackets.

But I won't go back to the days of "Yessuh," big smiles and giggles, stoop and bow. NO sir, no way! I put on the street jive and the parlor talk as I need to, but I got on my gangster armor. I get more respect from the racketeers than polite society. Even thugs like Billy Payne and that crazy Cal Mattox don't pretend to be anything other than what they are—a psycho in Cal's case.

Yeah, I'm as happy as a dead pig in mud. No man, black or white, wants this black cat to cross their paths. I'm the one the mob in Chicago sent out to do their dirty deeds. They didn't send the clean young men to be their assassins. They sent the one who could get it done and not look back. Killed my first man there, a man they called Roger Rock. He bled and bled. Who says you can't get blood out of a stone? I was like one of them old bloodhounds at Parchman. I had caught the scent, the whiff of death.

I'm just a soldier of fortune with sympathy for the devil. They say the bill's coming due, and I'm gonna have to pay my debts to him. But who prays for him? Don't he need it most of all? Don't I? It don't matter 'cause every time my palms itch, I know more money's coming into my hand. It's just me, my money, and my gun. My gun speaks to me, and I must please my gun.

He emerged from his musings, looked out his window, and saw a little cinnamon-colored girl splashing in a big puddle of water near his club. She was humming one of those old hymns his mama used to sing to him late at night.

"Hey! What you doing there? Who are you, girl?" he challenged as he walked outside.

She looked up at him, her pale-brown hands never leaving the brackish water. "I'm Jasmine. It's just me and Lizzie, my doll. I'm baptizing her. Pastor said I got to wash away her sins, make her white as snow," she answered.

"Make her white, huh? That's a good one!" He threw back his head, laughed maniacally, and slapped at his heaving chest until he caught his breath.

It was then that he noticed the swarm of large, black mosquitoes emerging from their breeding water where the girl was playing, but none were biting her.

"Do you know who I am?" Streeter growled.

The girl looked at him with her large brown eyes—the serious and honest eyes of a child. "Uh-huh. Mama told me. She said you got blood on your hands, but she said it's not the blood of Jesus that washes away your sins, Mr. Pusher. It's the kind that will send you straight to hell. Gonna bust them gates wide open, Mama said."

Streeter stared at her from behind a sudden grimace. Her quick words had caught him off guard, stabbed him under all of his hardness, and sucked the wind out of his murderous soul. He felt a tightening in his throat before he turned on his heels and retreated to his office, swatting at hungry mosquitoes pursuing him, blood-thirsty squadrons of buzzing whines.

All who knew him thought him to be devoid of conscience—even the possibility of conscience—and as hard as the rocks busted up by the chain gangs of Sunflower County, but for once…The Pusher had no answer to the disarming innocence of a child.

CHAPTER FOUR

*"It's not easy…seeing the gray amongst the
black and white."—April Mae Monterrosa*

*"God make you a good man…founded in
patience, humility, and meekness…to flee
treason, by no means to be cruel…to take no
battles in a wrongful quarrel for no law…"
—Encyclopedia Britannica,
"King Arthur's Pentecostal Oath"*

Michael was recovering from his first eventful visit to the Rendezvous. There was an ugly knot on his head and a throbbing pain behind his right eye. He had some bruised ribs and two chipped teeth that the county's dentist would file and polish, but since the fight at the club, the word had gotten around the county that there was more to the young deputy than first met the eye. That made his partner happy.

Sarge had heard about Robbie's trick and needled Michael about Mary—the minnow swimming in the shark pool at the Rendezvous.

"I don't know what happened between the two of you, but Robbie is telling everyone that the girl told her mama that she didn't want to go to the clubs anymore. She said she was just going to date boys her age and look for a boy like Michael."

"'A boy like Michael…what a man!'" his partner said in a falsetto voice as he gave a sly wink. Then he rolled his eyes, teasing his fresh-faced partner, whose disarming grin and kneejerk affinity for the underdog made him an easy target. Michael's bleeding heart worried Sarge.

Michael endured all the ribbing with good cheer and was up early on his first day off after the incident at the club, raking his curly brown hair with the giant comb that Pearl had hidden in last year's Christmas stocking—something to help him always look his best.

He had always tended to his hair and head, earning him a nickname of "Possible." When he was a little boy, Pearl had given him vague instructions on personal hygiene. She told him to start at his toes and to wash as high as possible—an oblique reference to his privates. He thought she meant his head. After all, that was as high as possible. When folks asked him why he scrubbed his head so obsessively, he said, "Grandma told me to always wash possible!"

Hence, the nickname of "Possible."

So, ribs taped, hair combed, and a big splash of Brut applied, "Possible" slipped off to Memphis to take Dixie Lee to Pasquale's Pizza in West Memphis and then to see *Love Story* at the Malco Theater.

Over dinner, they caught up on their separate lives, laughed, held hands, and had eyes only for each other in the crowded restaurant. He told her about life as a deputy: the club, the fight, and young Mary.

She seemed to withdraw when he told her about Mary's story, and a dark cloud settled over their table…a grayness he could not penetrate.

"You once rescued me. You're always rescuing damsels in distress, aren't you?" she asked coldly.

"She wasn't a damsel, Dixie, just a kid of thirteen or so— maybe a damsel in waiting. She was like Dorothy trapped in Oz. Someone just needed to tell her to click her heels three times and whisper, 'There's no place like home,'" he answered.

"Some of them are thirteen going on forty," she snapped.

"I know, but this one wasn't. She soon might've been, but she wasn't yet. What's wrong, Dixie?" he asked.

"I don't know…I'm sorry. I really am," she said, biting her lower lip.

They didn't say much on the way to the movie. Tired from a late shift and a long drive, he drifted off to sleep during *Love Story* and woke to find her with her head on his chest.

He looked at her and asked, "What?"

"Just listening to your heart beat. Do you know that it skips a beat sometimes? Is that just because of my nearness?" she asked in a little-girl voice.

At the end of the tear-jerker, she turned to him and smothered him with strawberry kisses. That fluttering in her voice, the rosy flush of red on her cheeks, and those big, leaking blue eyes punctuated each caress. They lived, loved, and played pretend in a private world they had created in Washington—one fading by degrees.

"See, Michael? It's just like Ali MacGraw said. Love means never having to say you're sorry!" she said.

Michael wasn't so sure about that, but a letter addressed in her distinctive handwriting and drenched in her favorite cologne arrived in Tupelo after their date.

Dear Michael,

Come back when you can. I'm still wearing the smile you give me when I see you! I won't say that I miss you, but just 'tu me manques.' That's French for you are missing from me. Missing you comes in waves, and tonight I'm drowning.

I was wandering when you rescued me in DC and then I got lost in you, but it was like being found, you know? You invaded my heart, and weren't repulsed by what you saw in my dreadful dreams. You brought the balm to calm and starve my gnawing fears.

There's an arrest warrant out for you in Memphis for stealing my heart, Mr. Deputy. You could destroy me, but I trust you not to. Cheri says she just knows that we'll be married one day.

I miss you...maybe too much, I think. I may not be your first love, but I want to be your last.

Dixie Lee

She had become his weakness, and he had given her his strength—a questionable exchange of power.

An old friend from the FBI days in Washington called to check on him and asked, "How's your life?"

Michael knew what he meant and answered, "She's fine."

He worried about her. Tiny brackets of stress and restlessness had formed fine lines around her eyes, an outward indictor of internal conflict. He feared that she could only fake it for so long, and then the lure of the dark side—the wild side she had exhibited in Washington—would return from wherever it had been temporarily consigned.

They had agreed to date other people when Michael couldn't get up to Memphis, a plan fraught with danger. He thought that she felt she was never enough for life, or that life was never enough for her. He sometimes saw the restlessness in her eyes when she didn't think he was looking.

In an echo of the searchers in the new hippie counter-culture, she had once told him that she had everything she'd ever wanted but one thing. When he asked her what that was, she said, "I don't have a clue."

He imagined that a day might come when he would look into her eyes and see nothing left there for him, no chances for tomorrow, no words left to save fragile love, nothing but the word *"finished."* But not now…not yet.

* * *

Race…Michael had led a sheltered life as a child, and he hadn't thought much about it.

The races were apart in the South—estranged, he'd heard someone say, like when a forced or arranged marriage goes bad, but they don't actually get a divorce because the lives of the parties are so intertwined. They need each other. They just don't live together anymore but behind strict divides. It was a tough life for black folks, living on the margins.

The two cultures were symbiotic, mutually dependent, coexisting through domestic work, sharecropping, and other labor contracts, but they could've been on separate planets. There were polite greetings on the street, and a lot of "How y'all doing?" and so on, but there was little real understanding of people who lived just over the hill or down the street and went to different schools.

There were so many unspoken taboos, and everyone just tiptoed around that big ole pink elephant in the room, pretending they didn't see it. The whites and the blacks agreed on that color, but they didn't talk about pink. Some just stepped over and around the elephant and the invisible people, the poor whites and blacks and those broken on the shoals of a lost world.

When he was a boy, Michael heard someone say how poor he was, but Michael didn't feel poor. He asked Pearl, "Grandma, are we po' folks like in that song we heard on the Grand Old Opry radio show?"

Pearl told him, "Son, we have fishing and hunting, tall trees and blue skies, truck patches, gardens, and God. We aren't wealthy by the standards of the plantation or the city slickers, but we aren't poor, either. Some of those folks are the poorest people I know. They have so much money and so many toys, but it won't buy them happiness."

She smiled that Pearl smile, popped the top on her King Leo peppermint tin, pulled out two sticks, and said, "We also have peppermint, Michael. How can they call us poor?"

Shortly after Michael was born on April 8, 1948, at the Tupelo hospital, other poor folks, Vernon and Gladys Presley, loaded up their car and moved to Memphis. Rumors were that Vernon might have been in some trouble and had to leave, but Pearl, with a twinkle in her eyes, told Michael that the real reason was that they decided Tupelo just wasn't big enough to hold both Elvis and Michael.

In 1958, when he was ten, a man came up the hill to the Parker house when only Pearl and Michael were home. Wayne Lindsey, a long, tall, skinny man with boney hands and large sweat stains under his frayed, white shirt, handed Michael a card and said he was an insurance salesman.

Michael looked at the card and said, "I don't know what insurance is."

Lindsey laughed, revealing dirty, yellowed teeth and breath that smelled like the rotten eggs Michael sometimes found when he gathered eggs for Pearl.

"Well, no matter, I'll just leave my card for your parents. Do you know about dragons, boy? Do you know what they are?" Lindsey asked.

"Do you mean the dragons that the Knights of the Round Table fight? I have a book about them. They protect the helpless, defend women, always tell the truth, and show mercy to their enemies…except those big lizards…er, dragons," Michael said.

Lindsey smiled like he had just smelled something and said, "No, not that nonsense, boy. That's all smoke and no fire, and we sure don't coddle our enemies. I am the dragon, little Mr. Parker…the Grand Dragon. Belonging to our klavern and fulfilling our oath is the Holy Grail. I'll come by and get you one day and take you to one of our rallies, and you'll get to see me in white with my pointy hat. Would you like that?" he asked.

Lindsey sat down on the porch, patted Michael on the head, and began to stroke his hair.

"We need young boys like you. We'll give you a home and be your real family. We'll show you what Scripture really means— not that watered-down stuff you get in church. We'll teach you about Communists and the darkies, about your destiny as a white boy…because we love you. Give me a hug, boy!" Lindsey said, his breathing growing deeper, like he'd been running.

Pearl was standing behind the screen door listening to the man. The door squeaked when she walked out onto the weathered wood porch, and it banged shut behind her.

She was always sweet to everyone, but that day…Michael saw a side of Grandma that he'd never seen. Cradled in her sweet, old hands was the family's sixteen-gauge shotgun.

"Mister, I've been listening to you talk to our boy. He's got a home and a family, and he is loved…but not the kind you mean. I got the family shotgun, passed down to me by my daddy, Captain Patterson, who taught me to shoot. It's loaded with some number six rabbit shot, and it ain't all smoke. It has plenty of fire. You best leave my boy alone, make like a rabbit, and hop on down the hill before you need one of your own insurance policies to cover wounded lizards," Pearl said.

Lindsey drew up to his full height and said, "Now, you wait just a minute!"

Pearl raised the barrels of the shotgun ever so slightly, aiming just south of the dragon's tarnished belt buckle.

Michael looked at Pearl like he'd never seen her before. His eyes got big, and his mouth dropped to his chest.

As the dragon-rabbit beat a hasty retreat, hopping and slithering on down the hill, Pearl winked at Michael and said, "What's up, Doc?" She quoted the "Wascally Wabbit" from the afternoon cartoons that came on right after the Hopalong Cassidy show they never missed.

Pearl propped the gun in the corner, sat on the porch swing, and motioned for Michael to sit beside her.

"Son, always stay far away from that white trash. They may carry the Confederate battle flag, but they aren't fit to tie Captain Patterson's boot laces. They have hijacked the cause. They are thugs and criminals. They want to hurt people like Alberta. She's been a part of our family, helping me for years, and she's cared for you since you were a baby. You know she loves you," Pearl said.

Years before, when Michael was still a small boy, Pearl had heard him utter a commonly used word to describe blacks, one he had picked up from adults.

"Son, that's not a nice word, and it's hurtful to Alberta when she hears it. Don't you ever use that word again. I know you hear others use it, but just because they say it don't make it right," she scolded.

It was the first time that anyone had told Michael that a word, other than cuss words, was wrong. It was a moment of lost innocence. It was like Adam and Eve discovering that they were naked. He sure didn't want to hurt Alberta's feelings. The jolly woman with the giant eyes and warm smile stayed with them in the daytime to look after Pearl. He loved her and talked to her for hours on end when Pearl was asleep. He never used the word again after Pearl's admonition, but he did ask Alberta a question one day.

"Alberta, why is your skin so dark?" he asked her, with not an ounce of guile or deceit—just his endless desire to know everything about everything.

Alberta smiled and said, "Well, I'm not sure. Maybe God gave us that to protect us against the hot sun of Africa."

Michael scratched his jaw in contemplation, and then with sudden revelation, he blurted out what seemed the obvious question to his child's mind: "Then why are you here in Mississippi?"

Alberta laughed and laughed, grabbed him to her bosom, and squeezed him until he thought his eyes were going to pop out.

That evening, Michael sat on the front porch shelling butter beans with Pearl and Alberta. Crickets and tree frogs were singing a salute to the restful evening shade, and the soft glow of twilight had fallen over Parker Grove. His tiny record player was playing The Platters' song about heavenly shades of night and togetherness at twilight time.

Pearl rocked in her chair, her apron full of beans, as a whippoorwill's plaintive call echoed through the hollows like a disembodied spirit, giving pause to little Ike, the skittish puppy at her feet. He was named for President Eisenhower.

She said, "Michael, did you know that night and day, dark and light, the moon and the sun all bumped into each other back at the dawn of creation? But they didn't fuss, because they all had a place in God's heavens and earth, and they needed each other to light the vaults of the sky, to populate the land, to rest, work, and be fruitful, and to serve as signs to mark sacred times. When they bumped into each other, they just got together and called it twilight time. There was harmony. And God saw it all and said, 'It is good…very good.'"

She stopped shelling her beans, smiled that kind Pearl smile at Michael, and said, "Harmony, Michael."

And Alberta said, "Amen, Grandma Pearl! Amen!"

* * *

Michael was taught to say please and thank you, just like Captain Kangaroo advised, to always respect his elders (except that dragon fella), and to address older folks as sir or ma'am.

One day, Michael said "Yes, sir" to an old black man.

A red-faced white man nearby heard him, walked over to Michael in front of the old man, and said, "You don't ever say 'sir' to him, boy! You hear me?"

All the rules, exceptions, and contradictions were confusing to a kid growing up in the South of the '50s and '60s. When he asked Pearl about all these rules, she told him to pay the naysayers no mind and just follow the Golden Rule, the only rule he would need in life.

When Michael picked cotton alongside black folks, he watched them when the sharp boles cut their fingers, and he saw that they bled red just like him. He loved the songs they sang, and they laughed when he tried to sing along with them on the spirituals, blues tunes, and odes to hard times. It would influence the music he gravitated to as an adult—songs that would bring comfort in the days of thorns and trials.

Michael graduated from an all-white high school and really knew no black people except Alberta. When he went to Washington to work for the FBI after high school, he was still insulated. D.C. was a segregated city. There were no people of color working in the Identification Division of Hoover's agency in the mid '60s.

After his time in Washington, he worked part-time as a doorman and ticket taker at the Lyric, the local theater in Tupelo, and the audiences were divided. Blacks and whites had separate entrances to the theater, with blacks seated in the balcony and whites on the main floor. Michael collected the ticket stubs, trying to keep the peace and smooth ruffled feathers when disputes arose, using his best peacekeeping tools—his ready smile and free tickets to the Highway 78 drive-in.

When Michael took a break from college and part-time work to fund his last two years of college, he was hired to work as a teacher's aide in adult education at the Itawamba Junior College Vo-Tech Center in Tupelo.

He was assigned to administer tests to high school graduates who had enrolled in secretarial courses. He gave a simple math test to young black girls fresh out of Carver High School, the all-black high school before integration. It was the same school that Michael and his fellow high school drummers had tried to emulate when they heard them in Christmas parades—until the band director had a hissy and ordered them to return to a nice, safe, sedate cadence.

The test Michael oversaw had 120 questions, but the teacher had structured the test to be graded as if it were only one hundred problems. That gave a break to the students. They could miss fifty answers and still make seventy for passing. When Michael graded the papers, the scores were in the minus range... minus ten, minus fifteen, and so on. That was when another cartoon lightbulb went on over Michael's head, and he realized that maybe the argument for a fair system of "separate but equal" wasn't so fair and equal after all.

He was sent into the projects in North Tupelo to sign up students for classes to be held in mobile classrooms that would be pulled right to the front doors of the residents of the new housing projects. It was there that he saw too many single-parent homes— homes that were only houses without fathers. He had never seen that before, and though he didn't fully understand the implications or causes, he thought that it couldn't be good for intact families or for the country.

But what really made it personal for Michael was the day he was assigned to help Tupelo policeman Marvin Bowen learn to read and write. Despite his illiteracy, Marvin had been pulled from the back of the garbage trucks and hired as a police officer to break the color barrier and to appease the minority community.

Marvin was a tall man, a gentle man and a gentleman, with a light that framed his face and drew you to a sparkle in his brown eyes…but he couldn't write tickets or file reports. His employment could have been called progress—but another term for it was emotional usury. And although some cynical politicians may have tried to use it for their own designs, it brought Marvin into Michael's life. God used that new friendship to pry open the door to Michael's heart and allow him to see that pink elephant in the room, to move past it, and to be set free.

There was an immediate connection and fondness between the two men. A lasting friendship was formed as the two men hunched over a table at the Vo-Tech Center for hours on end, working on basics that Michael no longer took for granted.

Marvin was a quick study. He learned to read and write. He was promoted and opened the door for others who would follow him.

"Lancelot" was forced to think, to consider and reconsider, to mine for truth, to guard against the "Wascally Wabbits" of life, and to armor up against the dragons.

* * *

While driving to the sheriff's department, Michael saw Marvin waving from his Tupelo patrol unit. He thought of those days in the small classroom, his chair hitched up beside Marvin's as they worked the lesson plans and phonetically formed the words that would empower Marvin…the bonding of the two men and the first incisions of the long transplant surgery that placed a servant heart into Michael.

Michael pulled over to the curb, and Marvin came alongside his unit.

"What's up, Marvin?" Michael asked, beginning a running joke between the men.

"I pulled into a white service station the other day playing George Jones on my radio. It drove them crazy!" Marvin said with a smile.

"Well," Michael said, "I stopped at a black station, and I was playing James Brown. It drove them crazy, too!"

Marvin took him to a special diner called the Steer Shack, near what had been old Shake Rag. He said it had the best steaks in Tupelo. When they walked in the café, everyone looked up at them briefly and then continued their meals. Michael was the only white customer in the restaurant.

They ordered their steaks and talked about Michael's internship while they waited.

The cook, a big, sweaty man named Wolf, brought them two giant steaks and plopped them on the table. Michael always had everything well done, but the slabs of meat were so rare that they were bleeding.

Michael stared first at the plate and then at Marvin. Marvin pursed his lips and raised his left eyebrow.

"What?" Wolf asked, the massive muscles in his tattooed arms bulging.

"Well, I asked for well done," Michael said.

"If it's still moving too much for you, Deputy, I'll take it back to the kitchen and kill it again," Wolf said.

"Well..." Michael began.

As fast as greased lightning, the big cook reared back and stabbed the big slab of meat with a huge steak knife he was carrying. The point of the knife pierced the steak all the way through and cracked the plate, and just as quickly, Wolf withdrew the knife and put his hands on his hips.

Marvin and Michael jumped back and almost fell out of their chairs.

"Is it dead enough now?" the cook asked.

"Oh, yeah!" Michael said. "Dead as a doornail! Thanks!"

The cook glared at Marvin and asked, "You got something to say?"

"No, sir, my steak's just right," Marvin said.

The psycho-cook smiled a sick little smile that looked more like a case of indigestion than culinary hospitality, and then he said, "Now that's what I like to see, happy customers. Well, dig in then. Eat like you like it."

It wasn't a request, and the two cops began to saw on their steaks with gusto.

"Uh-huh, that's better. Y'all come back soon," the cook said as he walked back to the kitchen to subdue another steer.

Marvin and Michael looked at each other, trying to stifle laughter, and Michael whispered, "Best steaks in Tupelo, huh?"

CHAPTER FIVE

*"I don't want nobody to moan. All I want
my friends to do, come and fold my
dying arms."—Josh White,
"Jesus Gonna Make Up My Dying Bed"*

*"Clouds of mystery pourin' confusion on the
ground. Good men through the ages trying
to find the sun."—John Fogerty,
"Who'll Stop The Rain"*

"Michael, the times are changing; isn't that what Bob Dylan sings? I'd like to meet him someday, maybe invite him to sit in with my old band, play some harmonica. He ain't no great shakes as a singer, but he's a great songwriter, and it all seems to work for him in these strange times.

"Styles come and they go. Someone asked me if I had bought a new suit. I told them that I had…twenty years ago. Why do people we don't know tell us what's stylish and what's not? Why not me or you? I guess I'll keep my suits until they come back in style again," Sheriff Simpson said.

He sighed and shook his head.

"I used to think that I understood the country, but no more. These days, I think I might understand this new world if I could jump up to the moon to get a better view of the earth," he said.

The sheriff told Michael that he needed a favor. He was hiring Thomas "Big Tom" Jackson, the former defensive end for the Detroit Lions, to be the first black deputy in Lee County. He was doing it for many reasons, not the least of which was to capture the black vote in his reelection campaign, and he wanted Michael to be Jackson's partner.

"Michael, I know that I can count on you. Some of the other deputies would not be comfortable with Tom riding with them, but you are young and easygoing, one of these new centurions we hear so much about. I need you to do this for me if you will," he said.

"Sure, Sheriff, no problem," Michael replied.

When Deputy Jackson walked into the department that morning, a hush fell over the office. Everyone stopped and stared—not just because he was black, but because he was a really big guy with massive shoulders. Even Earl, the radio operator with narcolepsy, woke up to say, "Well, I'll be doggone!" and then "Boy howdy," which is Southern for Amen.

Michael drank milkshakes with raw eggs every day just to try to gain a pound or two to hold up his britches and gun belt; he felt small and frail next to his new partner. The county's seamstress had to drastically alter the department's smallest uniform so the skinny kid from Ole Miss wouldn't look like he was playing dress-up in adult clothes.

At the other end of the spectrum, Tom's chest strained at the pearly buttons on the largest deputy shirt available, and the sight of a black man in the South with a big .38 Smith & Wesson hogleg on his hip was something different indeed—and mighty threatening to some.

He bounded over to Michael, extended his big hand, and proclaimed with a hearty laugh, "Hi, Mike! I'm Tom. So you're the one they dumped me on!"

No pretense and a great sense of humor.

Michael liked him immediately. He extracted his small hand from Tom's giant mitt and said, "Well, Tom, it's now or never. Let's check out a car, put up the bat signal over Gotham, and go patrol the county to root out crime and/or evil!"

On their patrols, Tom was open and matter-of-fact in filling Michael in on the lay of the land. He said that the sheriff needed some help in the black clubs in the county, and in a twofer deal, a power broker in the black community told the sheriff that he would work to deliver the black vote if the lawman showed him some respect.

Tom looked at Michael with his infectious grin and said, "Hello, my name is Respect!"

Tom talked about the glory days at Grambling under Eddie Robinson, and how he later had blown out his knees in the pros. "So I had to find some honest work to do. Seems I've gone from chasing running backs to chasing lawbreakers," he said.

"I worked a little muscle for some of the clubs 'round here, maybe delivered a little hooch for folks that peddle it to make money and to keep some consumers in our community happy. That's the only place some folks find what passes for happiness, don't you know? So, I ain't done nothing too bad!" he said with a big grin.

They talked football and life, and ignored the stares they got everywhere they went. Michael stopped a car in Verona that first day, and the man was giving him a hard time…until the giant presence of Tom loomed large behind him.

The word went out far and wide, and everyone asked their neighbors, "Have you heard? The sheriff has hired a black deputy, and he's working with that college boy!"

Michael liked the big guy and told him that maybe going into clubs (like the Rendezvous) on the weekends might not be the best idea just yet—at least not until the furor died down. Michael told him that he wasn't sure either of them would make it out alive.

Charles Evers came to town on a campaign swing when he was running for governor, and Michael and Tom were assigned to work security for his event. Evers looked them over and said, "You boys are quite a sight to see…living, breathing billboards for progress!"

After his speech, Evers sipped a cold Coke and talked with the deputies about his past. He admitted that he had walked on the dark side after World War II and had worked for organized crime in Chicago in order to survive, but he had since seen the Light.

"Every saint has a past. Every sinner has a future, boys!" he said. "You boys are a walking testimony to things we all got to get past."

It was ironic that Evers was running against Bill Waller, who had unsuccessfully prosecuted Byron De La Beckwith, the man thought to be the murderer of Evers' brother, Medgar. Waller was campaigning on the push for a new state department to fight drugs in response to Nixon's new war on drugs. Some wanted to call it the Mississippi Bureau of Narcotics.

After the political rally, Big Tom was quiet for a while as they patrolled the byways and backroads of the county.

He finally looked at Michael and said, "Mike, we got to be careful. Heroes come and go. We don't have to set ourselves on fire to warm the world. You're looking to live the American dream, while I'm trying to escape the American nightmare. For all of us who ain't with the program and playing their 'us versus them' games—that's me and you—there's gonna be hell to pay before it's over."

Michael thought for a minute and asked, "Did I ever tell you that I met Charlie Pride?"

"No, I don't think so," Tom said.

"I wasn't into country music that much, but I met him on an Ole Miss field trip to Nashville. You know he's from Sledge, Mississippi?" Michael asked.

"Yeah, I heard he was," Tom said.

"Do you know, I thought he was white?" Michael asked with a quizzical grin.

Tom threw his head back, laughed, and slapped his knee three times with his big hands.

He looked at Michael and said, "You got to be kidding me!"

"No, really I did. The day I met him, Charlie saw the surprised look on my face and said, 'I get it all the time. My folks say, How come you look like us but sound like them? Then your folks look at me and ask, How come you sound like us but look like them?'"

It was the perfect story to begin Michael's second real friendship with someone who once would have been hidden by the big, pink elephant.

* * *

The crackling static of the police radio and Earl's distinct voice interrupted their musings as they navigated the county's dirt roads. They were still sharing stories and getting to know each other as they served court summonses and checked for fugitives on outstanding warrants.

"Michael, y'all get on out to the Playhouse on the county line. There's been a murder there—one of the working girls. Sarge and the other units are on their way. Sarge wants you to help with the crime scene and interviews. Oh, uh, you too, Tom!" Earl said, still unaccustomed to Tom's presence.

"What's the Playhouse? I haven't heard of it," Michael said.

Tom turned to Michael and said, "That's where people— black and white—drink, sing, dance, gamble, play chess and crass— all kinds of board and bedroom games—and carouse with people they wouldn't speak to on the streets in the sunshine hours. It's the palace of golden girls, somewhere under the rainbow where bad dreams come true...an illusion where sharp razors hide behind dazzling smiles and skillful operators. Delirium reigns there; perdition beckons. It's The Pusher's place."

"Who's The Pusher?" Michael asked.

"James Streeter, someone a puritan like you don't ever want to mess with if you can help it," Tom said.

When Michael and Tom pulled up to the Pink Playhouse, Lee units, constables' cars, and the car belonging to the local Mississippi Highway Patrol investigator surrounded the garishly painted club like an invading army. One deputy was busy wrapping the building in yellow crime-scene tape.

On the outside of the club, old, wet newspaper made a soggy mess on the walkway, and the remains of beer cans and whiskey bottles littered the approach to the front door. Cigarette butts covered the area just outside the door, and someone was already collecting them for forensics.

As they entered the club of bright lights, hard liquor, and soft women—an integrated world where the races mixed and played—a strong odor of stale food, liquor, intimacy, and death swept over the deputies.

Michael noted that the tables in the outer dining area were covered with plates full of dried peas, hardened and shriveled like black gravel. The serving platters were filled with cold puddles of grease, congealed around the remainder of what appeared to be roast beef. Green flies swarmed around the food and the neon lights.

Then he saw the girl on the floor, soaked in blood and already outlined in yellow chalk. Her face had been smashed, she had been shot between the eyes, her throat had been cut, and her head was almost severed from her body. She was shrunken and diminished by loss of blood, flattened against the floor.

Michael could see that underneath the layers of makeup and the hush of death, she had been a pretty girl—a pretty girl who would take her beauty to the grave. He also saw the telltale signs of needle tracks near her wrists.

She had the thousand-yard stare to nowhere, the look of the dead or the near-dead who see something off in the distance that the living can't. There was an overpowering stench of urine and fecal matter, and her black hair had lost its sheen and looked like a bad wig in the morning sunlight spilling over the room. A giant cockroach ran from beneath her and wiggled its antennae at Michael. There was a deafening stillness, screaming in protest at the approach and penalty of death.

A wave of nausea swept over Michael, sweat beaded on his upper lip, his throat filled, and he wanted to throw up. This was not the sanitized crime photos of college textbooks.

Sarge looked concerned and asked, "You all right, rookie?"

"Yeah, I'll be fine," Michael said, trying hard to swallow his Adam's apple.

"We got ourselves a mess here. Someone cut up this kid. She was just seventeen, but she had a fake ID listed to Star Smith showing her as twenty-one. That's how she was able to work here at what they call a...gentleman's club. They hide behind legalities, and there's nothing we can do.

"Who knows what her real name was, but her working name was Stardust. They called her Star. I think they know more than they let on about who did this, but these girls are all scared of the man who owns the place—and of us. They probably won't tell you anything about this or their real business here, but start interviewing those other girls over there," Sarge said.

Michael looked away from the dead girl, nodded, and walked up to a group of the club girls. He stopped before a petite girl with cinnamon skin and kewpie-doll eyes—saucers beneath long, curled lashes. He took out his notepad.

"What's your name?" he asked.

"Magnolia," she answered passively.

"I need to ask you some questions if you don't mind, Magnolia," he said.

She looked up at Michael and then looked again when she saw Tom.

"Did you know Star?" Michael asked.

"Yes," she said placidly.

"Did you see what happened?" he asked.

"No…just found her this morning." she said with matter-of-fact delivery.

"Do you know anyone who would want to hurt Star?" Tom asked.

"No," she said flatly. Then she amended it by saying, "But that don't include a lot of jealous men who loved her madly."

"Do you know who Star was with last night?" Michael asked.

"No," she said without hesitation.

"Are you afraid to talk to us?" Michael asked.

"No," she said quickly, but her eyes betrayed her.

"Why do you think that someone would want to kill Star?" Michael asked.

She stepped up to him, nose-to-nose, coolly inspecting him with emotionless, chocolate eyes, and said, "Well, 'cause they wanted her dead, I spec. Ain't that why anyone kills someone? You gonna come to the funeral, lawman, or you just here for the visitation and the laying on of the dainty white shroud?

"There ain't no more sing-songs of laughter left here for you to record, Mr. Policeman…no more silver needles in her arms. What she was is now nothing more than a wisp of smoke. She was wild, sweet, and true. Her warm lips have gone as cold and hard as pebbled snow, and she's a million miles the other side of the Milky Way, riding the tail of a streaking comet. That wind outside is just her whispering along her way, trying to get home before ole St. Peter locks the gate."

From a table near them, Magnolia grabbed a glass of stale whiskey that had cigarette ashes floating in the amber liquid. Her eyes never leaving Michael's, she downed it in three gulps. It took three more hard swallows to keep the toxic mix down. Then she belched like a volcano about to erupt and wiped her mouth with the back of her hand.

"Now y'all go on outta here and leave us to mourn and bury our dead," she said.

As she stepped away, she shook his hand with gusto and quickly palmed a scrap of paper into Michael's hand.

At that moment, James Streeter burst into the club. He was loud, angry, and volatile. Michael stepped to the corner of the room and curled the note up against his chest as Sarge greeted Streeter and told him that it would be better if he left while the interviews were conducted.

Streeter then spied Michael and Tom.

He bellowed, "Well, what have we here…Mutt and Jeff, Laurel and Hardy, and Amos and Andy all rolled into one!"

He looked at Michael's partner and said, "Hello, Tom. They assign you to babysit this child?"

"No, sir. Michael's my partner from Ole Miss…and my friend," he said as he squared his massive shoulders.

"That a fact now?" Streeter said.

"I'm Deputy Michael Parker," Michael said, extending his hand, which was refused.

Michael felt a tightening in his jaw muscles and at the back of his neck. He dropped his hand and said, "Mr. Streeter, do you have any idea who might have done this? Someone who likes to cut up girls, or maybe a pimp who likes to use them to get rich, perhaps?"

Streeter's eyes narrowed, and then he laughed.

"You worried about this black girl, Deputy? She was just cheap whistle bait, a morgue-candidate-in-waiting, a gimp and a junkie. Don't nothing but death stop a junkie from being a junkie. She was gonna die one way or the other, moving bed-to-bed. Leave it at that," Streeter said.

"I don't think we can do that, Mr. Streeter," Michael said, beginning a stare-down with Streeter.

"Yeah you can. You just don't know it yet. It's done all the time by men in suits sipping martinis at the chamber of commerce— men who have hijacked your idealism and naïveté and repackaged it into something they call 'the greater good,'" Streeter snapped as he stepped close to Michael. Streeter's putrid breath reminded him of the smell of that dragon fella he'd met as a child.

"Look, boy. We get lots of folks here, from my community and yours…folks all torn up inside. Some are from your churches and country clubs, proper folks in town and hillbillies straight out of the woods. They sneak in here on hot Saturday nights and want to be set free. They put their faith on hold until they get the sin outta their systems. They just can't be who God and America wants them to be—at least not seven days a week. They live like the devil on Saturday night, and repent on Sunday, when they use that get-out-of-jail-free card. Isn't that how it's done? Fake it till you make it?

"No matter. If they don't get some relief, they'll just eventually bust…but that makes work for men like me and you, don't it, Deputy? Some of those tortured souls from your tribe—I call them our poor 'honky-donkeys,' honking their car horns for their favorite girls and braying out of both sides of their mouths."

He let that settle and watched Michael for the impact of his challenge.

"Deputy, let me tell you how it really is—not how Ole Miss says it is. You are walking in a right-handed world but brushing up against the underworld, the left-handed universe. The conformist in you sees vulgarity and depravity, Mr. Parker, but you are gonna find yourself intrigued by the darkness. It...he...is whispering to you right now."

His mouth formed a sick, taunting grin.

"You may even want to visit toy shops like mine to see the pretty, broken toys...if not to play, then to put them back together—to save them. Cause you're a fixer, aren't you, boy? You want the world on your terms as you think it should be, not as it is. You gonna be one miserable pilgrim, always running 'round trying to clean up other folks' messes.

"Accept it—people just can't change who they really are. The heart is wicked, who can know it? Isn't that what the Good Book says? So they come to me and my angels for distractions to assuage the merciless guilt that plagues them. Love is dead, Deputy. So they come here from far and wide for the other L words...lust and liberation," he said.

Michael watched as the coroner pulled the sheet over the dead girl, and the other girls began to moan and wail in a haunting chorus that made him shudder involuntarily. He turned to Streeter and asked, "You think she felt liberated by the blade that cut her throat?"

He looked at Michael for a long, pregnant moment and finally bit his lower lip and nodded.

"You come on back anytime, Deputy. You never know what you might find at the end of these dirt roads," The Pusher said. "Tortured honkies like you are always welcome here."

* * *

While the body was on its way to the morgue, the deputies finished their interviews. They stepped outside to escape the dust that filled the air from the fingerprint boys and to avoid the reporters from the *Tupelo Daily Journal*, whom Sarge had finally allowed into the club.

Dark clouds full of wild winds rolled in, sweeping the soiled plain clean and sweetening the air as the hard rains began. It was just as the local weatherman on WELO predicted.

Tom looked at Michael and asked, "What did the note say?"

Giant raindrops began to slap at the earth around them with a bass rhythm, turning Mississippi clay into mud as Michael said, "I'm not sure what it means, Tom. It only said, 'The whitest boy I ever seen.'"

When Michael arrived home in Parker Grove that night, the storm was still raging as the phone rang. It was Dixie Lee.

"Whatcha doing?" she asked in her whispery, husky voice.

"Not much," he said wearily. Then he laughed and said, "My behind is dragging so far behind me tonight that I had to unlock the door and turn on the porch light so it could find its way home!"

"Poor baby…you don't sound so good. Have you had a bad day?" she asked.

"Yep, it's been an ugly time," he answered.

"Then tell me something good; say something beautiful," she said.

So he just whispered her name softly and gently.

Dixie Lee…

Then silence. She wasn't there. The temperamental country phone service yielded to the storm and died suddenly, just like Star.

The lights went out.

He sat in the dark, his drifting mind knitting images of dead girls…trying to sort it all out, to feel something—anger, sadness, determination, helpless resignation.

The lights flickered in a strobe-like sequence. A driving rain beat at the door, and the wind rattled the windows with a *woo-woo* banshee wail. Cars went by, loud motors changing to a minor key as they faded away. The lights went dark again, and Michael drifted toward the deep sleep his body was demanding.

  Then the lights popped on again and jolted him from his fitful nap.

  Startled and not knowing where he was at first, he switched on the old black-and-white TV. He sat before it, illuminated by the glare of the fluttering flare of rolling images on Tupelo's only TV station. A skinny televangelist with a crew cut was talking about rain falling on the just and unjust, about the times when pain just won't stop pouring buckets of wet sorrow over our lives. His mouth always seemed to be pursing for a twitch or sneeze when he talked, and something about him was unsettling.

  The preacher looked at the camera with intense eyes, right at Michael, and said, "A woman saw me on this station late one night, and she called and asked if she could talk to me awhile. She finally asked if she could meet at church where her boss wouldn't see her and find out that she was hanging out with the 'Jesus peddlers,' as she put it. She told me of her pain, of the storms and trials in her life."

  The station's one camera moved in real close to the old preacher. His eyes crinkled at the corners, and he paused and swallowed real hard.

  "She's dead now. Star died a violent death, but the last time I saw her, she was trying to give up the life of sin that had burrowed into her soul. She was sad. She was living in a prison of depression. She was scared of someone. She told me that she had been boiled by Beelzebub and fried in his fire," the preacher said.

  "She was drowning in her storms and asked me, 'Pastor, can you stop the rain?'

  "I said, 'No, child, but I know the One who can.' I led Star to Him just late yesterday afternoon.

  "She's with Him now, where there's no depression...on the sunny side of Heaven, where it'll never rain on her again."

  As the background music began, the preacher closed his Bible, folded his hands, and said, "We close tonight with the Carter Family's 'No Depression.'"

"I'm going where there is no depression to a better land that's free from care. I'll leave this world of toil and trouble. My home's in Heaven. I'm goin' there."

The flood and the fury stopped, the moon broke out full and yellow, and Michael lowered his head. His heart and soul hurried to a private place, and he began to gently whisper some of Mort Dixon's lyrics as a eulogy for a girl leaving the oldest profession and going home. It was a song for a girl Michael never knew, slain in the slums of broken hearts and tumbled into a grave with her secrets sealed forever on her silent lips.

"Pack up all your cares and woes, here I go, singing low. Bye, bye, blackbird. Where Somebody waits for me, sugar's sweet and so is He. No one here can love and understand me. Make my bed and light the light. Jesus, I'll arrive late tonight."

CHAPTER SIX

*"When the darkness appears and the night
draws near...Guide my feet, hold my
hand...lead me home"—Thomas A. Dorsey,
"Take My Hand, Precious Lord"*

*"From childhood's hour I have not been as
others were; I have not seen as others saw...
I could not awaken my heart to joy at the
same tone, And all I loved, I loved alone."
—Edgar Allan Poe, "Alone"*

When he wrote of the murder in his notes to his Ole Miss professor, Tim Charles had counseled him, "You're like the hero in the old novels, certain to try to do the right thing as you see it, rushing in to rescue the damsel that the villain has tied to the railroad track, shouting 'Unhand her, you fiend!' And you write about it all in a way that will inspire some and embitter others.

"But you'll always be dancing close to the line, struggling between being too heroic or too depressing, too much of a spoil-sport. You're setting yourself up for a fall, because to keep up the intensity you'll have to dance faster and faster and eat up your reserve. It's a pace that few can keep up for very long.

"People are always ready to erase years of good over one mistake. No amount of accolades and 'attaboys' can overcome one 'aw shucks.' When the day comes that you can't deliver, your critics will smell the blood in the water. They will be unforgiving, because you led them to believe you cared more than they did, and when your obsessions give the impression of superiority, they will resent you for making them feel inferior. There is an end to everything, so what will you do, oh lord of language, when that day comes and all are against you...when the words fail you?"

* * *

The sun was shining as Michael followed the blowing winds down into the valley and across Town Creek, which was swollen by the heavy rains. The sunlight sparkled like diamonds and danced on the rushing waters, lighting Michael's path and the hard road to Star's funeral.

He didn't really know what he expected to find at the service. Was he attending out of respect for a life prematurely interrupted, or was it just his cop-curiosity to doggedly follow the cold trail, solve the puzzle, and answer the nagging challenge of "Riddle me this"?

The arrangements were handled by Lawson's funeral home in Tupelo, one of the unique black businesses formed when blacks had been at the mercy of white morticians...coalitions designed to take care of burial services for their own. The funeral parlor was downstairs for visitations, and the funeral director's living quarters were on the second floor.

But the site for the funeral itself was Zion Baptist Church on the east side of Skyline. On his way to the small, black church, he passed an old, dilapidated building on the right side of the road, and he began to think about the sorrows of yesteryear and their intrusion into the present day of mourning.

Michael saw that the rusted mailbox in front of the neglected office front had almost been overtaken by tall weeds. The box sported faded emblems of hooded men, and it matched the look of the building that had once been the local headquarters for the Ku Klux Klan, an organization that had fallen on hard times.

Most of the land on Martin Hill and in the valley east of Tupelo was owned by Leon Smith, the father-in-law of Jake Billings, leader of the local KKK klavern. Jake was married to Leon's daughter, Velma, a volatile woman who had once pulled a knife on Michael and a friend over a sports dispute at a basketball tournament in Shannon.

No charges had been filed in that incident, just as none were filed when her husband shot and killed a black man in his store on West Jackson Street in an argument over a penny. The man accused Billings of shorting him one cent, and Billings, who dealt in guns, produced a pistol and shot him dead. By the time police arrived at the store, a gun had found its way into the hand of the dead man, likely produced either by Billings or sympathetic police.

Michael had stopped at his store for a Coke once, before he knew who he was. Billings was a nervous man with darting eyes. He had a haunted look and the persona of a tortured man. Just before Michael left for Washington to work for the FBI, he learned from local agents that Billings had burned crosses in front of their homes in Tupelo to intimidate them.

The same week that Michael began his internship at the Lee County sheriff's office, Billings and other Klan members were arrested en route to Fayette to kill Mayor Charles Evers. Billings possessed a small arsenal, including a submachine gun and many pistols and shotguns. It was his last hurrah. The Klan was in decline, and by 1970, only a few hundred members had remained in the state—maybe fifty of them were hard-core.

Billings had established a new, violent splinter group, the Knights of the Green Forest, headquartered in Tupelo, but it was quickly marginalized through the efforts of FBI agents. They impersonated United Klan officers and penned letters suggesting that Billings was an FBI informant. A former Klan officer, encouraged by the FBI, openly declared the Klan to be populated by "booze heads and dope heads"; he also called it a "money racket to take in poor, innocent people" and a scam run by "gangsters and psychopaths who belonged in a mental institution."

A contract was issued to kill the man. When he found out, he said, "Like their partners in the Dixie Mafia, once they own you, there's no escape."

Paranoia seized Klan members. Some state police officers, who were found to be members, were finally fired by the governor. Many Mississippians feared the Klan but shunned the Klansmen because of their violent ways. Isolated and skittish Klan members began to suspect even their brethren of being FBI informants.

They looked and looked again, wondering, "Who's really under that sheet?"

In one more confirmation of the ties between the Dixie Mafia and the Klan, Billings' lawyer on the Fayette arrest was Reggie Morris from Columbus, the same lawyer whom Sarge had pointed out to Michael at the Rendezvous Club, calling him a shill for organized crime.

Morris had breezed into Fayette to say that the case against Billings was "undoubtedly not only the weakest case I have witnessed, but this is the first case where there is no case at all." Morris became the preferred mouthpiece of men who made up the compact of violence in the South.

Evers responded to Morris by saying, "The mere fact that Billings got a hearing was great. The fact we gave him a hearing—period—is above and beyond any justice we've ever gotten. We've never got that kind of justice. I know the trial was fair and just."

All of the old memories had come flooding back, connecting the dots and illuminating this moment. It dawned on Michael that he was on his way to the funeral for a black girl in a church built on the land of Klan sympathizers, and that the sign in front of the former Klan headquarters said "Future Halfway House for Broken Souls." He was overcome by the irony and lost in thought...*Hate never wins. Love triumphs in the end.*

Judging by the cars in the church parking lot, the home-going for Star was sparsely attended at the Zion Baptist Church. As he walked toward the front of the chapel, Michael could hear the strains of gospel music, and when he entered the foyer, a sincere, boyish usher wearing a bow tie approached him with an appropriately reverent countenance.

He looked at Michael, the only white attendee, and asked, "Are you a friend of the family or...a relative?"

"Just a friend," Michael answered.

"Then you may seat yourself on this side of the church; we have plenty of room," said the young man, who still had the dry cleaning tag on the pocket of his black suit.

"Oh, here's your program, sir. You are late, but we could arrange a last-minute viewing before we roll the body out, if you'd like," he offered.

"No, thanks," Michael said. "I've already had a private viewing."

As Michael found a place near the back, where he could see all who came and went, there were already shouts of joy and moans of agony mixed in the murmurs of those who crowded the front pews. There were old eyes and young eyes, people on walkers and new babies in strollers, vocal in the throes of teething. These home-going services were occasions of loss...but also ones of rejoicing, because the deceased were bound for a better place.

Michael glanced at the flyer and looked at the schedule for the service.

Home-going for "Miss Stardust"
Musical Prelude
Processional
Prayers
Songs (Hymns of Comfort)
Funeral Readings (Scripture, Poem, Prayer)
Acknowledgements
Reading of Cards & Condolences
Reading of Funeral Resolutions
Obituary Reading
Eulogy or Tribute
Final Viewing
Benediction
Recessional and Interment, or Committal

Sitting on the first pew on the right were James Streeter and all of the girls from the Playhouse. Michael always thought that some of the worst sinners sat in the front pews, "hiding in plain sight," he called it...those loud voices that unconvincingly sang "I'll Fly Away," a sign that they doubted that they ever would.

The girl named Magnolia turned and looked at Michael for a long time. He noticed for the first time that she had an elfin snub of a nose on a pretty face. He also thought that her features didn't seem as harsh as they had the day she challenged him at the murder scene.

Streeter turned to see what she was looking at, and Michael thought that the pulse at her neck became more prominent and the veins at her temple stood out. She turned away, chin on her chest, tears running from her eyes, breathing hard, and stifling a sob.

Streeter looked big and hard, solid as the trunk of the giant oak tree in Parker Grove where Great-Uncle Billy had napped and died of an epileptic seizure. As Streeter stared intensely at Michael, challenging and defiant, Michael wanted to look away first but willed himself not to. It was a measuring game of chicken, but finally, Streeter just nodded and looked back at the pastor walking up to the pulpit.

Across from the Playhouse entourage, Michael saw an older couple. The man had his back to him, and the small woman wore a black hat and a dark veil that entirely covered her face—a look reminiscent of Jackie Kennedy at the funeral of her husband.

The pastor began to pray as a recording of Mahalia Jackson began to play on the tinny sound system. She was singing "Take My Hand, Precious Lord," the song written for her by her mentor, Thomas A. Dorsey, the Father of Gospel Music. It was the same song she sang at Martin Luther King, Jr.'s funeral.

That hymn was followed by her rendition of "Move on Up a Little Higher."

The door to the church opened, briefly flooding the darkened interior with sunlight. A figure moved to the dark side of the church, opposite Michael, and huddled in the shadows with his hat pulled down over his face.

As the service began, some of the mourners began to shout, wail, and grow faint. It grew more intense after the casket was closed, and a sea of handheld fans attempted to stir the heat.

Dr. Andrew Graham, a young pastor with a thin mustache and flawless skin tones somewhere between russet and raw umber, seemed to draw heavily from the emotion and substance of Dr. King's speech in Birmingham after the tragic church bombing. Different circumstances to be sure, but another young life had been cut short, and all of the bereaved deserved answers.

"This afternoon we gather in the quiet of this sanctuary to pay our last tribute of respect to this child of God. She came and went, leaving a hole in our hearts and in this lost world that she walked through. Dust to dust, ashes to ashes, she has left us now, as we must one day leave."

The mourners signified their agreement as they testified and said, "That's right, Yeah, and Amen."

"Star's death speaks to us today, and to all those who seek anonymity behind the closed doors of our churches and the hard, high walls of government institutions—ones that allow predators to prey upon young girls like her. She is speaking to us from beyond, pleading for temporal justice, and she is saying that she and the other lost lambs are worthy of our love and forgiveness."

And the mourners said, "Thank you, Jesus. Yes, Lord."

"And these politicians who cut deals and allow this wickedness to exist, those who line their pockets and look the other way…yes, they will be held accountable—if not now, then in the courts of heaven."

And the crowd grew sorrowful and emotional and said, "Yes, Jesus. They can't hide."

The stern pastor looked right at Streeter and wagged his finger.

"Are they afraid of the gangsters? Are you afraid to know who killed this girl and why? Why do girls like Star take this path to achieve the American dream? Who is it that uses them and robs them of purity like a thief in the night?"

And the congregation asked, "Who, Lord? Who would do it?"

"God will make something good out of this grief. Listen and watch close for His purpose and His divine threads in this heavy burden and smothering blanket of pain. As Dr. King said in Birmingham, tragedy can bring new light to a dark city.

"And so I stand here to say to all assembled here, we must not turn away from Christ and feel all is lost. We must not become bitter and bad like the assassins and murderers who have sold their souls to the devil. Get behind us, Satan, with all your whispering temptations to walk down your dark path."

"Yes, that's right," the Amen chorus shouted.

"We must not seek revenge, though someone has committed a foul deed. We must pray for him. Even this man, as hard as it may be to accept, given the gruesome nature of his crime, can be reclaimed by Jesus Christ. Even this man, even this dark stain on his soul can be washed as white as snow by Jesus. Let's take him down to the river and wash his soul, brothers and sisters."

He had the crowd in the palms of his hands. The pastor was at a fever pitch, his voice rising and falling in a cascade of emotion, and the moaning from the pews was overwhelming.

"Repeat after me, all who grieve for Star, as I read from the twenty-third Psalm: 'The Lord is my shepherd; I shall not want. He maketh me to lie down in green pastures: he leadeth me beside the still waters. He restoreth my soul: he leadeth me in the paths of righteousness for his name's sake. Yea, though I walk through the valley of the shadow of death, I will fear no evil: for thou art with me; thy rod and thy staff they comfort me. Thou preparest a table before me in the presence of mine enemies: thou anointest my head with oil; my cup runneth over. Surely goodness and mercy shall follow me all the days of my life: and I will dwell in the house of the Lord forever.' Amen."

All said, "Amen."

"Death awaits us all—all those who grieve today and those who wrestle with the awful sin we have witnessed. Death is the great equalizer, and time is running out. Do you know Jesus? Will you accept Him? Is there something that you know about this girl's death that you need to release?"

His words had snap to them, but they also possessed a hypnotic lure to confess before it was too late.

He paused, and his face softened. He looked toward where Michael sat and said, "Then, unburden yourself! Set yourself free, and you shall be free indeed. Speak the truth to the Lord's avenger among us today. Jesus, Jesus, Jesus!"

At that moment, the man in the shadows looked suddenly at Michael and cupped his hands over his ears, as if the name of Jesus was too much for him to bear. As he jumped up and ran for the door, his red eyes met Michael's for a moment, and Michael thought, *The whitest face I've ever seen.*

The preacher ignored the loss of one spectator-mourner and began to come down from the mountain to calm his sheep.

"I hope you can find some consolation from our faith that this is not the end. Star is no longer trapped in that blind alley; she is on the road to Christ and eternal life. We've been up to the mountain top, and we've been down in the valley; we've been in the cold winters and the scorching summers, but the God of the mountain top is still God in the valley. And the God of the good times is also the God of the bad times…and it is there amidst our triumphs and our tribulations that He speaks to us and heals us.

"Seek Him today with all of your heart. Say 'Precious Lord: take my hand, lead me on, help me stand. I can't make it without you.' You are never alone, and some sense of purpose in this tragedy must be found.

"Good night, sweet princess. And may the flight of angels take thee to thy eternal rest. God bless you all."

Amen.

The crowd echoed him…Amen and amen.

Michael moved quickly through the front door. He looked left and right and all around the parking lot, but he saw no sign of the man who had run out.

Streeter walked up quietly behind Michael, startling him.

"What's the matter, Deputy? You see a ghost or something? You here to get saved or to save the lost? I confess each time I sin, so there's no need for me to confess anything to you, Officer. And I don't need no Baptist dunking me again, no Methodist sprinkling me, and no priest dousing me with his holy water," he said as he puffed out his chest and bragged in front of his girls, who giggled and cooed.

"Life's just this big stew; everything's connected and joined…now and then, things just float up to the top and you skim them off to use again, or you grab your pistol and kill them before they poison the whole pot.

"You know that girl you seem so concerned about? When I took her to the hayloft for a roll in the straw, we were just two more animals in the barn. It didn't devalue her, but it didn't elevate her status or value, either. That's only for sentimentalists like you, Deputy. You better loosen up them tight red-white-and-blue shoe-laces that are cramping your stroll and take a walk on the wild side.

"I bet your arm is just worn down to the nub from patting yourself on the back about how pure you are. If you want a friend in this old world, Deputy Dawg, you better get a dog. Frosty the Snowman has a better chance of saving my girls from hell than you do!" Streeter taunted.

The Pusher herded his harem toward a waiting limo and shot one last jab over his shoulder at Michael: "Ain't you heard? They done retired the devil—gave him a pension and a solid gold watch. Politicians took over his job of stealing souls. They're so much better at it!"

As he leaned against the limo door, he smirked and said, "Just look at you, Peace Officer! How you gonna keep the peace looking like some kind of 'Pauper Officer'? Here…get yourself some decent threads," he said as he snapped off several bills from a roll of money and flipped them at Michael.

The money fluttered to the ground around Michael's feet like errant butterflies, and Streeter taunted him. "Pick up your money and keep moving, Deputy. That's the secret...outrun the Grim Reaper," he said.

Just then a vortex formed, containing dust, debris, and pine needles. It whipped across the parking lot. The whirlwind picked up the money, swirled around Streeter's face, and drove the girls into the limousine. He spat, coughed, and swatted wildly at the rotating dust-devil cloud around his face. The grit pelted him, stung his eyes, and filled his mouth and nostrils...the money stuck to his face like flypaper.

Michael said, "Don't look now, but I think he's gaining on you."

CHAPTER SEVEN

"Call them the Dixie Mafia. You play ball
their way, or you don't play at all."
—Crazy: Discover the Legend

"Well, I stand up next to a mountain, and
I chop it down with the edge of my hand...
'Cause I'm a voodoo child..."
—Jimi Hendrix, "Voodoo Child"

A soft tap, tap, tap. A louder knock, knock, knock.

Someone somewhere was using a tack hammer, then a claw hammer, to chip away at The Pusher's soul. The hammering he heard as he was waking matched the sledgehammer pounding on the anvil of his brain, just like that old Anacin commercial.

James Streeter was hung over. Slow-death-the-morning-after was what he called it. There was a roaring in his ears that surged in angry waves when he breathed. His throat was parched, and it tasted like a family of polecats had died in his mouth. His body pleaded for water, even though he was nauseated. The smell from the basement lab didn't help. That's where the boys were cooking up the bad medicine for the clubs.

Music still played from the all-night party in the bar that adjoined his office. The musicians greeted the early tangerine sun with a rendition of "The House of the Rising Sun." They tweedled the high notes, tortured the catgut strings on their guitars, and tickled the ivory keys of the old barroom piano parked in the corner of the dining room.

Streeter wrestled with a night of bad decisions. He'd been on the road all night driving back from the Gulf Coast. The Pusher had gone soul-surfing in Biloxi to find Richie Partlow, a hapless wannabe gangster with a heavy shelf of brow and a crooked nose. The word was that whatever needed to be done, you could count on Partlow to "go low." He was a useful hanger-on, but he was also a man who had those loose lips that sink ships.

The Gulf Coast operation was much too lucrative to risk someone upsetting the apple cart, and Richie had been talking freely about some local police who burglarized stores for the mob, supplied fences with high-quality diamonds, and protected call-girl rings.

He found Richie leaving the home of "Junkie Jane," as she was known. She was his girlfriend, or so Richie thought. She was a stripper and a needle picker, and she would swallow a doorknob if she thought it would get her high...but he was in love with her. Richie probably would have forgiven her even if he had known that she'd called local Dixie Mafia bosses to tell them when he would be at her place—but this was the same genius who suffered eye problems and told everyone that he had a detached rectum...

Streeter was asked to drive down from Tupelo to...take care of it. He was the out-of-town fixer, so all of the local suspects would have airtight alibis when police looked hard at them. One of the high-profile gangsters was in a very public poker game at his club, and another was having dinner with his priest in Pascagoula.

Streeter waited in the shadows and subdued Richie at gunpoint. Then he bound him, locked him in the car trunk, and drove him to a garbage dump outside of Gulfport. Streeter wrestled to get his mark out of the car. Richie was heavy, and his guts were roaring and grumbling trying to digest the last supper that he and Jane had enjoyed.

The Last Supper! The Pusher smiled. He liked that.

Streeter finally rolled him out of the trunk and thumped him on the head, and while the man was still alive, Streeter sewed his lips shut with heavy-duty fishing leader. He wanted to make a point and leave a message for whoever found Richie: "Silence is golden."

When the man woke to find himself bound and his lips sewed shut, he looked up at Streeter with wide-eyed terror and began a muffled and weepy whimper.

The Pusher told him, "It's nothing personal, Richie, but you shoulda kept your mouth shut while you were alive. You got greedy. Pigs get fed, but hogs like you get slaughtered."

The man began to cry, to twist and turn and thrash about, tears seeping from his wild eyes. He soiled himself just as Streeter pressed his .22 pistol against the man's right temple and ended his misery with one quick shot.

Streeter began to talk to the man with the fixed stare of forever and justify death, even as the final death rattle of air escaped his victim. It was The Pusher's farewell to his mark, who could no longer hear him, a rambling confession and defense of the life of a killer.

"I've killed maybe a dozen men and two women, but they were all players and knew the game. I've gouged the eyes out of some who saw things they shouldn't have seen, but I've never killed children. What kind of beast do you think I am? Sorry, buddy, but I'm like James Bond...I've got a license to kill," Streeter said.

As Streeter stood over his victim, a mottled-brown stray dog that ate at the dump began to bark and bark after the report of the pistol and his judgment sermon to the dead. So Streeter shot it, too. It yelped once and fell dead.

"Two mutts for the price of one," Streeter said out loud.

He had a long drive back to Tupelo, time alone to drink bad whiskey and think about many things—what he'd just done, the death of Star, that stinking little deputy at the club and his big, black sidekick. But mostly he thought about bloody pitchforks and the deal he had made with the devil. He looked up to see that a red cloud was over the moon, which seemed to be on fire.

If I'm to believe these preachers that dog me, I will one day be like ole Richie—whimpering and whining and begging for my life, even as Lucifer is firing up the bellows of his furnace.

He arrived in Tupelo just as the first hint of dawn peeked over the dome of the Lee County courthouse.

It felt like he had just laid his head on the pillow when someone started banging on his door. The bright morning light sliced through the blinds, stabbed at his bloodshot eyes, and drilled into the pain centers under his brows. He only wanted the pain, thirst, and noise to stop…particularly the hammering out front.

He staggered to the front door in his birthday suit, naked as a jaybird, a tiny blood spatter on his cheek from the night before. He peered through the peephole, trying to focus through bloodshot eyes. There stood Tony "Ace" Connelly, owner of the Ace of Diamonds club in Memphis. Ace, originally from Baton Rouge, didn't look like a happy man on a social call. He looked like a boss on a "counseling mission"—a nice term for a litany of threats and ultimatums.

Streeter decided to let him stew a bit before opening the door. While Ace fumed outside, The Pusher pondered the state of the mob in recent times.

It ain't been a good year for what the government calls the Dixie Mafia. Ole "Towhead" White was gunned down in Corinth. Then George McGann and Gary McDaniel were found murdered—executed. That made three of the four men that Buford Pusser named as the hit men who killed his wife, Pauline. Only one on the list still living is my old friend Kirksey Nix, who I do favors for on the Gulf Coast.

Then that heist went wrong in Meridian, not to mention the planeload of drugs from El Salvador that the "Confederate Air Force" boys lost south of Calhoun City. And then the Mexican police wanted more money, double-crossed us, and arrested some of our mules crossing the border at McAllen, Texas.

The business is getting lots of unwanted attention. That government guy, Rex Armistead, compared us to La Cosa Nostra and claimed there were bodies in every well in Mississippi due to us. He called us the Dixie Mafia. That's when the name stuck. No one ever thought of that until he said it, and the newspapers picked it up. It's just the FBI trying to get more funding. Why, we ain't no Mafia—just friends helping friends. It's just a Southern thang.

He sighed. *Better let Ace in before he busts a gut.*

"Well, howdy! Look what the dogs done drug up to my doorstep here in the All-American City!" Streeter said.

"You took your own sweet time answering the door!" Ace growled from beneath Groucho Marx eyebrows and deep-set, bitter eyes.

Ace looked away suddenly. "Man, you're naked. I didn't drive down from Memphis to see your Southern exposure. Who answers their door that way early in the morning?" he complained.

"Excuse me, sir. Let me get my robe," Streeter said in a mocking tone.

That's what you get for listening to your snitches, those little mice that gnaw away at the marrow of profit and the deeds of real men...run squeaking to the king rat.

When Streeter returned to the den with his robe and two cups of coffee, Ace was seated on the couch, smoking a cigar and looking out the window.

"Tupelo's a nice little town. The revenue has been good. It's peaceful, not too many hassles, and we want to keep it that way," Ace said, sipping on the coffee.

He stopped, looked at Streeter, and asked, "Everything go well on your trip? I hope you had a pleasant journey."

"Yes, it was a fruitful vacation. I heard that song about words on the way home. You know the one that goes, 'It's only words, and words are all I have.' Well, there won't be no more words," Streeter said.

"James, I gotta ask you about this girl, Star, that was killed," Ace said.

"She wasn't nothing...just another needle freak that liked too many men," Streeter said.

"No, James! She was more than that. She had a benefactor in DeSoto County who had a thing for her, and he isn't happy. He's making waves for us in Memphis, and our friends in Corinth and McNairy County are not happy. We've been looking into making a move into DeSoto for our gambling operations. We're trying to get out ahead of our competition, Sonny Walker, who wants to move in there, too. Things just haven't been going too smooth lately with the death of George and Gary.

"Pusser is out as sheriff in McNairy, but he's still nosing around. We hear that some kind of movie about him and us is in the works. Our friends in Nashville and Biloxi think we may have to do something about him," Ace said.

"Man, it was probably that freak of yours, Fredrick, who killed the girl. I told you that I banned his rough stuff from the Playhouse. The girls were afraid of him," Streeter snapped in a loud voice.

"No, it wasn't him, James. He has an alibi. He was passed out in one of the rear rooms of the Bottom of the Blues Club in Memphis. Super Fly verified it," he said.

Connelly paused and leaned toward Streeter in a gesture of confidentiality…or a deliberate intrusion into his private space.

"Some think that you could have done it yourself, James. We hear that you were sweet on her, but I'm not judging you. I just came down here to tell you that these things must never happen again! You understand?" Ace said, raising his voice.

"What you saying, Ace? You gonna buy me an asbestos suit from your tailors in Memphis so I won't incinerate when I bust open the gates of hell? Or are you threatening me with a cheap burlap bag and concrete blocks when your boys drop me in the muddies of the Mississippi? If you gonna kill me, do it now and do it right!" Streeter said, rising out of his chair, fists clenched so tightly that his knuckles seemed to be cracking.

Ace rose to look him in the eye and said, "No, James. If that were the case, I wouldn't be here. The Tiller boys might have been waiting for you on a dark bend of the road on Highway 45 last night when you were driving home from Biloxi, or maybe Freddie and his switchblade might have been lurking in the shadows of your garage when you got home. He's got swagger with that dagger, and he doesn't much care for you, you know?

"If you decide to fight us on this, you might live another twenty-four hours. If you ever decide to betray us and run like a scared rabbit, you know the boys will find you. It may take a while, but they'll find you. You might buy yourself a year at most. We don't care about your color, James—just the color of the money you make. The blood that binds us and our mutual fortunes is thicker than the water of your mama's womb. You got any complaints, just write 'em down and we'll read 'em over you at the landfill where we bury the bodies!"

Ace turned, walked to the door, and paused as he looked back at The Pusher, who was now shaking with anger...but also, fright.

"Keep up the good work, James. You're our top producer in North Mississippi. You have a new girl called Sparkle who used to be at my club in Memphis. The grieving official from DeSoto likes her, too. He will visit the Playhouse to see her at my invitation. When he does, it's always on the house, understand? Have a nice day," Ace said as the door closed behind him.

James Streeter went back to bed and dreamed that he was at the same garbage dump where he had left Richie. The Tiller brothers had taken him there to kill him.

Richie rose up from the refuse and pointed his finger at The Pusher and said, "He's guilty in the first degree!"

More of The Pusher's victims began to encircle him, caress him, and prepare him for the journey to perdition. The men bowed, and the women squealed in high-pitched shrieks.

They began to chant in unison, "Live men, dead men, fertilizer all."

"No, no!" Streeter cried as the hammers cocked on his kidnappers' guns. "Don't leave me here with the dead!"

He broke free of the Tillers, ran the gauntlet of the dead, and fled into the dark night. He ran and ran as fast as he could, gasping for breath. Just as he thought he had it made, he looked back to see if they were gaining on him. When he turned again, he was impaled on Freddie's switchblade.

As the dream life seeped out of Streeter, the maniacal Freddie cackled, "It's payday! Satan is waiting!"

Streeter woke up screaming in his bed as he climbed up and up, away from the vivid images of a bottomless pit that reeked of sulphur—a place of mirrors with a thousand images of his face, all in agony. The seagulls foraging in the garbage dump were still pecking his eyes out, and the dream image of the headline from the Times-Picayune was burned into his brain.

"Pulpy, Bloated Body Found in Gulfport Dump. Note on the Body Read: 'Moved to a warmer climate.'"

CHAPTER EIGHT

"Men seldom bridge the gulf...between
doing and saying...this agonizing gulf
between the ought and the is, represents the
tragic theme of man's earthly pilgrimage."
—Martin Luther King, Jr., Strength to Love

"Twas a sheep not a lamb that strayed
away in the parable Jesus told...And why for
the sheep should we seek and earnestly
hope and pray? Because there is danger
when sheep go wrong; they lead the
lambs astray."—C.C. Miller

Michael sat in the administrative waiting room of the draconian Whitfield State Mental Hospital near Jackson, reading an article in the *Clarion-Ledger*. He had been removed from normal patrol assignments and relegated to the transport details, taking citizens committed against their will to a dungeon masquerading as a hospital.

Whitfield had once been used by state police to imprison civil rights workers and threaten blacks trying to enroll at state colleges. Though there were individuals whose madness had overwhelmed their families and needed help, he wasn't sure that they would find it in Whitfield's antiquated warehousing mentality.

Michael had requested assignment to the Playhouse murder case and asked if he could interview all the employees again. The chief deputy, who didn't particularly care for college-boy interns, refused his request and assigned him to the Whitfield trail...a detail that no regular deputy wanted, a road to nowhere.

The long three-and-a-half-hour drive down the Natchez Trace to Jackson was bad enough, but on his first run, the woman behind the cage of his patrol car screamed, cursed him, and kicked the cage all the way. It seemed the trip would never end. Michael radioed ahead for assistance with the woman, but when he arrived, the poor woman was exhausted and soaking wet with sweat. He felt that he was the one in need of mental evaluation by the end of the trip.

On his second transport trip, Michael's passenger was a young woman who had attended his high school.

Barbara Cochran was tall and lean with long, auburn hair and delicate cheekbones. She had been a cheerleader in school—one of those girls who seemed to be unapproachable, because her beauty intimidated boys. Her wide-set blue eyes were always dancing in those days, though they looked dead to Michael on this trip. She had once carried herself well, with a self-confidence bordering on arrogance. That air and the girl with the bouncing ponytail were no more.

Her family had obtained a court order committing her against her will to Whitfield for a diagnosis of...nymphomania. Michael suspected that it was a convenient judgment that some people secured from compliant judges to subdue or break rebellious spirits in their families—particularly a family where "Big Daddy" was a prominent and pious member of the local community development board.

She was waiting for Michael when he picked her up the morning of December 27th, just as the sun was peeking out from behind a bank of pinkish, cotton-candy clouds. Barbara was alone on her front porch with her small, brown, leather suitcase, standing just behind three plastic reindeers and a jolly old man in red. She looked like a child, a waif waiting for the train to nowhere.

When she got in the car with Michael, she acted as if he had come for her on a Saturday-night date and offered up a Southern-style apology in a little-girl voice. "Hi, Michael. Daddy wished he could be here to see us off, but he's awfully busy at the paper mill, you know? He said to give his best to your family."

On the long drive, she came alive, reminiscing about high school days and asking about this boy or that girl. In the never-ending forested drive along the Natchez Trace, what drivers called the "Green Tunnel," she told him that she needed to use the bathroom. Michael knew that if he allowed her to get to the woods, she would be long gone. He told her to try to wait until the halfway store.

When they arrived, she went to the ladies room. He waited and waited. A park ranger walked by with a questioning "Now what?" look. Michael finally knocked on the door and said, "Got to get going, Barbara. You about ready?"

A little-girl voice from the other side of the door said, "I don't think I'm going, Michael."

Michael leaned against the door and closed his eyes, choking back the pain he felt for her. "Now, Barbara, if you don't come out, I'll just have to break the door down," he said.

He heard the lock turn, and the door opened slowly. She looked like a petulant child, leaking eyes and pooched lips, a lost lamb whose eyes seemed to bleed and plead, "Mister, I've lost my way. Can you help me find the way home?"

She looked up at him with broken blue orbs and said, "I'm not crazy, Michael. I was once as pure as the driven snow back when you knew me, but like Mae West said, I guess I drifted. I like to have a good time, but I'm not hurting anybody."

Michael nodded and said, "I know, Barbara. I believe you."

When they arrived, three burly matrons were waiting and came out to get her. Barbara looked terrified as they led her away, and she looked back at him with puppy-dog eyes that begged him to rescue her.

He wanted to shout, "No! There's been a mistake!" and run to rescue her. It was wrong to leave her there, especially just after Christmas, but he knew he was powerless to prevent it.

Back at her Lee County home, Christmas giftwrap was still in the family garbage cans, along with boxes and cards bearing names of loved ones—all discarded after the Norman Rockwell family photos had been made around the dinner table and the big, green, cedar tree in the den…discarded just like Barbara was today, just two days after Christmas.

He turned in the papers at Whitfield's main office and slumped in a chair to read the *Clarion-Ledger*. He wanted to look away from what he'd seen and been a party to. Drinking a Coke filled with salted peanuts, he read that the exploits of daring drug dealers, planes crashing with loads of cocaine, and tales of organized crime were big news. The expansion of the federal government's role in what President Nixon called the new "drug wars" had Mississippi officials talking about their own war on organized crime, though most insisted there was no such thing in the Magnolia State.

Politicians called for creation of a new agency to counter drug trafficking and the corruption of elected officials in a state suddenly awash in drug money. Impassioned speeches in the legislature cited the need for an agency of "Untouchables"—college students hired on merit, not political patronage or nepotism.

One legislator said it could be called the Bureau of Drug Enforcement or the Mississippi Bureau of Narcotics, a name that began its ascent in answer to another phrase in the new lexicon— the Dixie Mafia.

The paper had interviewed a state criminal-justice panel regarding the influx of drugs and the call by some for what would be close to a true state-police agency, which local authorities had always resisted…often for the worst of reasons.

Sheriff Benjamin Boseman, not exactly a pillar of ethics, was quoted in the article. When asked about agents empowered to enter his county and supersede his authority, he threatened to arrest any state agent who came into his jurisdiction; then he upped the ante by threatening to arrest the governor himself if he tried to interfere with "local affairs."

The sheriff said, "There's been sin ever since Eve bit that apple. People come kicking and screaming out of the womb…out of luck, in despair, and bound for perdition. All this harmless vice is nothing new; it's just the way it is. What we do here is we try to manage it—keep it away from the little white children, you see.

"We ain't got the manpower to regulate lust, so we just try to manage it and get these undesirables to keep their sinful substances in the neighborhoods of the darkies, away from decent people. You might say we're doing God's work," he proclaimed.

Sheriff Boseman's pastor, Reverend William Thomas, was also on the panel, and the article quoted him as asking the sheriff, "Which god would that be, Benjamin?"

The sheriff forgot himself and said, "Now see, that's what I'm talking about. I got a new Cadillac in the garage. Mama's got pretty dresses. The kids are in private school. I got tailored suits and a diamond stickpin for my tie. Everybody's happy up here in DeSoto County...everybody except them dang prune-faced, pious Baptists!"

The article also went on to suggest a symbiotic relationship between the Dixie Mafia and the White Knights of the Ku Klux Klan. An anonymous federal agent said that the Dixie Mafia supplied weapons and explosives to the Klan in exchange for help with safe houses and drug smuggling, even though this was at odds with the Klan's publicly stated belief that the drug trade was a Communist conspiracy to destroy America.

Michael finished the article, took a last, long swig of salty peanut-Coke, and walked briskly to his sheriff's patrol unit. As he hurried to the car, he cupped his hands over his ears, not only to drown out the shrieks of the poor souls confined to this remote corner of hell, but also to mute the insane asylum's radio, which still played Burl Ives singing..."Have a holly-jolly Christmas."

* * *

Rather than returning to Tupelo, Michael drove up the long, barren stretch of Interstate 55 to meet Dixie Lee for a quick bite of lunch in Batesville and to take his required intern reports to Tim Charles at Ole Miss.

Dixie was waiting at a small restaurant near the interstate. The smoky smell of BBQ was wafting over the parking lot as she bounced from her car and ran to greet him when he pulled up. The sun made her hair sparkle like spun gold.

"My, my…you look official in your uniform. Women like men in uniform, or at least that's what Mama always told me about Daddy and his army greens in World War II," she said. Then she hugged him so tightly that she made his voice squeak when he tried to speak.

It was hard to take his eyes off of her. She wore a royal-blue jumpsuit accented by silver bracelets and matching earrings. She had sparkle and sizzle and a full, vital mouth that begged to be kissed.

So, he did.

They ordered sandwiches and talked of yesteryears and current fears as they ate.

"Mama keeps asking about you, about us. She was glad that you came up for Christmas dinner with us, even for just a little bit. My sisters are crazy about you, almost as crazy as I am for you," she said.

She seemed distracted, watching imaginary winged entities drift by…like a little girl blowing bubbles and trying to catch them as they all popped around her. "We seem to be just hit-and-miss lately, don't we?" she asked.

"Yes, seems so. So much is happening," he said.

She took his hand and squeezed it until he thought it might break. Her nails dug into his skin, and the look she gave him almost made him want to look away. But her eyes nibbled at his heart and eroded all the distance that had been between them lately.

"What?" he asked. "What's wrong, Dixie Lee?"

"Oh, I don't know, Michael. I might be bad for you," she said, averting her eyes.

"What do you mean, Dixie? What's going on?" he asked.

"Nothing…nothing really; I just get a little antsy when I don't see you very much. But I'm just being silly and selfish, aren't I? We've got all the time in the world—a million years of sunshine and lollipops, don't we?" she said as her blue eyes grew misty.

"This is the time to be in love, isn't it, Michael? You can feel the world moving beneath our feet! Is it too soon, or is it too late?" she asked.

When they left the restaurant, he lifted her chin, stared into her plaintive and uneasy eyes, and kissed her once more. He held her close for a moment and then stroked her cheeks and brushed her hair.

She smiled and said, "You know, when you put that deputy hat on and walk around in those cowboy boots, you kinda remind me of Clint Eastwood in *Coogan's Bluff*...but skinnier...well, sorta, kinda, maybe," she said, tilting her head to the left and then to the right as she squinted and used her hands to frame his face like a movie director.

She reached up to him, took off his hat; she brushed the hair from his forehead and softly stroked his cheek. "When I see you like you are now, I relax and stop fighting these thoughts in my head," she said.

Then she was gone.

He watched her drive away and thought about what she said. He remembered the dark moods that had consumed her in Washington and how those same shadows clouded her eyes once again. At times, she seemed to long so desperately for the numbing narcotics of the world and its distractions that he thought she might inject the temporal toxins intravenously if she could.

There are fewer exclamation points between us and no commas for peaceful pauses. There seem to be only question marks. It seems we are mired in what and why, and her words of love have begun to sound like an uncomfortable second language...but it will always be too late and too soon to leave her.

* * *

Michael cruised down the streets of Oxford, the broad avenues lined with giant oaks and ancient Victorian-style homes, and the backstreets with cramped apartments housing struggling students.

He turned onto University Drive and, as he entered the campus, he felt a wave of nostalgia wash over him. He felt the bittersweet pang of separation from Faulkner and football…from the innocence and sanctuary of the hushed halls of academia. The quiet incubators of reason and discovery seemed tame but essential to understanding the world he had entered.

His time at Ole Miss was nearing its end as more legions of new students were arriving, naïve as he had been and just as certain that they had all the answers to the great mysteries of life.

He climbed the creaking wood stairs to the upper floor of Bishop Hall and the rear office space of Tim Charles, Criminal Justice Studies Chairman. His bearded professor and friend rose to greet him with his infectious smile and hearty hello.

"Well, the prodigal son returns to the doorstep of my humble office…and in uniform, too! How are the sour hours of life in the real world soaking in, Deputy Parker?" he asked, vigorously shaking Michael's hand and arm like someone pumping the handle of a country well on a hot Mississippi afternoon.

"Have a seat. I've been reading your reports. I went to sleep reading one of them last night. They're not dry like most I read…more like novellas. You might be a writer one day. Who knows?" he said.

"Well, I don't know about that, but writing helps to make sense of it all," Michael said with a shrug of his shoulders.

"I sense that your bubble may be bursting—idealism and naïveté colliding with reality, maybe? Like that moment when a man falls for this beautiful, idealized image of a woman he's met, and then sees her without her makeup and picking her nose…after she's put her teeth in a glass!" Charles said, laughing at his joke and slapping his desktop.

Michael laughed too and said, "Well, it's not at all like the textbooks. No offense."

Tim leaned back in his squeaking office chair that sounded like worn bedsprings. He tugged at his beard and then put his hands behind his head. "You know when I had that first pang of disillusionment—when I thought it was all hopeless, and we were on a fool's mission?" he asked, turning very serious.

"I was a young investigator sent to investigate the murder of a toddler. There was this unwed mother, and her new boyfriend was at her house. Her son, Tommy, began to cry, and the boyfriend told her that he was leaving if she didn't shut her brat's mouth.

"The girl got up, calmly walked to the bedroom where her son was, picked up a pillow, and held it over this little chubby-cheeked boy's face until he got quiet. When I arrived, she told me that she'd had to do something or her boyfriend would have left her.

"She said, 'Tommy's just napping. He just took a long nap. He'll wake up, and when he does, we'll have a new daddy—a real family.' Those moments can just mess up your mind and crush your belief in any good or order in the world...but you can't let that insanity get in your door and take root," he said quietly.

Charles picked up his pen and wrote a big red A on each of Michael's reports, underlined the grades, and punctuated them with exclamation points.

"Oh, you remember Carl from your sophomore class? He just wrote to say that he went in on a drug bust at a flop house. He opened the door to a bathroom and there sat a naked woman. He flushed red, stammered, quickly turned his back, and said, 'Oh, excuse me, ma'am. I'm sorry.'

"Right then, she flushed six ounces of heroin down the toilet. Poor Carl said, 'Now if you're gonna do that, I'm going to have to look at you.' He was lucky that she didn't blow his brains out when he turned his back. Don't let your chivalry get you killed, Michael," he warned.

Charles let out a long, whooshing sigh of exasperation and shook his head.

"My friends in the highway patrol have given me a tip... one that might interest you. Mob-cons out of St. Louis have been in Jackson working a scam out of the Sun and Sand motel. They have local boots on the ground—some willing recruits set free from Parchman Prison by someone in the governor's office who called it an 'early work release,' a kind of 'goons-for-gangsters' work program.

"They target black families. They march up to a house, government-like briefcases in hand, and tell the owners that just before Bobby Kennedy and Martin Luther King were killed, they had come up with a plan to help poor folks put siding on their homes. They make it very personal and intimate and tell vulnerable people that they are on the list to get the siding at the express wishes of Martin and Bobby.

"People usually ask these fakers if they're sure their name is on the list. The Mafia boys say, 'Oh, let me check to make sure.'

"They pick up an official-looking walkie-talkie to radio 'the government' and check to make sure. Of course, he's really just calling another guy down the street.

"'Hey, did Bobby and Martin have the Smiths on their list?' he asks. The guy radios back and says, 'Oh yes, the Smiths are at the top of the list.'

"They tell the families that to receive their free government siding, they just need to sign over a warranty deed on their homes, and that will give the government the legal authority to start on their free siding," Charles said.

Michael shook his head. "You've got to be kidding! Folks buy in to this?"

"Yes! Hundreds of scams are worked in the state every day, and good, trusting people drop their guards and believe people who say, 'I'm from the government, and I'm here to help you.' These are emotional times, and the players are expert manipulators of emotions…and my sources say that they are on their way to Tupelo.

"Now, I know from your reports that you want to investigate that girl's death, but this little tip about the boys who think they're bulletproof might be tailor-made for an enterprising young deputy who might run up on them in Tupelo. Who knows?

"There are many opportunities in your little corner of Internland—master grifters, swindlers, forgers, gamblers, burglars and fences, moonshiners, and drug runners. As a matter of fact, I was told that one of the smugglers just ditched his plane in Davis Lake and waded ashore near Houston, where he was picked up by the Harland gang. The stretch of highway from Tupelo to Corinth, where you work, is the number one auto theft corridor of the country. They steal 'em. They strip 'em. They move 'em.

"Some of these boys learned their trade in Chicago. That's why old-timers call Corinth 'Little Chicago.' Others came out of Phenix City, Alabama, and left there when the going got rough in the '50s.The criminal-political machine there didn't just blur the line between the law and the lawless. They destroyed it," Charles said, caught up in the throes of a lecture to a class of one.

"In Phenix City, there were clubs, brothels, and gambling houses everywhere. Cops were handing out money for the machine to buy votes…kinda like some around here hand out pints of whiskey on Election Day. It was government working hand-in-hand with the mob—hard to know where one ended and the other began…or if there was any difference.

"The city revoked all gun licenses, and the police confiscated pistols and rifles from the law-abiding citizens so that only gangsters had guns. The syndicate went after anyone who opposed them and even firebombed homes. Then a reformer got after them, got elected, and got gunned down.

"The governor sent in the National Guard and machine-gun-toting state troopers. Local police were disarmed by the military. That had never before happened in America. They removed judges, patrolled the streets, and raided clubs. A remarkable number of indictments were handed down—740 of them, actually. That's when some of the mob decided it was time to move on to Corinth, to McNairy County, Tennessee, and to the Tupelo area. Some stayed, but some just passed through after meeting local women and leaving their bad seeds behind. And so, on it goes," Charles said.

He paused and let out a big whoosh of breath.

"Now, will you experience something that openly corrupt? Probably not. But you're going to find a few of your brothers in blue engaging in some selective enforcement of laws, some hassling of suspicious folks in town under the guise of good policing, planting evidence and 'drop' guns on people they shoot. It will all be done in the name of the greater good and proactive police work policing, but they'll actually just be shaking down rival out-of-towners to protect their local benefactors. They want those checks to keep coming—the ones from grateful, syndicate lawyers in silk suits. That's why we work so hard to train you boys to be a hedge against the old ways," he said.

"Some of the old guard in the thin blue line never believed the oath they swore to protect and serve, while others just become lost and decide to say 'Me, too! Me, too!' They want to get theirs after they lose the faith and see the real game. They get a little taste of 'look-the-other-way' money to support lifestyles they can't afford on a cop's pay or to satisfy nocturnal desires that their childhood-sweetheart wife can no longer fulfill. Then, even if they want to get out, they can't. Some try the rest of their lives to find their way back, and they detour down that long, dark road to tortured, sleepless nights, drowning at the bottom of a bottle with cold steel against their foreheads," he said.

He exhaled a long, deep breath of sadness and world-weariness.

"Did you know that a local grand jury indicted Highway Patrol Investigator Charlie Conn in Grenada last year? Not a straighter arrow than Charlie, but Lady Liberty is not always blind, Michael," Charles said.

"And what did he do? What was his crime? Just protecting black kids when the schools were integrated, that's all. They could indict you one day, Michael, and find you guilty of idealism. And all who know you…well…who would doubt it, and who would defend you? No one! Remember that, but know that it's just part of our calling," his professor said.

He smiled broadly and said, "That's the end of the lecture but something that needed to be said."

"You sure know how to cheer a guy up," Michael said with a smile.

"Michael, you don't have to always be the hero," he said quietly.

"I know," Michael answered.

"No, you don't, but that's okay. I didn't know either at your age," Charles said.

"Aw, you're going to do some good and have some fun— hit a lick for what's right, too. You boys and girls are the new generation...not yet tainted, though the system will try to tempt and turn you. We need good young men and women in law enforcement, but sometimes I'm torn. Maybe we shouldn't recruit idealists who want to be heroes into jobs like these. I'm not sure it ever ends well for the idealists," he said.

Charles stood up and shook Michael's hand. "You know, it's a fine line, Michael. You have to stand just far enough away from the muck of the criminal culture and the fire so you won't get burned but not so far away that everything goes cold on you and you get no leads.

"And that line will always be shifting and moving on you. Lots of cops never figure it out. They think they do, but it catches up with them, and they cross into the forbidden zone, rationalizing that it's the only way. Then it's the bottle, the pills, or nyloned flesh to cloud their mocking and accusing minds and to numb their cowardly hearts. Some go quickly; others just cut their own throats slowly by the lives they live, and they just waste away. Don't let any of that happen to you!" Charles pleaded one last time.

"I won't. I promise," Michael said.

Michael thanked him and turned to leave his office.

Charles called out to him as he walked down the hall, "Oh, and one more thing! Remember that your partner will never let you down if your partner is Jesus! He's the only one you can trust in a world where folks want to have their devil's cake and eat it, too."

As Michael left the campus, the shadows were falling on the Grove. The trembling bugler was sighing, the debaters had retired from their oratory, the pursuit of knowledge was hurrying to retire behind the gates of busy dorms, and the lure of hypo- thetical and theoretical musings had given way to the urgency of a new reality.

He was the fledgling standing at the edge of the nest, the campus cocoon where people did lots of thinking about…thinking, and Tim Charles was encouraging him to jump and soar.

The professor he had come to admire and respect was whispering, "Geronimo!"

* * *

Michael drove to Tupelo, turned in his government car, and changed into civilian clothes. Just as the sun was pinking up the sky and shadows were caressing the Lee County landscape, he drove to the pauper's cemetery near Mooreville, where they had buried Star Smith in an unmarked grave that he found only by signs of the fresh turn of earth.

He stood at the foot of her final resting place. A flock of cawing crows flapped lazily by, the howling wind creaked the surrounding pines, thunder drummed a salute to the solemn moment, and far away, the harmony of coyotes barked a hymn to the rising moon.

He wasn't sure why the death of one troubled girl resonated with him to the extent it did. Perhaps it was her short ride from cradle to grave. Maybe it was because even though she was no angel, neither was he. Maybe it was because no one else seemed to care that someone had stolen all she had and erased her from the world. The writing was on the wall, but Michael couldn't read it. The answer was blowing in the wind, but he couldn't hear it.

But he had thought about what Tim Charles had said about fidelity to truth and justice. So he brought buttercups from Pearl's garden and planted them there so that each year when the spring arrived, there would be a sign of hope and resurrection, a cry of victory—the grave had been conquered!

As he was digging a hole for the flowers, he scraped back the leaves and pine needles to find a crude sign and epitaph someone had left for Star: "Too young to die, too old to live."

He drove away in search of Tim's St. Louis gangsters as the night birds began to serenade the dead and the blanket of night fell from the heavens, settling over the forgotten ground like a gentle comforter.

CHAPTER NINE

"You can get much farther with a
kind word and a gun than you can
with a kind word alone."
—Al Capone

"Just giving them the message, 'You're not
welcome here.' "—Ken Fairly,
Mississippi Bureau of Narcotics Director

The radiance of the Holiday Inn's unique sign lit up the night sky in Tupelo, competing with Christmas trees adorning the windows of neighboring storefronts.

The motel's yellow star exploded with mesmerizing, pulsing, electric energy, and the Vegas-like arrow pointed weary travelers and sullen St. Louis gangsters toward a night of motor-court rest and beds with magic fingers for sore backs.

The cheddar-cheese moon peeked out from behind a stream of white clouds and winked at the first TVA city. The thundering melody of an old DC-3 workhorse shattered the silence of the night as it approached Tupelo's small airport.

Giant moths fluttered around the lone streetlight at the back of the motel. A nighthawk screeched above in search of its nightly meal, and a lazy armadillo—a "possum on the half shell," as locals called them—wandered lazily across the asphalt parking lot, which yielded no grubs. The armored throwbacks to another time had crossed the river from Louisiana, much like the grifters from Missouri that Michael sought, but no one had accused the armadillos of hawking aluminum siding.

Michael drifted through the rows of cars with his lights out, shining his flashlight on the tags of each car. Then he saw them, just as Tim Charles had predicted: two cars with Missouri plates. They were carelessly parked with their tags out, showing no respect for local police, who checked lodging sites to intercept unwelcome visitors to the city and to deter practitioners of the oldest profession.

He wrote the numbers on his pad, pulled into an alley, and slid way down in his bucket seat to become invisible and wait. He pulled the collar of his jacket around his neck and slipped on a coonskin cap that Pearl had bought for him when she took him to see Davy Crockett as a boy. It was snug, but the one-size-fits-all still worked, and it was the appropriate disguise for a long night of bear hunting on the wild frontiers of Tupelo.

He thought about his decision to go off the official grid and trust only a few friends at the department in this adventure.

Sometimes you just don't ask for permission; you just do what you must, and ask for forgiveness later if it all blows up in your face.

The streetlight partially illuminated the rooms near the suspects' cars with a foggy, gray light. Shadows of the bugs around the night-light cast eerie images across the lot, and Michael turned on his radio just as Art Roberts began his countdown of the top three songs on WLS in Chicago. The whole landscape seemed to be supernaturally serene and frozen in time.

He thought about all that had happened to bring him to this moment. Being a deputy was not a forever identity, he decided, but it was something that fit him like a glove for the moment.

Just as it began to rain, he looked up the hill at a lighted billboard. It bore an image of Jesus descending into the world. The words beneath it said, "He came on a rescue mission—for you."

Michael was drifting in and out of a fitful sleep where the world was jeering at him. He was fighting fatigue, as well as a chorus of whistles and insults in the scenes from the dreamscape, when he was awakened. The door to one of the motel rooms suddenly opened, and out stepped James Streeter, the owner of the Pink Playhouse. He shook hands with a burly man and drove away in his Cadillac with front side vanity plates that read— "Tupelo Tiger."

Just as a boiling lemon sun burst over the roofline of the motel, the visitors from St. Louis emerged from their rooms—four men and one woman.

One man, who seemed to be first in the gangster pecking order, looked like a *True Detective* magazine version of a mobster, a cartoon sketch of brutality. He exuded a primal, shark-like visage of terrifying emptiness. He had slack jaws, a vicious pit-bull scowl, opacity of the eyes, and a twisted nose. His thick, black hair grew low on his forehead and was slicked back with heavy pomade. Michael began to call him "Jimmy," for the gangsters James Cagney played in the movies. The other men seemed to be lesser, younger versions of mobster number one.

Michael watched them through his field glasses as they loaded the cars. He could read their lips and caught some of the coarse language of men prone to violence and devoid of mercy. These were the men who crushed skulls, lived by a code of blood, and punctuated their casual conversations with guttural growls. They recited crude gut-buster jokes guaranteed to get laughs in the strip joints and nightclubs of the St. Louis Mafia.

Michael couldn't catch all of their words, but what he got was enough...too much. From the way they moved, spoke, dressed, and carried themselves, he tagged them as men without the full range of human emotions. They exhibited only the extremes of emotion—juvenile laughter to brutal anger—born of lives lived amidst nonstop indulgence of the senses, with nothing in between.

The woman who accompanied the men was twentyish and tall with a wilderness of bottled-blonde hair. Her black roots were showing in the long hair piled high in a pyramid on top of her head in a sort of beehive style. Her cheekbones were set high, just under deep-set, dark eyes that gave her a hollow-eyed look. Her wide mouth bore too much lipstick and an air of pouty petulance—a poor man's Jayne Mansfield.

She moved slowly, as if walking through molasses, and her body language showed deference to the men—particularly the one who appeared to be the boss. She had the look of one of the girls scooped up from Mafia strip clubs, but on a downward spiral of drugs. When she hit bottom, they would discard her, because they viewed all the girls as expendable merchandise with no intrinsic value. Michael pegged her as the one brought along to add a feminine presence in order to sell wives and mothers on the siding scam.

The group pulled out of the parking lot of the Holiday Inn and headed toward the homes along North Green Street in Tupelo, a primarily black neighborhood. Michael followed at a discreet distance, though the tourists from Missouri appeared to be lackadaisical about security and careless in watching for tails.

One car with two men peeled off into a cul-de-sac about a half mile down the street from the modest wood-frame house where "Jimmy" and crew were headed.

Jimmy, the second man, and the woman parked and walked up to the sidewalk of the home, where an elderly black couple was sitting in a swing. After some greetings from Jimmy, the couple left the shade of their porch to walk out to the sidewalk gate to talk with their visitors.

Michael watched through his binoculars as the pitch was made. He could almost hear the smarmy words, and he saw the surprise and doubt on the couple's faces, then the fake call on the walkie-talkie to the boys down the street to make it all appear official. He saw the old man go to the house and return with their deed.

Then Michael drove up behind the Missouri car and exited his Mustang. He walked up the street toward the sidewalk siding convention. They all watched him as he approached. He was smiling, but anger was stewing in Michael like a pot over a flame—quick and sharp, like a knife cutting into his gut.

"Hello," he said to Jimmy as he approached the leader of the group. "Where y'all from? Oh, Missouri plates, I see. What are you folks doing in Tupelo?" Michael asked.

"Who wants to know?" Jimmy asked, looking at Michael with a mixture of annoyance and contempt.

"I'm chairman of the local Welcome Wagon, Deputy Parker with the Lee Sheriff's Department, and I just want you folks from the Show-Me State to show me your hole cards," Michael said, flashing his badge.

"We're conducting federal government business with the Knowles family here, sonny boy. You better just run along and police your little hick town," Jimmy said with a sneer of contempt.

His blonde companion, who reeked of alcohol and had a jaundiced look, gawked at Michael through a haze. Up close, her wrists were pale and shallow with the sharp edges of bone evident. She was not a positive model for the ad that claimed "Blondes have more fun."

"I just thought that I should inform our local folks that you weren't sent by the government. You were sent by the godfather to cheat good people out of their homes," Michael said.

The man bristled, turned to face Michael, and forgot the act for a moment.

"You all bark and no bite now, aren't you, poodle? Do you know who I am, Bubba boy? And how many men had to die for me to be me?" the brute threatened as he stepped closer to Michael.

Michael's amiable persona and affable smile faded. His eyes darkened, and his voice took on a sharp, mocking edge.

"Yeah, you're Jimmy Evil—the big slob who can't speak a sentence without using four-letter words, the guy who substitutes talcum powder under his armpits for baths. You're the cheap hood who splashes on dime-store cologne, goes to the girlie clubs that your buddies run, and smokes a big cigar that gives you that rancid breath. You're the little boy who thinks that stogie is a sign of masculinity when the hookers fall all over you—the same girls you pay because no real woman would look at you twice," he said.

Michael's audacious challenge just hung there in the tension-charged air like a rotting, dead skunk frying on a hot highway in a Mississippi summer—the carcass that no road crew wanted to touch. The old couple scurried back toward the safety of their front porch as the man appeared ready to burst with rage.

Michael saw savagery rising in him—a beast ready to attack with startling violence. It was all the man knew, and it was something shocking to the genteel couple now watching it all unfold from the shelter of their porch. Ruthlessness had long ago supplanted anything but a visceral, violent reaction to any threat.

The blonde withdrew from harm's way, and the other male companion began to move his hand inside his coat.

Michael's right hand—and his gun—had always been in his jacket. He moved the now visible point of his concealed pistol toward the face of the second man.

"Think!" Michael said. "Think about living. Think about dying!"

Both men measured Michael, still unsure that this pup had what it took to derail their plans. But they stopped suddenly and stepped back when they saw the imposing figure and smiling face of Tom Jackson come around the corner of the Knowles' home. He was carrying a double-barreled shotgun loaded with buckshot, both hammers cocked.

"You need some help, Michael?" Tom asked with his booming baritone.

"Whew! I thought you'd never ask," Michael said. Then he turned to address the visitors from St. Louis.

"Before you boys irritate Tom and cause his finger to spasm on that hair trigger, forcing him to have to explain to the game warden why he was hunting skunks out of season, I suggest you allow him to collect those nasty pistols you have under your coats. Then we'll radio your friends down the street," Michael said.

Tom took the revolvers the men carried, along with a tiny .25 he found on the woman. After that, encouraged by Michael, Jimmy's companion clicked his walkie-talkie and said, "Al, you there?"

Al didn't answer, but Sarge did. "No, Al is otherwise detained, as my college friend would say."

Michael looked at Jimmy and said, "I'm going to make a deal with you. Give me all the deeds you've already stolen to homes in Tupelo, get out of town, and never come back. You do that, and we'll just forget this unfortunate incident ever happened. Otherwise, it's the smallest, hottest, dirtiest cell the county has that you'll share with the toughest black inmates we have...and news spreads fast about outsiders cheating local folks and disgracing the good name of the dead."

Jimmy was seething and grinding his teeth, but he was trying to find bargaining ground. "We gotta go back to our rooms to get our stuff," he said.

"No, you don't. Someone's already there handling that for you, collecting all those warranty deeds you swindled out of people down in Jackson, too," Michael said.

"You can't do that! This is America," Jimmy snarled.

"I'm glad you reminded me. Your descriptions, tag numbers, and names will be sent to every police station between here and St. Louis. Some highway patrol units are just coming up the street, ready to escort you to the state line, blue lights flashing, sirens wailing...first-class parade courtesies for valued visitors. Welcome to swift justice—which is more than you deserve. Step away from your car, and deposit all of your briefcases on the hood of my car," Michael said with a smile.

"I won't forget you!" Jimmy threatened. His eyes were filled with hate, ageless and evil.

"Thanks! Be sure to write soon and often. It gets boring here in our hick town," Michael said with one last, self-indulgent barb of contempt for the human vultures who gave the birds a bad name.

As the state cars pulled away, Tom followed them in his patrol car. They disappeared over the rise, where Sarge waited with the other "siding specialists." Only a few trusted friends in law enforcement had been invited to the siding soiree.

Michael walked back to the house, up the walk to the porch, and handed the deed to the old couple.

"Folks, here's your deed back," he said.

The diminutive lady with silver hair and weathered skin stepped forward to take the paper.

"My, my, young man…that was like some kind of movie. Thank you! I'm Clara Knowles, and this is my husband, J.B.," she said.

She had an angelic smile, wore a black dress, and had her hair pulled back into a tight bun. Her skin was the color of the brownies Pearl used to bake on chilly winter mornings, and she reminded him of an older Cicely Tyson.

Her husband was a quiet man—a watcher who wore a poker face that was hard to read. Michael suspected that he normally deferred to his wife, at least in public.

Clara studied Michael for a bit and said, "You sure slayed the Philistines, son. You got the jawbone of a donkey under your jacket?"

Michael laughed and said, "No, ma'am, not the last time I checked."

"Are you the deputy who went to the Playhouse to see about that girl who died?" she asked.

"Yes, ma'am, I was one of them," he said.

"You the man that planted flowers on her grave?" she asked.

"Why, yes, ma'am, I am," Michael said, surprised that anyone knew that.

"Why'd you do that?" she asked, with her left eyebrow arched into a big question mark.

"It just seemed the right thing to do. I dug up some bulbs from Grandma Pearl's garden in Parker Grove, something that wouldn't die but might endure," he said.

She looked at him for a long time and said, "Why don't you come on in and let's talk?"

She paused as she turned toward the door and softly said, "I saw you at the funeral. You know…the girl you know as Star Smith was Star Knowles, our daughter."

A stunned Michael followed the couple into their home.

When they were seated, the old lady looked at him for a long minute or two, so intently that it made him squirm.

"Magnolia is my niece, Star's cousin. She told me about you, that you seemed different. She's not as tough as she pretends to be, but she loved Star and tried to take care of her cousin. Star was beautiful but had a limp; one leg was shorter than the other. The more Star tried to fit in, the more she stuck out. Kids can be cruel, and some never grow out of it.

"One day Star and Magnolia just up and ran away from home as teenagers, looking for Mr. Right to fix everything. They found Mr. Wrong, the one they call The Pusher. He passed them around to his friends, like the ones you just run off, and then he convinced the girls that they were tainted—that there was nothing left for them in life but his business that peddled damaged goods. He robbed those sweet girls of their innocence," she said, tears welling up in her big, sad eyes.

"I don't know if he killed her, but he might as well have," she said. "The last thing she told me was, 'Mama, I sleep with my TV on, because I know that someone will slip up to my bed to kill me one night. I just don't want to hear them when they come for me to end it all. I want to pretend, and I want it to be quick. I don't want to have time to think about death and all the wrong I've done, and when I slip off to slumber, I don't want to wake up in this wretched world, Mama.'"

"I'm so sorry," Michael said, hanging his head for a moment. "How long had she been addicted to drugs?"

"Is that what he told you? She was many things, but she was not an addict. She was a diabetic and had to give herself injections every day. If you saw needle marks, it was from the insulin shots and those pricks near her wrist she'd do sometimes to bring the blood to check her blood sugar," the lady with sad eyes said.

Michael's eyes went wide. "But the autopsy report didn't show that," he said.

"The county coroner's budget is tight; got to cut corners somewhere. I guess some deaths don't have the worth of others," she said with no trace of bitterness.

"Streeter would sometimes switch the insulin in her bottles to water when she wouldn't do all that he asked her to. She'd almost be comatose, since she was injecting water, not insulin. Then he'd show up, laughing and mocking her. He'd tell her that he'd give the insulin to her if she would beg him to live, and degrade herself in ways that I can't even bear to think about," she said.

Her husband, the quiet one, looked down and wiped his leaking eyes and nose with his handkerchief.

"Do you think Magnolia would talk to me?" Michael asked.

"Maybe so…we'll see. But right now, I'm more concerned with what God's showing me about you, son. The Shepherd knows His sheep and looks for those that wander away. He's looking for you, Michael," she said.

She looked at him again with an intensity that made him feel she could see right down into his heart.

"Are you saved, Michael?" she asked.

He stammered, looked at the floor for a moment, and said, "Well, I go to church now and then, but sometimes, organized religion is just a little too organized for me."

"But are you saved, son? You got a calling on your life, and He's looking for you now in His lost-and-found department. He's going to call you to walk on the water with Him, but there's gonna be a lot of sorrows in your tomorrows. You're going to need Him," she said, taking his hand and squeezing it.

"I think so. I hope so," Michael answered.

"Do you have a Bible?" the kindly old lady asked him, wet eyes boring into his.

"Yes, ma'am, somewhere, I think. My pastor gave me one when I graduated from high school and left for Washington," he said sheepishly.

She reached over to the end table by the couch and picked up a small King James Bible. "You take this one, son. It is a road map for your soul as you travel through this world. The pharaohs and Pharisees of these earthly temples don't want to love us; they want to own us. The highway of self will run out one day, and He will be there at the end of the road waiting for you," she said.

She took his hands and began to pray over him. He felt something, a spark of the divine, and for a moment he felt as if he was bumping his head on the gates of Heaven, via this extraordinary woman.

"I'm sorry we were too late to save your daughter, Mrs. Knowles," he said.

"Michael, you can't save everyone; even Jesus didn't do that while He was here. He was too late to save Lazarus. But he had a better plan and purpose then, and I'm trusting Him now for that plan and that purpose. We've seen a lot of wrong, but thanks to Jesus, we see that we got the same clothes to get glad in that we got mad in," she said.

As he stood to leave, she came to him and hugged him tightly. Michael was not a hugger, but he didn't freeze up or become uncomfortable as he normally did.

She looked up at Michael and said, "My little girl told me once, 'Mama, I just can't mean much to anyone anymore.' You didn't even know her, Deputy Parker, but you've already proven her wrong."

He drove away thinking about the day, about how he would explain it all to the sheriff if he asked, about the decision that he and the other deputies had made to recover homes rather than arrest the men. He hadn't wanted to risk losing the property to Mafia lawyers while families were on the streets.

But mostly, he thought about what Mrs. Knowles had said.

He pulled over to the side of the road to catch his breath and clear his fatigued mind. As he watched puffy white clouds drift by, he looked up at the giant pine tree above his car. Two limbs of equal length ran out from each side of the tree like a crossbeam. Though the trees should have been mostly dormant, he noticed that sap was pouring from a wound on the tree, already covering and concealing the hurt like a bandage.

He looked again and saw that the sticky sap had stained the tree, but it was not the yellow sap he had always seen.

The sap had stained the tree…red.

CHAPTER TEN

"To understand the world, you must first
understand a place like Mississippi."
—William Faulkner

"Lord, have mercy. Wasn't that a
mighty time? Tupelo's gone."
—John Lee Hooker, "Tupelo Blues"

Zip! Zip! Zip!

Like blurs in a southbound whirlwind, three luxury cars emerged from an early citrus sun and blew past Lee County's youngest deputy like he was parked on the side of the road.

Four days after Christmas, Michael was heading north toward Belden on Highway 78 to serve summons for jury duty. No one had said a word about what happened on North Green Street, and the sheriff's only comment was, "Had a big day yesterday, I hear. Good job! People are mighty pleased, some that might vote for us!"

Michael wheeled his patrol car around in a sharp U-turn to intercept the El Dorado, Mercedes, and Lincoln Continental that were all well above the posted speed limit.

The vinyl-topped, brown El Dorado Cadillac led the small convoy, and a long, black Lincoln Continental limo brought up the rear. In the middle of the mini-parade of opulence, sheltered by the two other cars, was a shiny, new gray Mercedes with four occupants.

As Michael drew near to the cars, he wondered if the big cars with out-of-state plates might be related to the gangsters from St. Louis.

He radioed the dispatcher. "Earl, I am following three cars with Tennessee plates, traveling east on Highway 78 at a high rate of speed. Stand by as I get the tag numbers for a registration check," Michael said.

The radio erupted with the sounds of an anxious Sheriff Simpson.

"Negative on that, Michael. Peel off and let that one go. Resume your regular duties," he said.

Scratching his head, Michael eased off the gas as the cars left him behind.

Before he had time to think about how unusual that was, Earl, never one to follow procedural jargon, radioed Michael in his usual informal manner.

"Hey, Michael, are you still out there near Belden? The animal shelter called. They say some crazy guy's there and won't leave. They want us to come and get him."

"10-4. Will do," Michael replied, still consumed with curiosity about the strange cars and the stranger behavior of the sheriff.

When Michael arrived at the animal shelter, the harried director rushed to meet him, pointing to the waiting room and a disheveled man who looked beaten down by life. The man was hunched over in his chair, wringing his hands, and raking his fingers through his long, graying hair.

"You got to do something, Deputy! We can't deal with him!" the fidgety director demanded.

"What is it that he wants?" Michael asked.

"You let him tell you. It's crazy. *He's* crazy," the director sputtered and stammered.

Michael walked over to the man. He recognized him from an article in the *Daily Journal* and had seen him around town with his giant board of protest anchored to the roof of his car. The IRS had moved against him and taken everything he had…his home, his business, and all of his assets. He claimed that he was on an enemies list for his political protests against the war.

His wife had finally left him under the weight of it all, taking their children to parts unknown, and no one would hire him now. He was a broken man, and pain radiated in waves from his fractured soul.

"Hello, sir," Michael said. "I'm Deputy Parker. You're Ralph Herndon, aren't you?"

The man looked at him with empty green eyes and nodded, robot-like.

"Well, Ralph, what is it that you want the animal shelter here to do for you?" Michael asked softly.

"I just need a thousand cats. Then everything will be fine," Ralph said earnestly.

"Wow! That's a lot of cats! What are you going to do with a thousand cats, Ralph?" Michael asked.

"I'm going to turn 'em loose in Washington! There's lots of rats up there wearing suits and ties!" Ralph said.

"I see," Michael said. "Well, how about I treat you to lunch at TKE Drugstore downtown, and let's talk about it over some BBQ and potato salad."

"Okay," Ralph said.

Michael walked over to the shelter director, who appeared exasperated. In disbelief, she asked, "You're not going to arrest him?"

"No," Michael said to the stunned director. "He's not crazy. He just didn't ask you for enough cats!"

After a lunch of Southern-cooked everything, Ralph agreed to wait until the shelter had sufficient cats to rid Washington of all of its rats. Michael told him that it might be a while and to call him if he needed someone to talk to.

As they parted, Ralph looked like a balloon, one drained of all its air, but with a fresh breath or two. He said, "Thanks for listening. No one will listen to me anymore."

Michael called a man he had worked for part-time in college and asked him if he had any delivery jobs open at the local Caterpillar supply house. When asked if the man had any experience with CAT bulldozers, Michael said, "Let's just say he knows more about how important cats are to this world than anyone I know!"

* * *

After his early lunch with cat-man, Michael passed the Travelodge motel on North Gloster and saw the same three cars that had passed him on the highway. Some intense men, who had the serious look of private security, were scouring the parking lot for danger and hustling two men and two women into the waiting gray Mercedes.

Michael pulled over to the gas station across the street and watched all three cars pull out and head downtown. He followed the cars and tailed them right to the back lot of the sheriff's department, where he lost sight of the caravan as the electric gate opened and closed. He passed by and parked out front.

When he walked in the front door, no one was to be found. Not a creature was stirring, not even the radio operator.

"Hey, where is everybody?" Michael called, but no one answered.

He walked toward the back where prisoners were processed, where he could hear the murmur of voices behind closed doors.

Just as he opened the door, he saw Earl fingerprinting a man—a very recognizable man in a black mink suit with a black shirt and white tie. He wasn't *in* chains...he was wearing chains around his neck and on his belt—chains that appeared to be real gold.

Everyone in the room got quiet, and the man looked up at Michael and said, "How you doing? I'm Elvis Presley."

Michael instinctively extended his hand, as all polite Southerners do, and Elvis held up his inky hands and shrugged apologetically.

"Ah, I don't think you want to shake hands with me right now," he said.

When he put his hands up, two guns were exposed. A .357 Colt revolver rested in a white shoulder holster under one arm, and a .357 Smith & Wesson was in the holster under his right arm. Both bore ornate, engraved handles.

Just then, the sheriff rounded the corner with Janelle McComb, who lived in Tupelo and wrote poetry for Tupelo's famous favorite son. Mary Edwards Carnathan was also there. She worked with Janelle at Mont's Tobacco, and had once lived near Michael in Parker Grove.

"We're presenting Elvis with a badge today. He will be a Lee County special deputy," the sheriff said when he saw Michael.

He turned to a couple behind him and said, "This is Shelby County, Tennessee, Sheriff Bill Morris and his wife, Ann, who came down from Memphis," he said.

Everyone stopped chatting and waved.

In the other room, Michael could see Priscilla Presley in a Western-style jacket with fringed cuffs. Two of Elvis's bodyguards stood near her. Tupelo police officer Guy Harris, a childhood friend of Elvis, was there with his wife and daughter, and Janelle's husband, Roy, was talking to other guests.

After Elvis cleaned his hands, official photographs were made in front of the lineup board, and the sheriff pinned the badge on the lapel of Elvis's coat. Janelle and Louis Spigner, a deputy, were snapping candid photos. Elvis asked one of the bodyguards for his briefcase, a brown Samsonite piece. When he opened it, there were sleeves full of money of all denominations.

Lee County's newest deputy watched as Elvis pulled out a small bag with drawstrings. "These are red rubies given to me by a queen of a foreign country, and these diamonds are from South Africa," Elvis said.

Elvis said that he had ordered a giant replica of a police badge, and he began to explain to the sheriff that he wanted jewelers to mount the stones in the replica. The sheriff had provided some finger foods for his event, but Elvis gave money to his bodyguards to buy food for everyone—hamburgers, cheeseburgers, and fries from Johnny's BBQ and the Dairy Bar in East Tupelo.

The sheriff walked back to the front with Michael and said, "Now you see why I didn't want you stopping those cars. We had to scramble to find a badge to present to Elvis. Louis gave up his badge for the occasion. It was short notice that Elvis was coming. He's kinda impulsive. They were all at the wedding of his bodyguard, Sonny West, last night. He gave Bill Morris that big, new Mercedes, and he just told everyone that they were all going to Tupelo.

"When he walked into the department today, he kissed all the women who were waiting here to meet him. Janelle presented him with a Good Neighbor Award and introduced him to Mary Carnathan. When he learned that Mary had twin girls, he asked her to bring them up to Graceland. Because he had a twin brother, twins fascinate him," he said.

He then began to whisper conspiratorially. "Elvis wants to run out to East Tupelo to see some relatives and Bill's grandmother. He wants me to help him lose his security detail so he can be alone for a while and maybe run over to Itawamba County to see Bill's parents.

"If you see any of the city police, don't tell them about this. Guy Harris is the only one from over there that he wanted here. He grew up with him. He doesn't want anyone in the city government to know he's here. We had to keep his visit very quiet. He's never liked the city fathers since that dispute over where the money went that he raised for the youth center in East Tupelo.

"Anyway, we may be scarce for a while, Michael. Just stay on call for us and patrol the county, and I'll relieve you before nightfall," the sheriff said.

With that admonition, the sheriff closed the door, and Michael stood alone in the hallway, wondering if it had all really happened. He thought of Dixie Lee, who loved Elvis. She would have been thrilled.

* * *

As the afternoon shift wore on, Michael seemed to be catching all of the calls, including an attempted breaking and entering near Mantachie. As he slowed to merge onto Highway 78 East, a familiar gray Mercedes—unaccompanied by the El Dorado and the Continental—passed him headed east. Elvis looked at him from the passenger side, did a double take, and looked again. He smiled in recognition and nodded.

It seemed that the sheriff had been successful, and Elvis had lost his security detail. Michael pulled out to go in the same direction, but he quickly lost sight of the Mercedes.

When he arrived at the gravel drive leading to the address of the attempted break-in off Highway 371, he saw a small, home-made sign marked with crude letters: "Welcome to our little patch of hell. Population 2, me and the devil."

As he neared the home, he could see the black marks on the white paint of the front door, made by something like a greasy crowbar. He radioed the address and a tag number on an ancient Ford, and it all came back registered to a Paul and Rosemary Walsh.

He walked around the exterior of the house, amidst the clutter of old tires, a rusted pickup on blocks, and an abandoned, rotting couch sitting beneath some pine trees.

He noticed that a front window panel was shattered, and some of the remaining glass had small holes in the panes. The glass shards were dispersed on the front porch in a manner that suggested the window was broken from the inside, possibly by pellets from a shotgun.

The complainant, Rosemary Walsh, walked out of the house to greet him with a dry, "Howdy. You the one they sent to catch this criminal?"

Rosemary was a pudding-faced woman with small, bitter black eyes and dirty, stringy hair dyed the yellow-green of the sewage ponds off Eason Boulevard in Tupelo. Her voice was like rusty hinges on an old door, creaking and squeaking her country twang, and she sported a prominent black eye.

"Yes, ma'am, I'm Deputy Michael Parker. When did you realize someone was trying to enter your home?" he asked.

"Oh, I was inside this morning, and I heard him out there with his crowbar, just a-prizing on the door, grunting and cursing. I just fired my little .410 shotgun out the front window, and he hollered and ran off...a little bird shot spooked that chicken," she said.

"I see," Michael said. "Mrs. Walsh, you live here alone?"

"I do now, ever since Paul went hunting on our anniversary, him and that dang ole hound he loves so much. That man has always been 'flicted, not right in the head. After I gave him and that mutt something to think about, I padlocked the doors and told him that he weren't welcome here no more," she said.

"Ma'am, are you saying that it was your husband who tried to force his way into the house?" Michael asked.

At that moment, a muddy pickup with oversized tires roared into the driveway. It was driven by a man in a red hat, and riding shotgun, head hanging out the passenger window, was a bluetick hound.

The man, wearing a camouflage hunting outfit, stepped out of the truck, slammed the door, and bellowed, "Ma, what you done? You dang near kill me with that shotgun, and now you call the law on me?"

Paul Walsh was a sour little fellow with the air of a boy-man who had probably not matured much since puberty—stuck on stupid with a low attention factor. His once-fiery red hair was receding. He had a stubble of beard stained by Red Man on his ripe jaw and a big band of fat around his middle. The sheriff's warning echoed in Michael's mind: "There are some strange brews cooking in the backwoods of the county—shiners and sooners. The shiners will shoot you to protect their shine, and the sooners might shoot just because you ride down into their hollows. Be ready for anything!"

As the man approached the porch and Rosemary with clenched fists, Michael rested his hand on the iron on his hip and said, "Whoa, that's far enough, sir. Let's talk this thing out…Mr. Walsh, I presume?"

The man stopped, spit a mouthful of brown juice off to the side, wiped his mouth with his shirt sleeve, and said, "Oh, I didn't mean no harm, Deputy, but she's just been treating me so mean."

"Why don't you tell me your side of this story," Michael said.

"She just went crazy the other day when I went hunting," he said.

Rosemary chimed in, "On our anniversary!"

"Well, I forgot," he said. "So shoot me! Oh wait, you already tried that!"

Michael sighed and said, "Just tell me what happened, Mr. Walsh."

"Well, I come home with plenty of wild game, a truckload for me and Mama to eat. Uh, say…you ain't associated with the game warden, is you?" he asked.

"No, just give me the details," Michael said.

"I come home to my house, and she won't speak to me and won't tell me what's the matter. She's just all swoll up like a tick on a deer's rump. Then Blue gets sick, starts to moaning, sneezing, eyes running, and everything. It was awful. I look on the porch and there is Rosemary laughing her head off. I ask her what was so funny. And, Deputy, she told me that she dusted Blue's doghouse with cayenne pepper. She's probably ruined Blue as a hunting dog! I told her that making my poor dog sick wasn't funny, and I asked her if her anger was satisfied, picking on a poor, dumb animal. She laughed and asked which dumb animal I was talking about. After that, she got quiet and just watched me and didn't say nothing, and then I began to feel sick myself," he said.

"She was laughing harder, and I asked her, 'Woman, what have you done?' Then she told me that she had swished my tooth-brush in the toilet bowl just before I used it! I ran off into the woods and puked my guts out until my toes went numb!"

Michael was trying not to laugh.

"Well, serves you right. I cried all day the day you left me…the anniversary of the day you told me that I was the prettiest girl east of the Mississippi and that you would always keep me high on a pedestal," Rosemary said, now softening.

"And my little joke gave you no right to hit me, either," she added.

"Aw, I'm sorry, baby," he said, reaching out to her.

"I am too, hon," she answered.

"Come here, woman. Let's swap some spit!" the romantic replied.

They embraced, and he held her tightly around the waist, his mouth just an inch or so from her snuff-stained teeth, the round of her hip pressed into his. Then he crudely fastened his lips onto hers. The lovers looked like two guppies, both now totally ignoring Michael.

At that tender moment, a gentle breeze whistled through the pines, a flock of doves flushed from the side of the house, ole Blue began to howl from the front seat of Paul's truck, and Michael could swear that he heard the strains of "Love Is A Many-Splendored Thing."

"Well, I'll be going now. Y'all take care," Michael said, clearing his throat. "Please keep the peace, call the vet about your dog, no more punching your wife, no more shooting shotguns at your husband, and Mr. Walsh, I'd suggest some serious gargling with a jug of Listerine after your toothbrush experience."

Walsh left his sweetheart's embrace and walked to the car with Michael. He stopped and looked back at Rosemary on the porch.

"Thanks for coming out. Sorry to bother you. She's a witch, Deputy, but she's *my* witch. What can I do? I love her. The first time I saw her, it was at a distance and a funny angle. I thought she was beautiful, but it was one of them octopus illusions," he said.

"An octopus illusion?" Michael asked with a smile.

"Yep, that's what it was, but it was too late when I realized it. The toothpaste was out of the tube. There's nothing left now but to live with her in *bliss and kiss* until death do us part—or until we're old and fat and all them phe-ro-mones have dried up. I read about them in that *National Enquirer* story called 'I Cut Out Her Heart and Stomped on It.' I guess we won't have nothing left to say to each other then, and it'll be time to lock up all of her shotgun shells and sharp knives," Walsh said with homespun philosophy.

"Sometimes loving her is like trying to hug a porcupine or squeeze a skunk. Marriage vows and promises are hard to keep, ain't they? That reminds me, I guess I had better take down that sign I made about our home being hell, huh?" he asked rhetorically.

He clamped his big hand on Michael's shoulder and said, "Deputy, despite it all, love overflows my heart. I'm just hubcap-deep-to-an-eighteen-wheeler in love with her."

* * *

After Michael bade farewell to Romeo and Juliet, he headed to the next call that awaited him in the Brewer community outside of Shannon.

Mrs. Dottie Farrar had requested a deputy come to her house, where she claimed a utility worker's neglect had caused her to trip and fall.

Michael pulled into the drive of the modest brick home just down the road from the Brewer Methodist Church. There was a South Central Bell truck parked in front of her house, and a somber-faced technician was working on a new drop line running to her house. Michael spoke to him, but he didn't appear to be in a sociable mood.

Michael walked up to the door and noted that there was a brand new Cadillac in the open carport. The curtains around the picture window by the front door were open, and he could see one of those new giant-screen, rear-projection televisions that he'd read about—the ones that carried hefty price tags.

He then saw a robust, fortyish woman with jet-black beauty-parlor hair, who he assumed was Dottie Farrar. She was scurrying around her house, cleaning, bending, and lifting objects—the very picture of good health.

When Michael rang her doorbell, he saw her stop and run to the back. She emerged a different person—stooped, with the gait of an elderly woman and sporting a neck brace. She walked slowly with the aid of a cane.

"Yes?" she asked as she opened the front door with a grimace.

"Deputy Michael Parker, ma'am. You called for someone to come out about an accident?" he asked.

"Oh yes, thank you for comin' so promptly. That Bell worker over yonder strung out some wire low to the ground without warning, and I tripped over it as I was gathering some fruit from our trees for my poor sick daughter," she said, scowling in the direction of the telephone man.

"I see. I hope your daughter recovers soon. Is it one of these flu bugs going around?" Michael asked of the woman with the exaggerated, *Gone-with-the-Wind* Southern accent.

"Oh no, De-pu-tee, it's the traw-muh and physical damage from the fish bone that lodged in her throat when we were eating some fish sticks. The settlement the manufacturer gave us will never truly compensate for her pain and suffering. Her life is just ruined. She is scarred for-evah!" Dottie said.

"I'm sorry to hear that. Is your neck brace from the bad fall you took this morning?" Michael asked.

"Oh no. That's from the auto accident that I had, an unfortunate encounter with that careless postal carrier. My ah-turn-nee… I mean my doc-tah told me to wear it at all times," she said.

"Especially outdoors…in public, I bet," Michael said.

"Why yes…oh, but indoors, too," she replied with a sweet smile and quizzical look. *Is this boy playing with me, trying to be the clever little deputy?*

"I see," Michael said. "I need to get some background for my report. Are you employed or just staying here today with your sick daughter?" he asked.

"Oh no," she said. "I can ne-vah work again after that tragic accident in Albertson's in Memphis. It's that big, fine supermarket, and I was shopping there one day and took a big fall… right in front of the bread section, where someone had mopped and left a puddle of water on the floor," she said.

She smiled and said, "I busted *my* buns right in front of *their* buns, you might say. I will nev-ah be able to be productively employed. Their insurance company was very kind to me."

"Well, you certainly have had some bad luck. Let me finish my investigation, and I'll be right back to give you that report you'll need for any court proceedings that might follow this unfortunate incident," he said.

Michael walked over to the telephone tech and asked, "Would you like to give me your side of the story?"

"I sure would! Mrs. Farrar called to say that her drop line to her house was down and her phone was out. I got here, and sure 'nough, the drop line was not only down from the pole to her house...it was just gone altogether," he said.

"Gone from the house and all the way up the top of that pole?" Michael asked.

"Yep...I've never seen anything like that. So, I attached the new line to the eaves of her house and had just walked over to the pole to reconnect it, when I hear this bloodcurdling scream and turn to see her sprawled in the yard, moaning and cussing me. There was no way she could've tripped on that wire! I ain't done anything, Deputy, and I sure don't want this on my work record. I need my job!" he said.

Michael said, "Just do your job, and I'll get back with you."

He walked out behind the house and looked around. Then he saw it in the tall grass beneath a giant, old apple tree—the long black line lying amongst the bee-infested spoiled apples. The drop line had been severed and bore the pinched, diagonal cuts of a wire cutter.

He returned to her front door and knocked.

Dottie came to the door and asked, "Do you have my report now? I'll need that for any civil mat-tahs that might come up."

"Well, not quite," he said as he held up the old drop wire.

"Do you have a pair of wire-cutters, Mrs. Farrar? I need to take a look at them and maybe send them off for analysis to compare to the marks on this wire," he said.

She paused for a long, pregnant moment. He could see the wheels turning in her conniving mind. "Oh now, Deputy Parker, one should not judge another, you know. That's what the Good

Book says. To each their own…'Bee to the blossom, moth to the flame; each to their passion, what's in a name?' as my favorite poet, Helen Hunt Jackson, wrote," she said with a proper, practiced smile.

"Yes, ma'am, but she also finished that poem with 'The trees in apple orchards with fruit are bending down.' I'm not judging you, Mrs. Farrar, but I am trained to observe fruits. That's when I found truth among all of your rotten apples, beneath your tree of good and evil out back," he said, his eyes never leaving hers.

The telephone man had reattached the line and had stopped to watch Michael. The man in the truck with blue-and-gold stripes was no longer down in the mouth. He was smiling.

But Dottie was not smiling. There was fire in her eyes, her tiny fists were clenched into red balls, and her genteel, syrupy drawl had disappeared.

"You think you're something, don't you, sonny boy? I saw that article in the paper on you, college boy. Ole Miss teach you to disrespect poor widows in your fancy classes?" she snapped.

"No, ma'am…just how to recognize a wolf in a cheat's clothing," he said.

She slammed the door in his face with a bang so loud that it surely must have made her daughter cough up that big ole fishbone.

The telephone man was grinning from ear to ear.

"Oh, man, that was one of the best things I've ever seen. It almost makes my worry worth it, just to see that. Thank you," he said.

"No, thank you for all you guys do to keep our phones working for rural folks who need them for real emergencies, for sons and daughters who are really sick. There will always be more victims of grifters like her—companies who pay up and then raise their prices and make the rest of us pay—but not here, not you, and not today," Michael said.

* * *

As the shadows began to fall over Lee County and the sun faded from pink to the blue of dusk, he realized that he had not seen or heard any other deputies in hours. Then the dispatcher said that there had been a mix-up.

"You're the only deputy on duty in the county until further notice, and we got word that there may be some trouble down at the wrestling arena near Verona tonight. The owner wants someone to come down. He says lots of wrestlers are coming down from Memphis, and there's some bad blood with some of the local promotors. I'll get you some relief as soon as I can find someone. Till then, it looks like you and me both are working double shifts," Earl said in that radio voice that seldom brought good news, but kept the shift interesting.

When Michael arrived at the wrestling venue, cars and pickup trucks were parked all around the old factory building.

Wrestling had spilled over from Memphis to Tupelo at a makeshift sports venue known as the Bear Trap near Verona on Highway 45 South. Pickups with rusted fender wells, bald tires, and tags from Lee, Itawamba, Monroe, Pontotoc, and Tishomingo counties were layered around a wrestling hovel consisting of plywood walls, old linoleum floors—premium prices earned a rat-gnawed, wooden seat at ringside, while rough bleachers sufficed for the cheap seats. The promoters figured that if the warring wrestlers tore the place down to the ground, not much would be lost, and it could be rebuilt at little expense.

The wrestling connoisseurs in their overalls, cowboy hats, and sack dresses continued to pour into the joint. Out front, a portable sign with a blinking arrow said, "Brawl in the Bear Trap. Check your guns at the door."

Michael walked through the crowd and heard patrons talking about a new young wrestler that might be on the bill—a former disc jockey from Memphis named Jerry Lawler. They gushed about how he had been trained by everyone's favorite, Jackie Fargo.

Inside, Michael spotted familiar faces, including Jerry Brown and Judy Montgomery. He had gone to high school with

Judy. Jerry was a local truck driver for Shumpert Truck Lines, and Judy worked at the Tupelo Water and Light Department.

The wild matches began with lots of huffing and puffing and fancy moves. The blue-jeaned crowd called for more...for blood. Like the spectators of the Roman gladiator contests, they were on their feet to cheer their favorites and curse the villains, "heels," as they were known.

Midway through the second match, some dirty moves were made just when the hapless referee turned his back, and one wrestler was banged over the head with a folding chair. A chorus of boos and jeers greeted the action and the ineptness of the inept-on-purpose referee.

The victim's partner, detained by the ref in the far corner, protested mightily. Frustrated, he suddenly brushed past the striped shirt, punched one of the tag-team members, grabbed the chair-wielder by his long hair, and threw him over the ropes right at the feet of Judy and Jerry.

A homemade spotlight followed the action and panned across Judy. She screamed bloody murder when the big man in boots and tights bounced over her and banged into the chair next to her. His opponent was in hot pursuit, huffing, puffing, and cursing as he chased his opponent past Judy and down the aisle, swinging at him with a giant broom in wide, sweeping arcs.

At that moment, an older man, who had driven in from Belmont for the big wrestling event, jumped out of the bleachers, brandishing a knife and swearing to even up the odds.

Jerry stood up and said, "Uncle Tommy, is that you? What're you doing? Give me that knife, and get back up in the bleachers. You're going to have a heart attack!"

As he was corralling Uncle Tommy, the event promoter ran up to Michael and protested, "That ain't in the script. Aren't you going to arrest that man?"

Michael smiled, shook his head, and said, "No, Jerry's handling it just fine!"

By that time, all four wrestlers were on the floor, fighting, swinging, and swearing. One grabbed a giant jar of pickles from the concession stand and hurled the jug at another man. The glass jar shattered, and pickles littered the floor. The manager of one of the tag teams tried to intervene, but he slipped on pickle juice and was slammed to the floor by an opposing wrestler, his fancy snakeskin suit ripped off.

As he was sprawled across the floor, covered in what looked like blood, his assailant stood over him, hand over his heart in mock reverence, and said, "He just shined himself to death in that suit."

Finally, the combatants were hustled out by private security, and Michael stepped in front of some angry patrons eyeing the referee, who was trying to make his own swift exit. In a far corner, a short, wide man had wedged a tall man against the bleachers and was trying to put him in a headlock as he mimicked his favorite wrestler and pounded him in an arching hammering motion, like chopping wood.

Before Michael could get to them through the crowd, it was over. The rowdy crowd filing out of the shabby building off the beaten track had hooted loudly, cursed fans of the black hats, bought enough Budweiser beer to float the *Titanic*, and gathered tall tales to tell and retell on the factory assembly lines. Some stories would be enhanced by the bad whiskey the storytellers had used to doctor their Cokes.

The two men who had been fighting walked out together... best friends again. All was forgiven. A man attempted to console his girlfriend, who was crying because her favorite knight of the ring had been injured and robbed of his tag-team title. Amidst the sobs that racked her body, she told him that she would never get over seeing "Big Bad Bubba" treated that way.

Her boyfriend supported her as they walked, patting her on the back and offering her some "tell-it-like-it-is, pull-no-punches" words of comfort.

"Darling, I know it hurts, but this too shall pass one day. It may pass like a giant, jagged kidney stone on fire and feel like barbed wire being dragged through your guts...but it'll pass, honey."

* * *

As he pulled away from the Bear Trap, a storm blew in. The cold wind dropped the temperature and rocked his car, and the rain began to fall in torrents.

The dispatcher broke the radio silence and said, "Michael, the worst of the storm just passed through Nettleton. Lots of damage. They're requesting backup, and you're still it. It's raining cats and dogs...Persians and poodles everywhere, they say!"

Michael ignored the bad joke and said, "10-4...on my way."

Trees were down across a major street in Nettleton, as well as a hot power wire, too. When he arrived, Michael donned his coat and rain gear to stand in the rain and direct traffic until the power company crews came and secured the road.

Michael finally returned to his car, still shivering from the bite of the icy rain, just as the dispatcher paged him. "Michael, if you're done in Nettleton, we got a prowler call in the Skyline community at 139 Skyline Drive. A woman there, a Miss Martha Rogers, says someone is outside her house, peeping Tom maybe."

When Michael arrived at the woman's house, he cut his lights as he approached the address and peered into the gloom for any signs of activity. He then panned the area and the woods behind her house with the spotlight attached to the cruiser. Seeing nothing moving, he parked and exited his car, now low on fuel from canvassing the county all day.

The drizzling mist-drops, remnants of the storm, appeared silver in the fringe of the headlights as he walked toward the house, Kel-Lite flashlight in hand as the shrill cry of a killdeer broke the silent night.

Martha Rogers, a young woman in her early twenties, came to the door in her housecoat, clutching it to her throat and glancing about with nervous eyes.

"Deputy Michael Parker, ma'am. You called about a prowler?" he asked.

She nodded. She was about five foot six inches tall, 140 pounds or so, Michael guessed. There was something about the look of her—the slope of her knitted brow above nervous green eyes, the curl of a long and convex upper lip above her prominent, chattering teeth—something that his police instinct warned might be more than nerves…maybe trouble instead.

She said, "Yes. I didn't actually see him, but I could feel him, you know? I'm here all alone and helpless. I just needed someone to check it out."

Michael asked her if there was any reason to think someone was stalking her, but she said no. He checked all of her doors and windows again but found nothing. He looked in the leaves and mud around all entry points but saw no evidence of anything that had been disturbed recently.

When Michael returned to the front door, he advised her to check her locks and to call the department again if she heard or saw anything suspicious.

"It just makes me feel so safe and protected that you came, Michael. Thank you," she whispered in an earnest tone.

Michael resumed his patrol, and thirty minutes later, the dispatcher called. "Michael, that woman called again and said she thinks she heard something. She asked for you…by name," he said, pausing for effect.

"I'm on my way, Earl. Give me about twenty minutes and then radio me to return to the station," Michael said.

"Will do, Michael," he said.

Michael returned to her house, and it was totally dark—no sign of life or light. He scanned the landscape with the spotlight again and saw nothing. When he knocked on the front door, he heard someone moving about in the house.

Finally, he heard her voice from behind the door. "Michael, is that you?"

"Yes, ma'am. Did you hear or see something?" he asked.

He heard the chain slip the lock, and then the door opened. There stood Martha Rogers—hair brushed, fresh makeup, and a sheer evening gown backlit by glowing, flickering candles all over her house.

"I'm not sure. I've been alone tonight in the storm, reading about Lancelot and Guinevere as the rain beat against my window panes. Then I just envisioned you clad from head to toe in glimmering, golden armor. You held your lance high, bearing my silken scarf in my private colors," she said in a mixture of a child-like coo and kittenish purr.

"You came to rescue me as the moon illuminated the tower room of the castle where I had been imprisoned for so long. I let down my braided hair to my knight, and you climbed up from the moat below, stepping over the stiffening bodies of the dragons you had slain just for me. You swept me away to a beautiful, green dale, and I showered you, my gallant knight, with sweet, perfumed rewards," she gushed with sly eyes and a shy smile.

She looked at him with a breathless, vulnerable, and expectant face framed by the flickering candles behind her. Her eyes bored into his, willing her thoughts to be his, projecting her silent words: "I feel this, and you will, too."

Michael could see the anticipation in her eyes, the swell of her lips, and the quickening of her pulse showing at her throat. He was at a loss for words when, just in the nick of time, he was rescued by Earl on his walkie-talkie: "Lee Unit 14, report to the sheriff's department immediately."

Michael answered quickly without appearing too eager. "I'm on my way."

"Secure your doors, Miss Rogers. Everything will look better in the morning when the roosters crow and the sun chases away the darkness," he said.

She stood in the doorway as he walked away. He could feel her eyes on his back as she called out in a soft voice, "It'll take more than the sun to burn away the creeping shadows that stain my barren soul, Michael."

She was a lonely woman, a desperate woman dreaming of a larger-than-life knight—not an ordinary man birthed in an ordinary world, but a once-upon-a-time man. He felt sorry for her and reminded himself that it could have been any deputy…that he was nothing special. But he was glad that he was the one who had answered her call and not someone who might have taken advantage of her.

All the bruising abrasions of life and the leaking loneliness had encamped around Martha. Needlessly hurting someone is hard to undo, hard to live with, and something Michael never wanted to do.

As he was driving away, the dispatcher said, "You gone from there now?"

"Yep, I'm headed in. What you got for me now?" he asked.

"Good news. We got deputies coming in after midnight. You can call it a day…a long day. The sheriff is sorry for the extra hours. That guest we had slipped away after visiting with his relatives and Guy Harris. His security men told us that he always loses them when he wants to be alone. It felt funny to be finger-printing Elvis Presley! Before he left the department, he asked the sheriff if we would give the rest of the food he had bought for the reception to the inmates in the jail. The prisoners were excited to know that the treat came from him, and some of them broke out into his old songs!

"He'll come back through to link up with his security. The sheriff and Louis are going to meet them at the Natchez Trace Inn. I hear that Sheriff Morris is taking Elvis to Washington tomorrow to maybe meet J. Edgar Hoover! They say Elvis just met President Nixon in the White House last week! Ain't that something?" Earl said.

The dispatcher was saying way too much on a radio frequency monitored on scanners by police junkies, bootleggers, and smugglers.

He said, "I heard that they stopped at a store for gas when they were headed to Tupelo and found a whole rack of his songs for sale…bootlegged. I guess he has to deal with bootleggers, just like we do. He didn't have them arrested, though. They just bought them all and then drove off to a side road, laid them all out on the pavement, and ran over them, time and time again. Ain't that something?"

"Yeah, Earl, that's something," Michael answered.

Michael pulled over to the side of the road on Martin Hill that overlooked the sleeping city of Tupelo. The sparkling streetlights and the lighted Christmas candles on Main Street lampposts made the city look larger than it was and somehow vulnerable to menacing intruders, as hundreds of slumbering dramas waited for a new day to dawn.

Time-out had been called on countless loyalties and betrayals, individual lusts and repentances, deaths and births, sunrises and sunsets melting away the days of the flesh, blood, and bone of brief lives…all meeting, blending, and forming the threads of a common quilt of life, revealing patterns of imperfect humans struggling to overcome the lesser angels in themselves.

The rain had ceased, and an eerie stillness had settled over Tupelo. He thought of tortured men and a thousand cats…of those who thought that wrestling was real and by defeating the heels in a fixed game, they could assuage the abuse they had suffered at the hands of real heels in the rigged game of the world.

He thought of the daily dramas of the Walsh household, lonely people like Martha looking for love, Barbara all alone in Whitfield…and he thought of singers who wanted to be deputies and deputies who wanted to be singers.

As he began his descent into the valley, he saw a lighted church sign on a hillside. It read: "I'm OK with rock and roll. I got my feet on the Rock and my name on the roll."

The rhythmic caress of fading thunder rumbled gently, and a shooting star streaked across the sky as he drove down into the city, singing a medley about hound dogs and teddy bears and not being cruel to hearts that are true…or broken.

It was all just a day in the life of a deputy in Mississippi.

CHAPTER ELEVEN

*"Thunder was his engine and white
lightning was his load. And there was
moonshine, moonshine, to quench the
devil's thirst."—Robert Mitchum,
"The Ballad of Thunder Road"*

*"'Stead of learnin' to live they are
learnin' to die."—Bob Dylan,
"Let Me Die in My Footsteps"*

"He's back there with Sarge and a visitor, but I wouldn't go back there right now if I were you," Earl said when Michael entered the department and headed for the sheriff's private office.

In the intervening months since Star's death, violence had escalated in the county's nightclubs. Sheriff Gill Simpson had become frustrated by his department's inability to curb the violence of the gangs within the restrictions of state and county laws. His frustration was exacerbated by the obstruction of weak-kneed judges who seemed reluctant or afraid to curb the excesses of professional criminals. He felt that he was spinning his wheels.

As Michael neared his office door, he could hear the sheriff shouting and using blue invectives that almost never crossed his lips.

"His daddy was a bootlegger in northeast Mississippi and paid out the money to get his boy out of every briar patch he fell into. Now Cal Mattox is the head mad dog in a kennel of thieves, shiners, dopers, pimps, and burglars—all fiercely loyal to only him. They'd do anything for Cal.

"We find the victims of his boys sitting by the side of the road—rolled, robbed, and spitting out teeth. Some of them were soldiers on leave from Vietnam. They survived the jungles and Communists, and then they came home to this.

"They usually won't talk, but we know who did it. Tourists, servicemen, competitors, and the gullible are all equal-opportunity victims for the Mattox thugs. They hit the convenience stores and mom-and-pop shops at night. And they just hijacked a whole truckload of beer from Cash Distributing and took it to a big warehouse they have. They'll store it all there until they move it.

"Some sheriffs have just rolled over in their counties and put their hands out, and others are afraid. Where's all that integrity they campaigned on? Where did it go? It was watered down, washed away by threats or by dirty money laid on their desktops and the hoods of patrol cars in midnight meetings on remote dirt roads.

"That's where the fine words melted away. The sweet-talking thugs and their greasy, unmarked bills led the lawmen to the bottom of the well, and they'll find out too late that one day it will run dry. But it won't be that way in Lee County—not as long as I'm sheriff!" Gill said.

He looked up and saw Michael in the hall.

"Michael, I see you out there. Come on in here. You know Sheriff Buford Pusser?" he asked.

The man who stood up to greet Michael was tall, maybe six feet six inches. Michael could understand why they still called Tennessee's youngest sheriff in history "Buford the Bull," a hold-over from his days as a professional wrestler. Before his term as McNairy County sheriff ended, he had often come to Tupelo to pick up prisoners held for him by Lee County.

His face was deeply scarred. From what Michael had heard, he assumed it to be the after-effects of the reported ambush in 1967, the same year Michael had returned from Washington to attend Ole Miss. Pusser and his wife, Pauline, were out for a ride in McNairy County, Tennessee, when Dixie Mafia hit men came alongside and opened fire, riddling Pusser's car and killing Pauline.

Sheriff Pusser took two or three rounds, and his jaw was lying on his chest, hanging from his face by a narrow strip of tissue. They found a part of his jawbone in the floorboard of his car. Some of his teeth were found on his wife's lap after they moved her body. They were covered by her brain tissue.

Michael had heard all the stories about the State Line Mob and their clubs, motels, and restaurants in McNairy County, Tennessee, and Alcorn County, Mississippi, where tourists were fleeced and then threatened with logging chains and a swift trip to the bottom of the Tennessee River if they went to the police.

He had heard many stories, some fact and some enhanced in their retelling, but whatever the truth, there was no doubt that Sheriff Pusser had looked death in the eye and bore the scars to prove it. In one year alone, he had dismantled eighty-five stills. There were people who loved Pusser, and there were those who hated him.

Michael also knew that Pusser had shot and killed Louise Hathcock at the Shamrock after she fired at him, and that some suspected him to be the real killer of Towhead White and two other men Pusser believed to be responsible for the ambush and murder of his wife, Pauline.

"Hello, Sheriff Pusser. Glad to meet you," Michael said.

"Just Buford now; I'm not sheriff anymore. Outlaws couldn't stop me, but term limits did. I'll run again as soon as the new incumbent is up for reelection," he said with a smile that was twisted due to the damage to his face.

"From what Gill tells me, I think some of my old adversaries or their associates are trying to muscle some sheriffs in your area. I got some big sticks if your boys need 'em, Gill!" Pusser joked.

Sheriff Simpson laughed and said, "May need some, for sure."

The smile evaporated, and the sheriff's voice had a hard edge when he turned to his deputy and said, "Michael, I was just telling Buford that Cal Mattox showed up here today and asked to see me. Walked in like he owned the place. He laid down one thousand dollars, cash money…just peeled the bills off slow and easy, counting, smiling, mocking, and never taking his eyes off mine. 'One hundred, two hundred, three hundred,' he'd say, snapping the bills and popping them like the shoeshine man at the Hotel Tupelo, licking his fingers before skinning each bill from that big wad of greasy money, and smelling each one, running them under his nose like they were Cuban cigars.

"He said, 'Smells and tastes mighty fine, Sheriff.' I just stared at him. I was seething…the audacity, the gall of the man to come into my office and try to buy me like he was buying favors in a house of ill repute in the red-light district.

"He promised to deliver the same amount to me each week in exchange for free rein…to keep you boys—my deputies—on a short leash and just let him and his band of burglars, thieves, moonshiners, and arsonists run free like the pack of rabid dogs that they are," he said.

He was rocking in his desk chair, and the springs were squeaking, accentuating every gesture of his hands, each inflection of his agitated voice.

"I grabbed my shotgun from under the desk, and I was shaking, my finger twitching on that scattergun's hair trigger. I could already see him plastered all over the wall and the news media asking how it was that I blew a man to bits in the office of the sheriff of Lee County.

"I said, 'Cal, I ought to kill you right here where you stand. You dropped right out of your family's poisoned branches, and the rotten apple hasn't bounced far from the tree. Now you get out of my office before my trigger finger overcomes my brain, and I blow your head off and buy you an express ticket to the lake of fire! I'll see you behind bars before I leave this earth.'"

The sheriff finally got control of himself. He sighed deeply and smiled a bit when he said, "He didn't much like that last part." Then Simpson nodded toward the door and said, "See you boys later. I want to talk privately for a while with Sheriff Pusser."

Sarge motioned for Michael to come with him, and as they left, he saw Gill take down his fiddle from the wall and ask Pusser, "Buford, do you enjoy some calming fiddle music?"

When they turned the corner down the hall, Sarge said, "I just got word from an informant at a local shop where some of the runners for the syndicate get their cars modified. Cal just picked up a souped-up 1968 Dodge Charger 440 Magnum with 375-horsepower V8 engine…special suspension and storage area for the hooch.

"He's making a run tonight from suppliers outside of Tuscaloosa to the Rendezvous. The club is closed, so they are going to run it in about nine. Some would take all the back roads, but Cal is so cocky that he'll run it right up Highway 45. You up for helping me set a trap? Tom and Matt will be in one car, and we'll be in ours. The sheriff will be proud if we can bring in Cal," he said.

As they walked outside, Sarge laughed and said, "There must be a truce between Mattox and Billy Payne, because I've heard that Cal had spiked some of his loads with Ex-Lax, thinking that Payne had cheated him. Lots of rushing to the outhouse for those ole boys!"

Nightfall came, and Sarge and Michael were set up on Highway 45 just south of Saltillo, near the county road Cal would have to take to get to the Rendezvous. Tom and Matt were just up the road but also south of the club exit. The plan was to catch the runner by blockading the road north and south of him.

"Will he be armed?" Michael asked.

"Any time Cal gets in that car, he's armed. It's a weapon to him. But yeah, he'll be packing, too," Sarge answered.

At 8:55, the deputies heard the rumble of the big muscle car, and then it passed the alcove where they waited in their car. They eased out behind him and radioed the other unit to get ready to block the road.

"Hit your lights now, Tom!" Sarge said.

The blue lights behind and ahead of the smuggler lit up the night. Both cars blocked the road. But Cal didn't stop. He gunned his car, ran off the highway, and clipped the rear of Tom and Billy's car as he climbed back up the mud embankment.

He hit four garbage cans on the side of the road. His tires were spinning and whining on the mud, but they got traction when he hit the paved road, and black smoke boiled from his tires. He regained control of his car and fired past the turn to the Rendezvous, heading north toward Corinth. Michael could hear the whine of his engine and the tires barking each time he changed gears.

As Michael and Sarge gave pursuit and passed the other patrol car, glass and garbage cans littered the highway before them. The cars, thousands of pounds of metal, hurtled down the highway, skidding and riding the dips and curves.

Cal lost control in one four-wheel drift around a hard left corner and crashed into a tricycle left at the edge of someone's drive. Sarge tried to stay with him in the slower patrol car and slid through the curve after him. Storefronts with windows like prying eyes, church steeples, homes, and store lights of flickering neon flashed by. Michael held on to what seemed like a hot ride on a roller coaster to hell as the car ahead veered on and off the highway, pelting the county car with showers of fine gravel and the inter-mittent thunk of large rocks.

They roared through Saltillo and then passed Guntown. Michael radioed ahead to the highway patrol for help, and Tom and Billy's car was now behind them as well. A pedestrian, trying to cross the road south of Baldwyn, looked up to see the big Dodge bearing down on him.

The man leapt to safety at the last moment. Cal had glanced back at the pursuing cars, turned just in time to see the man, and swerved hard to the left. He hit a telephone booth, demolishing it and pushing its mangled parts down the road for fifty yards before it broke free, tumbled end-on-end, and bounced off the road.

Yellow pages of a phone book from the booth filled the air and fluttered above the ground like errant butterflies. *No more... Let your fingers do the walking*, Michael thought as they whisked by the wreckage.

It was a light show in a sea of darkness along Highway 45. The smuggler's big Dodge roared through the countryside and blasted through red traffic lights in Baldwyn. His silver headlamps illuminated the road with illegal high beams taken from airplane landing lights. The strong search streams split the night and cast shadows on homes, churches, and businesses. The flashing radiance of the police cars in hot pursuit blued up the night and blinded Cal in his rearview mirror.

He scraped three metal mailboxes, and yellow-red sparks showered the road ahead of the patrol cars. Up and down the road's dips, rises, and curves, and past blind entrances from farm roads the three cars went, streaking by sleepy hamlets, hanging through the curves, and jumping hills as they tried to dogleg the sharp crooks in the highway. As they all jumped one rise, the second patrol car hit the unforgiving blacktop so hard that it bent the flywheel and disabled the car.

At times on the straightaway, the Dodge exceeded 125 miles per hour and became airborne on the hills like a winged ship gliding on an asphalt stream. Cal was smiling a demonic smile and shouted, "It was cat-and-mouse, you cops thought, but I'm the cat and you are the mice! Enough of this foreplay! Goodbye, suckers! Eat my dust!"

He pulled far ahead, and Sarge told Michael to try a long shot with their carbine to take out a rear tire before Cal killed someone. Michael leaned out the window to take one shot at the right rear tire, but a spark in the night suggested that the round struck the metal bumper above the tire.

Soon, all they could do was to catch glimpses of his taillights now and then. All the towns ahead had been notified by radio, and the highway patrol and sheriff's units south of Corinth had set up a major roadblock.

But when the Lee unit neared the roadblock, Cal had disappeared.

"He must have cut off at the road to Kossuth," Sarge said.

They backtracked and took the road, but the jet on the ground had disappeared. They went up and down the backroads

looking for him, but none of the wooded groves or sleepy hollows
was hiding a Dodge super-car. The chase was over.

"Cal's gone now, probably to sanctuary in Memphis," Sarge
said glumly. "They'll take him in and probably buy his load.
We've put out our APB. There's nothing left to do but go home."

When they passed the disabled patrol unit, the wrecker was
hooking up to tow it to the garage, and Tom and Matt hitched a
ride with them to Tupelo.

When the long-faced group of deputies walked into the
sheriff's department, disappointed and exhausted, there was a
message waiting for Michael—call Clara.

* * *

There was urgency in her voice when she answered.
"Michael, Magnolia will meet with you tonight at midnight, at the
graveside. She wants to talk with you, to explain things, and to
warn you."

"That's wonderful! I'll be there. But warn me? Warn me
about what?" he asked.

"You may not believe in prophecy, the gift of prophecy, but
she has it, and she has seen things about you. Just be there, son.
Don't be late, and keep your heart open to receive the things she
will share," she said.

Michael promised her he would be receptive to all that
Magnolia might tell him, but privately, he wasn't so sure about the
prophecy part. The only prophets his church had spoken of were
the long-dead men in the Bible. The closest that Jack King, his
Methodist pastor, ever got to prophecy was in one uncharacteristic,
fiery sermon. He was so agitated that day that his young twin boys,
sitting on the front pew with their mother, began to cry and said,
"Mama, why's Daddy so mad?"

Something spooky about midnight meetings, he thought.
Traveling down the dirt road, a bobcat bolted from the shadows
and crossed his path. A giant barn owl, floating moth-like in the
night, crossed the beams of his headlights, and as he pulled up to

the edge of the cemetery, a group of gray-brown field mice scurried from behind makeshift headstones.

He parked, walked to the graveside, and waited…and waited. Finally, as the night sounds were about to consume him, she emerged ghost-like out of the night. She was lean, almost gaunt, and bony at first glance…then not so. Her back was straight, and she had a tiny waist, maybe the span of two hands. Her shoulders and throat seemed to have symmetry of design. Her cinnamon face was pinched into a forced confidence, hiding a thinly veiled uncertainty.

Magnolia's dress flowed in the night breeze and seemed almost too large for her, like a child playing grownup. Her black hair appeared ethereal in the moonlight, a princess from another planet on the cover of a *John Carter of Mars* paperback book.

"Hello, Mr. Deputy. Thanks for coming here to meet me. The funeral home in Tupelo buried Star here so her killer wouldn't know where she was buried, to keep her grave from being desecrated. He looked for it, too, but they hid her in this forsaken land where troubled people rest and cry out for justice," she said.

"Thanks for agreeing to meet me, Magnolia. Please just call me Michael. Who is the 'he' you refer to?" he asked.

"Streeter, The Pusher, the destroyer," she said.

"Are you saying he killed Star?" Michael asked.

"Yes…I witnessed her death through a camera in the upstairs office. They use it to monitor the girls, and sometimes to record powerful customers so they can blackmail them later. Just before her last sunrise, she heard him breaking down her door. I watched it. There was nothing I could do. Star knew that her nightmares about death coming for her were real. All of her childhood nursery rhymes had ended. London bridge was falling down, falling down…fair lady," she said.

"What about the note you gave me about the whitest face?" he asked.

"Just to let you know that there was another witness. No, Freddie from Memphis wasn't the killer, but he saw it and knew that the mob would look at him as a suspect. He returned to Memphis to concoct an alibi and to wait for his revenge. He is a wicked boy with a savage heart, who serves the prince of this world...but he left here that night crying. He loved Star. Many men did. Streeter is the one you want, Michael," she said.

"Who is this Freddie you refer to, and where might I find him?" he asked.

"You don't find Freddie. He finds you," she answered.

"Would you testify to what you saw? Maybe we could get you into the federal witness protection program," he said.

"I would never live to testify. Streeter would find me, or the boys out of Memphis. The boss might even send Freddie, his favorite, crazy assassin, to track me down. But Streeter would torture or kill Clara and J.B. to get to me. I can't risk that," she said.

"I'm going to run, and they may look for me awhile, but the people in Memphis won't kill anybody to find just another trollop who skips out. I want to help you as best I can before I run away as far as I can, and I want to tell you about prophecy revealed to me, and how you changed my life. My decision to break free is all on you. You changed my life and opened my eyes, and I want to open yours," she said.

He ignored the part about prophecy and asked, "How could I have changed your life, Magnolia? I don't really know you."

"Big Billy Payne, who runs the Rendezvous Club, visits us from time to time, and he gets drunk. When he gets drunk, he talks too much. He told us that you embarrassed him and refused his generosity. He lost face in front of customers and some important people at his club that night. It may have seemed minor to you, but it was major to him. He hates your guts.

"That constable, Robbie, is on his payroll, and he told Billy the story about you and that little girl you saved...the baby that once could've been me. He wanted to hurt you, so Robbie brought him to see the girl's mother, the one Robbie is dating. Billy offered her mother $20,000 to buy the girl and place her in Streeter's care, to make the child work off her debt.

"Before she'd agree to take Billy's money, the woman brought your little waif here to show her around. She told her daughter, 'See, Mary, it's not such a bad place…lots of pretty clothes, plenty to eat, and a roof over your head.'

"I've seen so much in my life that I thought I was beyond the anger I felt that day. Little Mary had scared rabbit eyes. She was terrified…but strong. She looked at her mother and said, 'Mama, I just want to be a kid. I want to marry someone like the deputy and have kids. I just want to be a kid right now. Please let me, Mama.'

"The mother was ate up with guilt and looked at the floor, but her daughter said, 'I heard that preacher on TV talking about crowns in heaven from Jesus. I want to keep my head up, so my crown won't fall off, just like Mr. Michael told me at the club. I know that's what he meant. We got to keep our heads up, Mama.'

"After I heard that, I knew that I had to get out or die trying. You saved that baby's life, Michael. Mine, too. I came out here to talk with Star and saw you planting those flowers. I had given up on good, but you lit a candle in my darkness, and I knew that I had to run. He may find me. He may kill me. All I ask is that you see that justice is done for me…and for Star," she said.

For once in his life, Michael was speechless.

"You may not believe or think a trollop has anything spiritual that's worth sharing, but this is what I am supposed to tell you. A ghostly apparition waits for you in the dark. He is your destiny, but you will be his undoing. There will be fire in Columbus, death in Corinth, and a political mugging in Atlanta. The devil is waiting for you in a dark alley, and you will want to die, but Jesus is coming to pour His blood over you, and He will answer all of your questions. You will seek pardon, but Jesus is the only One Who can expunge your record. I don't know what it all means, but this is what I was told to share, and now I have," she said.

She stepped forward, hugged him, and said, "There will be showdowns and throw-downs, and it'll all begin right here by a forgotten girl's grave. Go out boldly, Michael. Gideon was outnumbered, too. Blow your trumpet and make a mighty noise for God."

She looked up at the night sky and said, "I woke up from a nightmare, where I was utterly and awfully alone, and wondered how I might escape this earthly prison, where there is nothing, and I felt that I was nothing. I'm going away now, to bloom wherever God plants me. If you need to get a message to me, Aunt Clara will know how to reach me."

Then she was gone.

He heard her car crank and saw her headlights as she moved down the dirt road. He wasn't sure what any of it meant, but as she drove away, the canopy of the heavens rotated above him. The big and little dippers seemed to collide. Orion was on the hunt, Pegasus spread his wings, and the star-speckled, Carpenter-spackled night sky ceased to glow and began to pulse, to whisper to him in hoarse, dry dictations—messages he couldn't quite understand, but prophecies that he knew he must one day decipher.

Deputy Parker licked his dry, chapped lips just as a creature of the night, a panther, screamed its distant soliloquy. An electric shiver crept up his spine. He pulled the collar of his jacket high and tight around his neck and stuffed his hands in his pockets as he walked away.

Just a human speck riding a pale blue dot, no more than a speck itself in the universe, hurtling through one of millions of galaxies—but the soul is essential glue in the cosmic equation, and the stakes are so high.

Michael never knew just how high.

CHAPTER TWELVE

"My baby done caught that train and
gone...you know I am to blame...I musta
did somebody wrong."—Elmore James,
"I Done Somebody Wrong"

"I used to advertise my loyalty and I don't
believe there is a single person I loved that
I didn't eventually betray."
—Albert Camus, The Fall

Trouble in Gangland...

James Streeter was holed up in a cheap motel in Booneville, a rent-by-the-hour dive and safe house owned by Billy Payne...but one that Ace Connelly and his boys were not aware of.

He had been missing from his post for a week. The Pusher had tied one on and awoke three days later in Billy's fleabag room with a hangover the size of Texas, a headache punctuated by crashing cymbals behind his eyes, and a roaring river of pain in his ears. He was also hot and burning up.

His bed linen was soiled, his clothes were dirty and wrinkled, and he had burned a hole in the bed covers from the ashes of a cigar that had carelessly fallen from his lips. He only had ten crumpled one-dollar bills left to get him back to Tupelo. Sparkle, the new girl who he'd brought with him, was gone, and with her, the bulk of his money.

Rolled, at my age, he thought.

The Jack Daniels was almost gone, too. He was on the skids. What was a gangster do?

He paused and stared through the haze of his fever dream into the dark corner of the tiny room.

"I see you there, Star. Where you been? I been looking for your grave. Why don't you say something? I went to your funeral and made nice with your mourners. I was the saddest one there. Really!" he pleaded.

"Well, maybe it's time to pack up and get out of this hick state, maybe drift down south to New Orleans, get back to my roots. What do you think? Just saddle up and go. Beats sitting here listening to my heart thump, drinking my life away, sitting here huffing and puffing like an out-of-shape dolphin. Everything's thinning out, growing dark. Ain't no color left in the world. It's all fading away, and I dread nightfall. Look at my hands. They're all covered with ulcers and sores. Did you put 'em there? I was gonna take you with me. I was! As GAL is my witness, we was gonna go to the Quarter and the bayou and find the mojo.

"But you pushed me too far. I made a mistake and lost my temper. I wish it hadn't gone down that way, but it did. It was an accident, so I can't be held responsible, can I? Now I'm sitting here, talking to your ghost. Did you know that I can see right through you?" he asked.

"Did you know that Magnolia has disappeared? Yeah, and to make matters worse, I lost my temper when I learned that she had disappeared. I grabbed that new girl from Memphis, Sparkle, and brought her with me. She made a smart remark, and I back-handed her. I knocked that tramp halfway across the room, and it left an ugly mark on her face.

"The way she looked at me…must've put something in my drink. She's probably with that john-politician from DeSoto right now, crying on his shoulder. I bet they both done run squawking and crying to the Ace of Diamonds Club.

"I got to fix things, or Ace will send the boys down from Memphis to chop me up and bury me at the landfill," he said, running to the window, parting and peeking through the thin curtains.

"What was that? You hear it? Sounds like them hounds chasing me again down at Parchman. What do you think Magnolia knows? Did you see her that night? Could she be in Memphis with Ace, too… right now, spilling her guts, ready to rat me out or putting the police on me?

"Who would Ace send? He'd probably send Freddie. Don't even have to pay him to kill. He likes it. I heard about him getting bored, needing the blood, and just traveling to cities at random, picking names out of a phone book, people he didn't know. He'd stalk them, watch them, and study their dull lives. They never knew they were about to be killed, and why should they? They were just working stiffs, coming home, sleeping, and doing it all over again. Who would want to kill them, except some freak like Freddie, out honing his craft?

"Oh, I forgot, he liked you, 'cause you were kind to him. You put a spell on that monster, for sure, but you were the best, weren't you? I'd like to go back to those early days when I took you and Magnolia in, just two girls out for adventure, destined to meet their pimp-daddy," Streeter said, pausing from his long dialogue with his visitor from beyond the grave.

He took a deep breath and mopped his brow. Sweat poured off him in buckets, and he was shaking uncontrollably.

"Then I go to your mama's house, Magnolia's aunt's, to try to fix it, to find her and make amends...nothing else, and there's that two-bit deputy opening her door and threatening me. I've killed better men than that punk with my cheapest Saturday night special.

"I told him, 'You ever come after me, you'd better bring the army, the navy, and the air force. I break men like you break wind, boy, and turn live men into dead men, and dead men into fertilizer. I tell these girls I love 'em, too. Don't mean nothing—means less than nothing.'

"Oh, but not you, baby. I meant every word I said to you. I did. You know I did. I talk too much. I'm just like a caged lion lately. I need to be let out, set free. Oh, I'm sorry. Can I get you something? I don't know. Do ghosts drink?" he asked.

The clattering and metallic rattling of the ancient air conditioner brought him back to a semi-lucid state and up for a breath of air for a moment. He looked at the giant stain from the leaky window unit that ran down the wall behind Star's image. He looked at her and the image with wonder. It looked like one of the American states, but he wasn't quite sure which one.

"Say, Star, is that heaven or hell behind you? You living in the fire or in the air? Is that where you been hiding from me? Say, is that flip-flops you're wearing? The Japanese think women reveal who they are through their toes. Is that what all the fashionable dead girls are wearing? I guess it's all good, 'cause flip-flops are high heels for Southern women, they say," he said with an almost girlish giggle.

"All that junk in my trunk, the accusing faces of victims... lugging it around can drive a man insane. Makes me jumpy and paranoid... You was always needling me, so I just assigned it all to you—made the madness you. And then one day, I shot you right between the eyes. I haven't heard the voices since then. It was great therapy...until now.

"You shouldn't have pushed me. You was still breathing, lying in my arms, staring at me. You wouldn't stop staring at me with your dead eyes...eyes accusing me, inviting me to come with you. So I tried to cut your head off to make you stop. What's a ghost need with a head anyway?" he said, endlessly rambling in his delirium.

With that, his eyes went wild and glassy. He seized his pistol from the nightstand, shouted, "Get back! Get back!" and fired five deafening rounds in the small echo chamber until there were only the dry clicks and snaps of the trigger. He was trying to kill Star again.

He attempted to reload, but his quivering fingers turned into ten thumbs. He fumbled, juggled, and dropped the bullets, and they rolled around the floor like errant dice in a game of chance. He dropped to his knees, trying desperately to find them before Star's icy fingers clawed at his soul and pulled him into the grave. He grasped at bullets balled up like roly-poly bugs, which mocked him and eluded his clumsy pawing.

He swallowed hard, foaming at the mouth, and his sphincter suddenly relaxed. He laughed an empty laugh and said, "I think I'm going to be sick."

His face went slack, his eyes rolled back up into his head, and he fell face first, mouth open, into the grimy, yellowed carpet of a motel that survived only through payoffs to the health inspector.

The Pusher, whom everyone feared, passed out in a pool of his own vomit, right at the ephemeral feet and curled toes of his accusing ghost, whispering one last guttural exhalation... "You was buried six feet under. Who woke you up?"

* * *

The night life was just beginning at the Ace of Diamonds Club in Memphis. The long bar, framed in ornate teakwood, was scrubbed, polished, and stocked, ready for the bartenders to fill the shot glasses and keep the booze flowing. Spigots would spew the beer that made Milwaukee famous.

The club was the place to be. The eclectic mix of patrons spoke to its universal appeal. It was the place to be seen in Metro Memphis and the favorite watering hole for the hardcore members of the Dixie Mafia.

Bouncers screened the party animals and early arrivals at the "buzz-to-enter" door, turning away anyone who was not a regular or did not know anyone "important." The FBI Organized Crime Task Force had been trying to infiltrate the club with undercover agents. The phones had been tapped, and the parking lot was full of gray government cars and men in cheap JC Penney suits, who were taking pictures and writing down tag numbers.

The band was twanging the guitars, tuning for the night's big show. Cockeyed women with charcoal eyes, darkened by their flirtation with the wild side, hung on the muscled arms of gold-chained Lotharios wearing big guns beneath their jackets. Syndicate enforcers and soldiers straight out of central casting were riding the rails of the violent life—thrill-seekers, never thinking about tomorrow and the short lifespan for men in their occupation. Their actuarial clocks were already ticking.

Tony "Ace" Connelly, a Cajun by birth, sat in the office of his club in Memphis. He circled one thumb around and around the other and slowly nodded to the agitated man before him, blinking mock sympathy via long, slow cat-caresses from the depths of his deep-set black eyes.

Ace pursed, pooched, and puckered his lips, and his shabby brows raised, lowered, and arched in acknowledgment of each complaint from DeSoto County Commissioner Joseph Sterns, a mousy and pasty-faced little man with rimless accountant-spectacles. Right by the commissioner's side, plastered as close as she could get, sat Sparkle, the apple of his eye—the spark in his libido who made him think she was worth risking everything—his marriage, his family, his reputation, his liberty, and even his life by dealing with people like Ace.

He had watched them on the cameras as they moved through the club toward his office, arms locked, giggling—two lovers, shoulder-to-shoulder and hip-to-hip, bearing a secret they thought the world didn't know but wanted to. They had the air of servants who would be masters, pretending they were much more than they were.

Sparkle had the high-heeled silver Cinderella slippers that clicked and clacked on the club floor. She was a gilded lily with a trim little figure and shiny black hair, which was swept up from the nape of a long gazelle neck and piled high atop her perfect head. She always smelled of jasmine, seemed to glow with a honeyed luminescence, and dressed to impress her older suitor.

She smiled up at her Joseph, and as he spoke bravely and sternly to Ace on her behalf, she turned to kiss him ever so softly, her lips barely brushing his cheek in a contrived caress. She manipulated him with utter confidence and looked at Ace with a sort of defiance, as if the commissioner's desire somehow imbued her with immunity or invincibility from the wrath of the syndicate.

Ace was lost in thought. *It's like watching a dummy and a ventriloquist. He is clearly the dummy, and she is yanking his strings and fueling his demands. She may have to be dealt with one day when we no longer need him, but not now. When that day comes, she'll learn that the pictures we have of them will be all we need to poison Cupid's barbs. Her stock will plunge, and her broker will scramble to sell high before the crash.*

Ace assured the commissioner that Streeter had been warned and that this would never happen again, that no one would abuse Sparkle.

The puffed-up rooster asked, "How can I be sure?"

Ace looked at him for a long time with the unblinking, challenging stare of unfriendly eyes, and then said, "Because I just told you so."

The commissioner took a step back and looked nervously at the floor after being reminded that he was petting a rattlesnake.

Ace smiled and said, "We will be moving Sparkle back to Memphis. Just as soon as we make our move into DeSoto Country—with your help, of course—and establish our networks of clubs with the Full House as our crown jewel, Sparkle will be the Queen of Hernando, with an apartment for an exclusive clientele of one—you, Mr. Commissioner."

He stood up, shook the hand of the mouse that wanted to roar, and said, "We have big plans for Mississippi and appreciate your facilitation of the relationship with Hal Davidson, who we think could very well be the governor of Mississippi one day. Now you kids run along while I tend to business. A generous line of credit has been opened for y'all, and I want you to have a good time and not trouble yourselves over this matter again."

Something had twisted and warped Ace a long time ago. No one was quite sure what it was, but many expected it was all balled up in that dreadful day when he had come home from school to find his mother and father dead—a gruesome murder-suicide scene.

He had given up on God and good after that, and instead went after everything he wanted with a vengeance. He could smile and play the business and social scene, but he had no mercy in him...no scruples and no ethics.

If anyone got in his way, he always said, "May God have mercy on you and all of my enemies, 'cause I won't." Behind that crocodile smile was a cold-hearted and cold-blooded crime boss who got what he wanted.

When the commissioner and his paramour left, he picked up his phone and said, "Suzy, get me Freddie on the private line—the one the FBI doesn't know about."

"He's on the line, boss," a squeaky-voiced Suzy said before she clicked off.

"Freddie, that Star was magic, wasn't she? And revenge is sweet, is it not? Why is the ground so red around Tupelo? It's because of all that blood it's gonna be soaking up. His get-out-of-the-coffin-free card has been revoked. The casket is empty and must be filled. The victims demand it, and the mourners are already mourning," Ace said in the rambling riddles of code-talk to his killer-for-hire.

He could hear Freddie breathing harder and faster, hyperventilating.

"Freddie, make it clean, but make it slow. Take him to a dark alley where no one can see. Leave a message for others, but don't mutilate him. We owe him that much," Ace said.

As Ace hung up, his intercom buzzed.

"Boss, there's a newbie here—a woman who says she came here once with Frank DeVaney, but he's not here tonight. She wants access on her own. What do you want us to do?" the bouncer asked.

"On my way down there. Hold on," Ace said.

Ace walked through the club, which was filled with the smells of spilled beer, stale perfume, fried food, and bodies dirty dancing with other bodies...the numbers players, the easy women, junkies, the horse players, women and men with white powder on their noses, gangsters in silk suits, glassy-eyed adolescents pretending to be adults—an amalgamation of sinners that would be a sermon-writer's delight.

But it was his life. Ace was so deep into this universe, he couldn't leave if he wanted to...not that he wanted to. Some teased him about Elvis's new hit, "Suspicious Minds," and told him that he was "caught in a trap and can't walk out." But the trap Ace truly feared was marriage, a wife, babies, a mortgage—conventionality. He thought there had to be much more than that between the headlines of "He was born" and "He died"—didn't there?

When he approached the front door, he saw that they had a young blonde pulled to the side. She was tall with blue eyes and fair skin, a sculptured throat, and an air of innocence. *Scandinavian heritage, maybe the type kings sent agents out to find or to kidnap once upon a time*, he thought.

She fidgeted with her hair, twirling ringlets in her long tresses with her fingers, shuffling left and right on her red, spiked heels.

"Yes, ma'am, I'm the proprietor. How might I help you?" he asked.

"I just drove over from West Memphis to hear the band and to dance a little," she said.

"You're not FBI, are you?" he laughed.

"Oh, no! I'm a secretary, that's all. I work for Frank DeVaney. Maybe I'll see him here," she answered.

Ace looked at her and then the bouncer. "Pat her down for wires and weapons," he said.

The bouncer went up and down her body, feeling, squeezing, and lingering longer than necessary, and then he rifled through her purse.

"She's clean," he said with a shrug.

"Young woman, you are in luck tonight. I was just on a call about the impending death of a dear, dear friend, and I am in a generous mood to help someone in honor of his memory," Ace said. A hint of a crocodile tear shone in the eye of a man whose soul had been compromised the day his parents died, the day a corrosive force moved in to occupy his heart—a force reminiscent of his favorite movie...*Invasion of the Body Snatchers*.

"Tell ole Ace the truth now, you hear? What did you cross the river to find in Memphis tonight, my dear?" he asked gently.

"I...I'm not sure," she stammered.

"Well, whatever it is, make sure you find it, and it doesn't find you. If it's a man you're looking for, about the only choices you'll find here are one who allows you to consume your garbage directly out of the trash can or another who offers all you can eat…right off the floor. And pardon me for saying so, but you look like the kind of woman many of these men dream about abusing on cold, winter nights," he said.

"Oh, I'm not looking for men. I have a boyfriend in Tupelo," she said earnestly.

"Well, you should bring him with you to the club," Ace said.

"No, sir, I don't think he'd come," she said shyly.

At that moment, there was a ruckus at the door, and the bouncer said, "It's that street preacher again, boss."

The young evangelist yelled from the open door, "Mr. Connelly, you're ruining lives, robbing girls of their innocence… just like this young woman you're talking to now," he said, pointing to the nervous girl beside Ace.

"You are a thief in the night, the son of Satan, and you are bound for hell," the pastor shouted.

"Padre, we don't peddle your salvation sandwiches here. This is a refuge for people running from hypocrites like you and the God my parents believed could save them—before Daddy blew their brains out all over Mama's brand new carpet." Ace turned to the bouncers and said, "Throw him out!"

Ace looked at the stunned girl and said, "Does that shock you, my dear? When you enter this club, you cross a line. This is the wild side of the street, and if Jesus himself showed up here, I wouldn't advise him to come in, because there are many here with the soul of Judas, and they all have thirty pieces of silver. Most of them would sell their own mamas down the river for half that… Still want to party tonight?" he asked.

The girl looked at the door and then at the glitter, the flashing lights, the neon dance floor, the dancers, and the "beautiful people"—the world-class sprinters in the Memphis fast lane. The steamy beat of the music was creeping up on her, invading her senses like a pied piper of gin and sin. She grabbed a grayish-white drink from a passing waiter's tray, downed it in one silver slurp, and said, "Yes. I have to know."

"Know what, Goldilocks?" he asked.

"If it's here…something that can fill that big hole in my heart," she said.

As he turned to leave her, he said, "Well, too bad about your boyfriend. In any event, have a good time. What's your name, darling?"

"Dixie…Dixie Lee Carter," answered the girl—the girl whom Michael Parker had cast in the role of princess in a play where he was the white knight.

* * *

When young Fredrick Hammel was overseas courting the Communists and playing both sides against each other in the Cold and Hot wars, he was invited to sit with a mystic in Cambodia, who spoke with him at length about life and the struggle between light and dark—what man reduced to good and evil. The mystic answered his questions about the devil and his many incarnations throughout man's brief history.

They joined hands to move to a higher plane, but the mystic suddenly jerked his hands free from Freddie, abruptly terminated the session, and left the room. He told his assistant, "I have touched the black star of mysticism many times, but to enter into that realm with Freddie caused evil to suddenly awaken from its slumber and to look right at me, when I had always been invisible on my previous journeys. To breathe the same air as Freddie is to inhale the toxic atmosphere of a putrid universe that smothers the soul. Never allow Hammel to return to our establishment. He is darkness born from darkness."

After the call from Ace, Freddie sat alone in his apartment in the midst of the Bohemian community that surrounded Memphis State. The room was darkened to accommodate his sensitive pink irises and deep-red pupils. He contemplated the gift given to him by Ace and the memory of Star, the one girl who had not been repulsed by him.

She couldn't heal herself, but she had wanted to heal him, to draw him away from the abyss. Through her, Fredrick experienced his first and only brush with what others called love. He knew that she was dangerous to him. She confused the demons within him when she talked of Jesus. He was a disciple of death in conflict, a gravedigger at his own funeral, but he could not turn away from her.

She made him squirm when she said, "The one you call your father below is a liar. How can you believe him? Some say that there are deeper hells within Hell; maybe that's what he has in mind for you. You better ask questions now, Freddie. I'm not sure you get to ask any questions in Hell."

Then she was taken from him. Part of Freddie, the nagging chorus, said it was best and inevitable, because he might've been the one called to stop her invasion of his darkness by killing her himself. But he knew that was a lie. She had been his last tether to sanity and to some nagging light at the edge of his madness...a light he remembered from what he now viewed as treasonous childhood dreams. But that had been in the saffron autumns, before the consuming shadows of his black winters...his last subversive memories of a Light that whispered louder than the screams of his darkness.

Now Fredrick was left alone again with the maddening voices he had heard as long as he could remember, his only respite coming from his sacrifices to the darkness that demanded to be fed.

He had progressed through the years. What had started with words—taunting, belittling, maligning—had escalated to physical acts—depriving, hurting, punching, striking, wounding, cutting, and...finally killing. That first night in the dark parking lot, it had been a young sailor on shore leave. The papers said he was drunk and trying to get back to his ship when he was stabbed thirty-six times.

Freddie was trapped in a duality of madness, villain and hero, avenger and reaper—an impossible conflict to reconcile. There was always a gradual disintegration, the gnarling of the mind, a decay…the aroma of rot…but he was Ace's go-to killer. And he was also the example other assassins referred to when pleading their case to those who knew their chosen profession—"At least I'm not like Freddie."

As Freddie contemplated his latest contract, he had nothing but contempt for the pedestrian hit men of his business who had the nerve to call him a savage.

They are nothing but miserable killers—just chop, chop… bang, bang, quick and dirty. No poetry, no grace in their death thrusts. They just want to get it over with. Nothing more than clowns and cowards donning their death masks. Have some respect for your victims.

On the nights when the moon was full and darkened by eerie shadows like ghostly gallows and guillotines, you could find Freddie stick-drawing 666 in the mud. He would recite Satanist Aleister Crowley's guiding rule of his cosmology: "'Do what thou wilt' shall be the whole of law," while soaking his pale feet in brackish pools of death, thinking of Star, and pausing to whisper— "Darlin'… darlin'."

* * *

Billy Payne counted and recounted the proceeds from another "Saturday Night Live" at the Rendezvous Club, and they were down…way down. Billy was a hard-boiled egg, but as the till grew lighter, he became sullen and more violent and disagreeable than usual. His once-firm mouth had developed a noticeable slackness. The pallor of his skin had taken on an unhealthy cast, and his fingers had begun to curl into what looked like a witch's paw.

Lee County deputies had been intercepting more and more loads of moonshine whiskey, and Payne's business was suffering. They waited in Nettleton for runners—and in Shannon, Mooreville, and Guntown, too. They seemed to know the routes and the schedules to a tee, and few jugs and barrels were coming in to fill the shot glasses and pint bottles at the Rendezvous.

Streeter couldn't be found. Ace wasn't answering calls. Cal was obsessed with Sheriff Simpson and took the last load into Memphis. It seemed as if it was all coming unraveled.

Payne walked outside the Rendezvous and pawed at the ground with his boots, staring into the blue-black of the sky.

Sometimes I feel like I'm in one of those Westerns at the Lee Drive-In. I'm some pioneer in the Wild West, surrounded by the Indians and the cavalry, and the cloud of dust is so thick from the horses and the fighting that I can't see who's winning. I don't know who to shoot at, and I'm bleeding and covered with splints and bandages.

Nothing seems to be working. I couldn't even get my revenge and have some fun with the college deputy by buying that little gal from her mama for Streeter's club. I tried to give her a little kiss to settle her down when they brought her to the Playhouse, but the little scamp began speaking in tongues and scared me to death. Now another one of Streeter's girls has run off, and rumors are that Parker knows all about what I tried to do to that kid.

Buzzy Hester is one of the best runners in the country, but when Sarge ran him in the ditch on that run through Plantersville, Buzzy went a little crazy. He jumped out and ran into the woods. Then he got a car and ran up into Sarge's yard in Saltillo later that night, whooping and hollering and firing his pistol at everything that moved. He killed one of Sarge's dogs.

Now he shouldn't have done that, but Sarge had no business coming in my club and dragging Buzzy out with a pistol under his chin, threatening to scatter his brains all over the hillside if he ever came near his house again. He made Buzzy believe he was about to die—made him get on his knees. Then he just shot in the air and walked away.

They say that Ace is angry and assassins may be arriving in Tupelo by the train load, but we all gotta do what we gotta do. Me and my boys are going to have to get serious. We are going to shoot them Dudley Do-Rights right out of their saddles.

* * *

There are all kinds of killers. The flavors of deadly are hidden in the nuances of DNA, the crevices of the heart, and the nooks and crannies of the psyche. Cal Mattox was a killer and junkyard-dog mean—a man who pistol-whipped his wife and terrorized his children.

He didn't flinch the night two hit men came to the Snake Pit's locked front door, broke it down, and shot their way into his place, yelling and cussing. They wounded Cal, but he returned fire in a fierce gun battle. Both of the assassins fell dead outside his store. The man who had put out the contract was Cal's partner-in-crime, later killed by the FBI.

Cal had been acquitted of every crime he was charged with. To some of the locals, he was a third-rate Robin Hood character with ready fists…a man who relished his reputation—the eye-averting fear he inspired and the groveling he saw when he decided to patronize his sniveling subjects in his bootleg kingdom. The populace either grudgingly admired him for beating the police, or they feared him because of his volatility, hot temper, and sharp tongue.

He had the survival instincts of a wild beast. But he was not a measured, calculating killer like Ace, nor driven by ghosts like Streeter, and certainly not an adherent of the satanic psycho-sadism of Fredrick Hammel.

Cal blew in from Memphis drunk and disorderly, the hammer of alcohol pounding his head, reeling from another bender as he rolled into his joint near Sherman. He was throwing back his favorite poison, Charter Whiskey, and holding court with the members of his gang to gloat about outrunning Sarge and Michael. His sycophants watched him warily, laughed on cue, and withdrew when his mercurial moods dictated discretion. He could be generous to the extreme or turn on his loyal band of ruffians without warning, but all of his flunkies and yes-men thought that their boss seemed to be in a good mood.

"It was like the old days and chases with local yokels, when I was running that slow-cooked white lightning up from Gulfport. Those Lee County boys ate my dust, too, and I rode the load of moonshine right on to Memphis after I lost them at Kossuth," Cal bragged.

"I sold the entire load and the car to Ace Connelly. Ace took the car in spite of the bullet hole in the rear bumper, compliments of the deputy...the one in the *Daily Journal*, the college boy. Ace said it gave the car character. I just took his big fat roll of fresh green, had a few drinks down on Beale Street, and boarded the Greyhound back to Tupelo. 'Leave the driving to us,' like they say. I slept like a baby.

"And who did I see there, lurking around the bus terminal in Tupelo looking for me? It was those same two deputies. They were sour—looked like babies sucking their thumbs, like somebody had shot their mamas or something. Sad sacks, for sure. I'd know 'em anywhere. Saw 'em that night when I passed those tin stars, all tucked back in that road waiting, thinking they was hidden and that I didn't know. I knew all right, but more than that...I wanted it. I relished it!

"Man...that was fun. They can't touch me...the world can't touch me! I'm invincible! That's what I told them at the bus station. I said, 'Howdy men! Y'all need to buy some new cars if you gonna run with the big boys!'"

Cal was laughing and slapping the bar at each punch line. He was riding a jubilant sea, floating on a cloud of euphoria, and he felt ten feet tall and...victorious.

"But always remember...those who cross me must pay. When I was in the navy, I dated a French girl named Clementine. Her name means mercy in French, but she had none, and I ain't got none either."

A wave of sudden generosity swept over Cal, and he lined up the shot glasses on the bar. "Step up, boys! Drinks are on the house. No, no—drinks are on the slow cars of Lee County!" he said.

As the boys bellied up to the counter, he motioned for one of them, Stanley Still, to follow him to the back room.

Stanley was a thickset man, heavy around the middle, with a bulbous nose and a web of small, broken red veins that spread across his nose and onto his ruddy cheeks. The skin around his eyes was dark-stained and puffy. He was fiercely loyal to Cal.

He was called "Standstill" by Cal, because Stanley was fidgety—always drumming his fingers, picking his nose, and constantly cursing, but he was all nervous energy. He couldn't be still, and he never got anything done. The nickname was a combination of warped affection and naked mockery, as Cal made Stanley his court jester and the butt of his cruel jokes.

Cal finished his bottle of whiskey and put his arm around Standstill. "Stanley, we got to do something about the sheriff. He refused my money, threatened me, and sends his underlings to chase after me. He must pay a penalty for saying no and for threatening me," Cal said.

"Standstill, you know we could learn a thing or two from them little Communist crybabies who are bombing everybody. I despise 'em, but I read their how-to books, and it's time for us to make a homemade bomb of our own—one that goes kaboom! Those kids say they gave peace a chance and then turned to the bomb. That I understand. I offered Gill a peace offering, more money than he'd ever make in his life, and he refused."

Cal reached beneath his desk and produced a box containing a crude candle bomb. He handed it to Stan and said, "He's driven me to this…to this bomb I'm giving you.

"Ride into his neighborhood like you belong there. That way no one will remember you. Don't look like a bum. Your collars are frayed, your cuffs are dirty, and you got a three-day beard shadow. Clean yourself up, so no one will notice you. Blend in, Stan. Here's some money to buy a gray jumpsuit to wear so you'll look like a meter reader or a phone man. The utility room should be easy to access. Get in there about 7:30 and light the candle. The bomb should go off about 8 a.m. His wife and kids will be out of the house long before then. We're not baby killers," Cal said.

Stanley just chomped on his cud of gum and nodded blankly, as he always did—a good soldier receiving his orders...never one to question, just do as ordered. He was scared of Cal, and their encounters always worsened his acid reflux from what doctors diagnosed as a hiatal hernia, which he called a "high-tailed hernia." He told his mama that Cal's scolding and all that acid in his throat just made him want to curl up into the "fertile position."

"Don't worry. It'll be like walking out to the pasture and shooting dumb animals or blasting fish in a barrel. He'll never know what hit him, but they'll all know who did it. They'll say that old Cal is no one to mess with.

"Ace and the boys don't want no trouble in Tupelo, but they sit high and dry up in Memphis. The sheriff ain't up in the middle of their business like he is in mine. Besides, death and explosives give me a rush—a sense of invincibility. Stan, with enough death and plenty of bombs, we could change the world... erase everything and start all over," Cal said.

"Oh," he added, "remember, the bomb goes in the utility room. His daughter has a pet monkey called Jo-Jo. That's where they keep it. I want to kill that monkey. That'll hurt him...stick it right to him. I want him to know that you don't monkey around with me," he said as he laughed and slapped Stanley on the back.

"Here's a bottle of fresh shine that'll give you courage and put hair on your chest. When you light the fuse, don't be reluctant. That's the key. I'm never reluctant," Cal said.

"Stop thinking, stop squirming. Just light the candle fuse and run like the devil is after you...like he's trying to get you to sign a long-term lease on a house in hell."

CHAPTER THIRTEEN

"I ain't no monkey man."
—Charlie Kyle, "Monkey Man Blues"

"The fact is, all gangsters live in dog
years…"—Drexel Deal, The Fight of My
Life is Wrapped Up in My Father

Dawn, morning twilight, had broken. The sun was just visible, the sky was showing an early tease of a fresh, robin-egg blue, and the dull-reddish arch on the horizon had faded.

A rooster crowed and crowed again. Sleepy people wandered out to get the Tupelo Daily Journal from their driveways. Mothers prepared kids to catch the school bus, commuters readied themselves for their factory jobs, teachers arranged lesson plans for another slate of classes, and techs and medics hurried to punch in at the medical center.

In the midst of the daily normalcy, there was a sudden jarring and disruption of sameness in the understory of life in Lee County…

Boom!

The explosion rattled windows, shook the good china out of cabinets, and startled the residents along Feemster Lake Road in East Tupelo. Mrs. Velma Young had just knelt down to clean out her flower bed, Janine White had arrived to clean many of the neighborhood houses, and Betsy Jones had finally rocked her newborn to sleep and laid him in the crib.

At first many of them thought it was a sonic boom from one of those jets out of the Columbus Air Force base, but the plume of smoke began to rise. Caught by brisk, early morning winds, the pungent odor of gunpowder and explosives spread quickly over the quiet community, and residents began to rush to their windows and front doors to see what had happened.

The bomb blast had ripped off the utility room door, blown out the windows around the kitchen and den, and set the roof of Sheriff Simpson's house on fire. Splintered wood and plaster residue filled the air.

The people next door to the sheriff's house called the fire department, and then they called the sheriff. The left side of the house had collapsed, blown away by a terrible force. Part of the roof was gone, and the rest was either charred or on fire.

It was a primitive bomb with a candle burning down into a jug of explosives, small by the standards of the Weather Underground and faulty in its design, but it was the opening salvo in Dixie Mafia Guerilla Theater in Tupelo. They became the authors of bomb number 4,331 that year in the United States, joining Communist sympathizers, antiwar extremists, and the Klan in employing terror by bombing...often killing in the name of peace, bombing to protest bombing, or instilling terror based on skin color...bombs made for strange bedfellows.

By the time the candle had burned down to the explosive, Stanley was far away in a plateless, stolen van that he later ditched. He had slipped up to the sheriff's house, jimmied the lock to the utility room, and set the bomb right next to the pet monkey. But before leaving, Stanley had mocked the tiny capuchin, rattled his cage, and poked him with his finger... He had paid a price for that indulgence of cruelty and was bleeding from the monkey bite to his right index finger.

As instructed, when Stanley lit the candle and made his run, he stopped to nail a hand-painted sign to the big pin oak in the front yard.

The sign, shaped like a cross, read—"Jo-Jo died for your sins."

* * *

Around the same time as the explosion, Mack Morrison, the tall, sun-browned chief deputy—who always wore what the other deputies called his Mountie hat—left his home early, driving his personal car to drop it off at the local Ford repair shop. He intended to serve some summons along the way at the Snake Pit. Cal Mattox was to appear before a judge for alcohol citations, selling liquor out the back door. It was a nasty bunch out there, but it was early, and he could legally serve the papers and then get his car to the shop before going in to work.

He had thought of asking Michael Parker to serve them, but he didn't know if their youngest deputy was up to that just yet. Mack was the oldest deputy on the force and known to be expressionless in the face of danger. Little fazed him. He and Parker got along fine, except for the dispute over the Whitfield transport assignment.

Morrison only had his walkie-talkie, and its range was limited. He had that squelched due to the early hour, so he had no idea what was happening at the sheriff's house.

There were cars and pickup trucks parked in front of the club when he arrived. He noticed that Cal was always more dangerous when he had an audience to entertain, but he assumed the cars probably belonged to men sleeping off the illegal whiskey that Cal had sold them the night before. So he walked up to the front door, bunched his broad shoulders, and grabbed the rusty door handle. But when he opened the door, he saw Cal and eleven men sitting at a large rectangular table, eating and playing cards. One of the men had an injury on his right index finger, and from the bloodstains on the bandage, it looked fresh.

Cal looked up and barked, "What're you doing here so early, Chief Deputy?" The muscles in his face and neck were jumping and quivering.

A giant, yellow tomcat at Cal's feet hissed at Morrison. There was a trace of strong perfume in the room, and a deadly cloud of silence fell over the club.

"I've just stopped by to deliver these summons," he said as he flipped the summons onto the table. Mack's wrinkled face and baggy eyes never betrayed any emotion. Everyone said that he possessed the true poker face.

"You've been legally served. See you in court, boys," the chief deputy said as he turned to leave.

Cal jumped up and produced a pistol, which he leveled at him. "You think it's that easy, do you?" he brayed. "Just waltz in here alone, showing no respect. Who comes into my club alone?" he asked.

All the other men became shapeless blobs and smudges on the canvas of danger—extras in Cal's theater. The chief deputy focused only on the gun, now aimed at his bowels.

The jukebox in the corner was playing something by George Jones. A big diesel rig roared by outside, drowning out the music, and a mockingbird heralded a new day from the chinaberry tree outside the window.

"I don't want any trouble, Cal. I've done my job. You'll pay a small fine, and the game will start all over again. You know the drill," Morrison said.

Cal walked slowly toward him, holding the gun before him. He brushed so close to the chief deputy that Morrison could smell the corn liquor on his breath.

"I ought to pistol-whip you and send a message to Gill. Whadda ya think, boys?" Cal asked.

The air seemed to tremble in anticipation of coming violence. The men all laughed, and one said, "Let me, Cal. Let me."

Cal grabbed the badge on Morrison's shirt and ripped it from where it was pinned, tearing the shirt. He tossed the star across the room, and it skittered along the tile floor. As the badge came to rest near the entrance to the toilet, he suddenly slapped the Mountie hat off the chief deputy's head and stepped on it with his boots, working the hat into the floor with his heel.

"We're going to keep your badge in case we ever get pulled over by the highway patrol and need to flash it to get out of a ticket. Now get out of the free state of Cal, and don't ever come back. If you come in here again to face twelve hard men, it'll be six men who'll carry you out in a pine box!" he threatened.

The chief deputy walked to the door and turned just as he put his hand on the doorknob. "You know Gill is not going to be happy about this," he said.

Cal threw his head back and laughed, and all of his gang joined in. "Is that right? Hear that, boys? Well, Mack, I think Gill is going to have his hands full for a while! Bigger fish to fry... deader monkeys to bury!" he said.

"There's wishful thinking in hell, too, I hear," Morrison said as he walked out the door.

Mack Morrison leaned on the hood of his car and lit a cigarette to calm himself. His hands shook as he cupped them around the lighter to shield it from the wind. The pant and moan of a distant freight train on its early-morning run split the crisp morning air.

He looked up at the steeple on a Primitive Baptist church on the distant hill as the Possum's song still whispered in his ear, "Walk Through This World With Me."

He picked up his walkie-talkie and said, "Lee 2 to Lee S.O. Come in, please."

Inside the club the meeting broke up, and Cal staggered to the backroom couch and passed out. He had indulged his murderous heart and defended his territory. So, calmed by the cold steel of the gun tucked under his belt...the animal slept.

* * *

In the South, old men always sat in front of local country stores, played checkers, and whittled wood until it became art. These ancient sages watched Buzzy Hester as he roared by their gossip-history stations in his maroon Road Runner.

One grizzled old man, who had to push his tongue up into his dentures to smile, had a saying about Buzzy: "He can get the smooth kick to top off your Mason fruit jar, but you gotta catch that boy to place your order. He's got the right car, 'cause he's like the road runner in the cartoon... *Beep-beep!* He's gone!"

Buzzy, who had a florid face, pimples, and a red mustache, was called "Tic" behind his back, due to the nervous tic in his right eye that made it jump and twitch constantly. Some said his twitchy-itchy, herky-jerky spasms extended to his quick use of the long guns he carried under his coat, the small guns in his cowboy boots, and the weapons hidden in every nook and cranny of the shiny muscle car he called "White Lightning."

He lived on the ragged edge of disaster, reckless and wild. Some said he had a death wish, but all agreed that he had a quick temper, evidenced by the men he had beaten, cut, or shot, and by the black eyes his girlfriend, Jeanie, frequently sported.

He told friends that their relationship was "complicated." He viewed her as a mistake, and he treated her with contempt…but the girl stayed. Jeanie was not exactly beautiful, but she had long, dishwater-blonde hair and large blue eyes that could swell into saucers like Betty Boop's cartoon orbs.

Buzzy told his buddies that she was no rocket scientist, but she had some strange hold on him. Yet he berated her for being nothing more than a good-time girl mooching off of him and every man who had been with her before him. He told her constantly that she was fat, when she was really anorexic. He insisted that she was going to seed on a downhill, fast track and would soon be relegated to selling herself just to live.

Buzzy, who was twenty-eight and broad-shouldered, had a square face that seemed to move up and down when he talked. He suffered from performance anxiety each time a run was scheduled. His tension would rise, and he would have to let it out so it wouldn't distract from his driving. So before each run, he used Jeanie as therapy—a punching bag. He smacked her around until her eyes wouldn't focus and punched her in the stomach until she threw up.

The owls were still hooting as Buzzy prepared to leave Nettleton, long before the roosters took over the morning shift for crowing duty. As Jeanie lay on the floor after another beating, Buzzy stood over her and said, "Gotta go, honey. Give me a kiss." He bent down, wiped the blood off her lips with a harsh smudge of his thumb, and gave her a long, hard kiss that made the battered girl wince.

"*Whew!* Baby, your breath is bad! You'd better gargle some mouthwash and put some makeup on that eye before you go to work. I ain't gonna have you lying around here unemployed. I ain't your welfare office, and I ain't your Uncle Sam—just your Sugar Daddy.

"You know...I love you," he said as he slammed out the front door and fired up his only true friend, White Lightning, and drove off into the early-morning gloom.

Just after he left, Jeanie lay crumpled in the floor, curled into a fetal position. She listened intently to the roar of the Road Runner, the squealing of tires, and the usual shower of pea gravel that showered the house when Buzzy peeled out of the driveway. She waited patiently until she heard the fading sounds of her tormentor running through the gears. At the distant bark of his tires as he hit third gear, she spit out a tooth and crawled snail-like, inch by agonizing inch, to the phone.

"Sarge, he just left," Jeanie said through whispered winces.

"He'll be coming down Highway 363 just after dawn, headed to the Rendezvous with a load of shine. He'll have that kid with him and lots of guns," she said through her broken teeth and bleeding gums.

She paused and added, "Big Billy Payne is telling everyone that unless you stop intercepting shipments, his boys are going to have to shoot you out of the saddle."

Jeanie got quiet, but Sarge could hear her breathing, so he waited.

"Waking up to see Buzzy lying next to me, looking at me with those serpentine eyes, is like sleeping with Lucifer or a rattlesnake without the rattle. He hates you, Sarge, so be careful. If you have to hurt him, hurt him a little for me if you get the chance...but don't kill him. I love him. God help me, but I do," she said, just before she rolled over on the floor and passed out from the savage beating that her true love had given her.

* * *

Buzzy roared past the sleeping towns and winked at the old town marshals who saw him and knew what he was up to, but figured it was not their business. They also knew that he would kill them, just like some men would squash a bug.

He swung by Houlka and picked up a kid named Chet Riley. The eighteen-year-old, who still bore the pimples of youth, idolized Buzzy. He had dropped out of school in the eighth grade and worked odd jobs for local businesses. Buzzy used him as a gofer to load the cargo and as chief hanger-on. Chet also got to relieve Buzzy on some of the long runs when his idol was just too smashed to drive—courtesy of his own product.

Buzzy was a high-maintenance sociopath whose narcissism needed to be stroked constantly. He felt entitled to brutalize Jeanie because it felt good and there were no consequences. A tiny morsel of shame that remained in him was nullified by Chet, who thought he could do no wrong. Chet's flattery and hero-worship built Buzzy up again so he could continue to violate societal norms while seeking excitement and pleasure through the pain and fear of others. In one sense, Jeanie was the yin to Chet's yang in the warped world of Buzzy Hester.

As they roared down the back roads, he regaled Chet with tales of all the men he had maimed or killed. "Chet, I found the genie in the bottle, and he taught me how to rub the magic lamp and kill without remorse—just erase them like magic…like make-believe," he bragged.

"That's great, Buzzy!" Chet answered.

"Uh-huh…you just dump bodies down a dark well and walk away. You never hang around to hear them hit bottom. It does give a funky taste to the water at first, until you get used to drinking with the dead," Buzzy said as he pressed the pedal to the metal and barreled down the highway like a man possessed.

At the same time Standstill was carefully loading his bomb for the drive to the sheriff's house, Buzzy and Chet were loading fresh-brewed poison at a Chickasaw County distribution way station near Houlka. They then crisscrossed the backroads through Okolona, Amory, Smithville, Fulton, and Lee County in a circuitous route to the Rendezvous Club to deliver the smooth, slow-cooked white whiskey.

Buzzy fancied himself an heir to the runners of old, busting blockades to supply the Confederate troops in Vicksburg or Atlanta. He looked at Chet as they zipped along and said, "This ain't crime, boy. This is war! And the troops need some fuel!"

As the car bounced around a bump in the road, the radio was turned wide open. The eight-track player thumped the car's speakers with Buzzy's ode to Jeanie, "Psychotic Reaction." The headlights illuminated a black blur crossing the road in front of the car. Buzzy hit the brakes, screeched to a halt, jumped out with a pistol, and blasted the poor creature with six rounds.

He jumped back in the car and said, "Ain't no black cat gonna cross my path. It's bad luck!"

Chet said, "Uh, I think it was a skunk, Buzzy."

"Close enough," Buzzy answered as he gunned the engine like a dragster on a quarter-mile strip, and the dirge for life with Jeanie played on..."I can't get your love, I can't get a fraction. Uh-oh, little girl, it's a psychotic reaction."

Since his run-in with Sarge, Buzzy was careful to avoid him. He kept his routes and times known only to a close inner circle of players in the syndicate—the bootleggers and ruffians who ran the Lee-Monroe-Chickasaw-Alcorn cooperative. He couldn't figure out how the word was getting out about the runs.

Someone asked him if Jeanie might be the leak, but he said, "Her? Are you kidding? She ain't got sense enough to come in out of the rain and has never had an original thought in her life."

Under the seat of his modified 1969 Road Runner was a rack holding a sawed-off pump shotgun loaded with 00 buckshot. On the seat beside him was a 9mm Browning pistol with a clip of twelve rounds—minus the six for the skunk/cat. In his waistband was a snub-nosed .38, and his ankle holster held Billy's favorite "sneaky pop gun," as he called it...a .32-caliber automatic.

Just before the first light broke, Buzzy shot the gap at Peppertown and roared past Mantachie on Highway 363. He gunned the Road Runner, hugging curves and roller-coasting over every bend and break in the road like a kid at the county fair, each bounce and skid punctuated by a loud—"Yahoo!" Turkeys, possums, and raccoons wandered onto the dark path of the bootlegger. Some made it. Some didn't. The sound of the skulls busting on Buzzy's front bumper made Chet sick to his stomach.

* * *

Sarge called Michael after Jeanie's tip and said, "It's time for us to spring the trap."

They lay in wait in the shadows of Highway 363 just south of the Rendezvous Club, where 363 joined what was called Jim Parson Road.

The morning sky was as black as a crow's wing, and the only natural light came from the moon playing hide-and-seek through drifting clouds. When the clouds parted, the silver moon peeked through the trees to illuminate puddles of water along the road like footlights bordering a stage.

Sarge seemed distant and pensive to Michael. He was brooding and taking inventory of his life.

"Michael, you saw Johnny Cash in Memphis last year, didn't you?" Sarge asked.

"Yeah, it was a great concert with Johnny, June, the Carter Family, Carl Perkins, and the Statler Brothers, too. Johnny introduced Tex Ritter, who was in the audience that night," Michael said.

"I love Johnny Cash and hope to see him before I die," Sarge said with a note of resignation.

Michael looked at him but didn't challenge the gloom pouring out from Sarge. He just let him talk.

"You know, Michael, there was this girl once. I met her on leave from basic training when I was eighteen. I was in the bus station in Mobile waiting for my Greyhound to come in. She came in alone and had this look, like a lost lamb, you know?" he asked.

Michael nodded.

"We began to talk. She was maybe sixteen, long legs and hair like that doll, Raggedy-Ann, and a million freckles. There was something about her...something I still can't get out of my mind. I think she might have been a runaway. I sat by her, and the time flew by. So many stories swapped. She loosened up and didn't seem so scared anymore. She laid her hand on mine, and when I looked into those blue eyes, I thought that maybe I was in love," he said and then got real quiet.

"Before my bus came in, I kissed her, and the world began to spin around. Then the Greyhound to Tupelo arrived, and as I got up to leave her, she held my hand so tight that I thought she might never let go. I looked back as I stepped up into the bus, and she was still watching me, eyes pleading, begging me to stay," he said.

Sarge sighed and said, "You know, I never told her my name or asked hers. Isn't that crazy? So when I think about her, I just call her Rose, like that old song, 'Sweet Rose of Alabama.' I think about those might-have-been moments, and I wonder if she's still out there somewhere...and if she still thinks of me."

He looked away quickly to hide his face until the last of the moon betrayed him and bathed his wet face in a soft, silvery glow. Then the footlight puddles suddenly lit up with the first orange glow from the sun. Michael felt he was listening to another episode of Ralph Edwards' show..."Sarge, this is your life!"

Just as the rays of the sun winked over the horizon and Sarge's unexpected vulnerability overwhelmed him, Michael thought of Dixie Lee with the gamine smile, the eyes that became dreamy dares, and the lips that could swell and pout at the drop of a hat. He wondered if she, too, was frozen in the terminal of time, just out of reach.

He turned to Sarge and said, "I bet Rose still dreams of you, Sarge, the kind young man that might have been."

"Yeah, well...sometimes you have premonitions," Sarge said as he pulled out a gray handkerchief and honked his nose.

"Anyway, I read an article in my Army magazine about this thing they used in the days of the Roman chariots and later in the military in World War II...a long strip with spikes to stop the advance of the enemy, to injure feet and later to puncture tires. They called them *caltrops* or *crow's feet*. I figured that if they slowed the enemies then, they might shut down a fast bootlegger car. Got to thinking about it after Cal outran us all the other night," he said.

"The old blacksmith at Saltillo made one for me—an imitation of what I saw pictures of in the magazine. There's no traffic out here this time of the morning, so when we hear the Road Runner coming, we're going to pull that strip out of the trunk and lay those spikes right across this curve on 363. I won't have Buzzy getting away this time," Sarge said.

Their windows were down, and the early-morning quiet was broken by the distant engine whine of an approaching super-car, punctuated by the staccato, muffled roar of Buzzy's glasspack mufflers about two hills and hollows away.

Michael jumped out to help Sarge pull the long strip of nails from one embankment to the next; there was no way to pass them without hitting that strip. Their car blocked Jim Parson Road, and the strip covered 363. Michael had never seen anything quite like that homemade roadblock.

They returned to the patrol car just as the Road Runner topped the ridge and became airborne for an instant. The tires touched down on the blacktop pavement and slid sideways into the sharp curve at eighty. Buzzy saw the patrol car at the same time Michael hit the blue lights and cranked up the ear-splitting wail of the siren.

Smiling, he passed Sarge and Michael's position, and with one hand out the driver's window, he began firing the Browning. The windshield on the patrol car fractured, and spider-like cracks ran across the glass. Shards of glass peppered the deputies.

Still smiling, Buzzy hit the strip of spikes just as he down-shifted to first gear and floored the Road Runner to sprint away.

There was the roar of the engine and then a loud screeching as the brakes locked up and the car began to slide on the pavement.

The hollow spikes did their job, and the tires blew out with a one-two-three *boom!* A whooshing sound followed as the air escaped the tires, and then the repeated *flop-ah, flop-ah, flop* of the deflated tires hitting the road. White Lightning almost turned over, but instead slid sideways into the ditch, leaning against a large embankment of sticky, red clay.

The impact and the jarring drop onto the rims of the wheels opened a small crack in the transport tank beneath the trunk, and moonshine began to seep onto the remote road—first a trickle, then a steady stream of the liquid gold that men were willing to fight and die for.

The radiator was busted and made a hissing, tinkling sound as Buzzy snaked out the driver's window, throwing the last two shots from the Browning in the direction of the deputies. The shots hit the driver's side door where Sarge had taken cover, the impact of the shots making a plunking-pinging sound, like someone dropping marbles in a can.

Chet barreled out the passenger side with the shotgun, and Sarge yelled, "Get the kid, Michael! I'll take Buzzy!"

Chet was running and falling, firing the shotgun wildly. Just as he fired the third round at no one in particular, he stepped onto a muddy patch, and the recoil caused the skinny kid to lose his balance. He landed on his rear but popped up running, without the shotgun.

Michael was right behind him, and they left the life-and-death drama of Sarge and Buzzy behind them as they disappeared from view over the rise.

Buzzy was slipping and sliding down the side of the road, hugging the embankment and the tree line for cover. He had twisted one ankle, and his gait was a cross between a run and a hobbled hop.

He had emptied the Browning but produced the .38 revolver. Out of breath, he stopped now and then around each contour in the road to squeeze off a shot when he saw Sarge rounding the bend.

Sarge jumped into the ditch and into a prone position each time to fire rounds from the carbine he was carrying. One round whistled by Buzzy's right ear, making a sharp *speeyong* ricochet sound off the tree behind him.

* * *

Michael had overtaken Chet near a thicket of pines and made a perfect open field tackle, wrapping his arms around the back of Chet's knees. He went down like a sack of potatoes, and all the air in him came out with a big *whoosh!*

As Michael rolled him onto his stomach and wrenched his hands behind his back to cuff him, he heard the gunshots from down the hill. He snapped one bracelet on Chet's right wrist and dragged him to a thin but sturdy pine and chained him to the tree.

Then Michael began to run back down the hill in a stumbling, lurching sprint, as fast as his feet would carry him. The closer he got, the louder the reports of the weapons and the more difficult it was to tell where the fight was taking place. The shots and shouts seemed to come from every direction in a carnival of illusion.

He yelled, "Sarge, where are you?" His voice echoed down the hollows and returned to him…the only answer he received.

* * *

Buzzy had made his way up and over the slope of the road and down the other side to the shallows of a roaring creek running through the woods. He jumped into the water, flopping and splashing his way down the creek.

Four vultures suddenly appeared and were making a slow, lazy circle over the potential scene of death.

Buzzy stopped and squeezed off some shots with the ankle gun whenever he saw movement in the tree line above him. Each time he fired the .32, it sounded like a sharp, metallic version of someone popping the cork out of a bottle.

Sarge was moving along the ridge to execute that tried-and-true plan of all Western movies...he was going to head off the desperado at the pass. But just as he was maneuvering above and in front of Buzzy, he lost his footing and came crashing down the hillside, tumbling head-over-heel, out of control, and banging into trees and stumps.

Buzzy, who was looking behind him, heard the commotion and turned just as Sarge bounced off the slope and into the water at his feet. Sarge was bruised and bleeding and had lost his carbine and his service revolver.

Sarge was gasping for breath from what felt like broken or bruised ribs. He half sat up and winced in pain as he squatted in the water. Then he saw Buzzy.

Buzzy wore a dull smile, a wiry cat's-got-the-canary smile. His shirt was soiled, and his pants were wet and dingy. His head was wet from sweat, which was also pouring from his underarms.

The circling buzzards above the men seemed to drop lower in expectation.

Sarge's mind was racing. *So this is how it ends.*

Buzzy took two steps toward Sarge and towered over him, the .32 never leaving the ten-ring area. Then he raised the barrel to aim right between Sarge's eyes and said, "Got the drop on you, Sarge. I'm going to miss you."

He could already see the hole he would put right between Sarge's eyes. Everything seemed to slow down. He squeezed the trigger. The hammer snapped forward, and the pin struck the primer to create the spark that would ignite the gunpowder and cause the explosion to propel the bullet out of the small gun and into Sarge's head.

Buzzy could already hear the explosion and feel the slight recoil of the small pistol as a glint of silver in the air hurtled toward Sarge to explode his head like a melon. He knew that the extractor would grab hold of the rim and eject the empty casing from the gun. This was his last round, but it was all he needed.

Except this time, none of that happened—just a snap and no discharge.

Buzzy looked at the gun in disbelief, and Sarge willed himself forward for one desperate, bull-like charge. As he hit the gunman, the force knocked Buzzy backwards onto a bed of rock, and Buzzy's head bounced off the rock...not once, not twice, but three times. Blood from the back of Buzzy's head bathed the rocks in red and turned the silver-blue water to crimson.

Michael came sloshing down the creek at that moment, knee-deep in water, and shouted, "Sarge? Sarge? Are you all right?"

Sarge had picked up Buzzy's gun from atop one of the rocks and just sat on his haunches, looking at it and at Buzzy.

"Yeah, I'm okay," he said.

Michael was out of breath, and he was gasping for air. He stopped near his partner. He looked at Buzzy sprawled over the jagged rocks, his skull leaking blood, and then back at Sarge. "Something's going on in the county. The radio was erupting as I ran by, and they were calling us," Michael said.

Sarge didn't answer. He had ejected the last round in the chamber and held it up before Michael, who knelt beside him.

"Look at this, Michael," he said as the water began to seep from his eyes. "A gun leaves unique marks on cartridge cases, except there are no marks on this one. It not only didn't fire...it left no markings. It was as if there was something—or Someone—between the firing pin and primer cap at the rear of the cartridge."

Sarge looked at Michael and said, "I've been running on empty for too long, Michael. I've been mean, and I was sometimes wicked when I fought the wicked...but this is a miracle, a second chance at redemption. This was God. Only God could put His hand between the pin and cap and not leave a mark."

They heard a commotion above them and saw someone at the top of the ridge silhouetted against the morning sun, leaving him in shadow for a moment. The profile of a featureless entity seemed to emerge from a doorway to nowhere.

But it was Tom, and he shouted to them, "Are y'all okay?"

"Yeah, we're going to make it, but better call an ambulance for me and the coroner for him," Sarge answered, pointing to Buzzy, who lay motionless on the rocks.

Tom stood there for a moment, backlit against the light, like the pale rider whose name was Death, the companion of the grave.

He said, "Oh, Lord, Michael! God help us, Sarge! All hell's broken loose! The chief deputy was roughed up at the Snake Pit, the sheriff's house was firebombed, and Jo-Jo's dead!"

Michael and Sarge looked at each other in disbelief.

Buzzy suddenly came to life and began to murmur from his cradle on the gray-brown rocks, one standing on end behind his head like a headstone.

"What, what?" he asked groggily.

"Oh, I remember. The bough broke and down came Buzzy, cradle and all," he said.

Sarge and Michael stood over him.

Buzzy looked up at Sarge and smiled. "It was Jeanie, wasn't it? Got to admire that girl's spunk. Give her 'White Lightning' and all I got. You are witness to my last will and testament. Tell her I'm sorry, that I just couldn't help myself."

His eyes fluttered, closed, and then opened again.

The black vultures began to land one by one, staying a discreet distance, all bowing their heads as if giving thanks for the meal they were about to receive.

Buzzy saw them. His eyes were wild, clouded by the visit of a stranger to his heart—fear. "Make them birds go away! Make 'em go away!"

Michael shooed the big buzzards, and they lazily took to the sky, flapping away on the early-morning updrafts to continue their one mission in life: to clean the earth of carrion—out with the old and in with the new—to make way for life.

Buzzy's panic ceased, his rapid breathing slowed, and he calmed as the winged undertakers disappeared over the wooded ridge.

"It's subtle, you know? You never realize it until it's too late. They lure us with their bread crumbs, as they herd us to our sleeping place, and then we slumber forever and wait for more to join us," he said through a hoarse, dry mouth.

"Who's that skeleton with the long sling blade over there? Y'all see him, don't you? Sarge, do you smell smoke?" Buzzy asked.

He winced and whispered, "My dead self will be waiting for you, Sarge."

He made a gargling sound as he gave up the ghost, and the final death rattle of air escaped him. Buzzy learned that all the praise of his court jesters and the plaudits of those who feared him were counterfeit tokens of no currency when his guns were silenced and his black heart ceased to beat.

The one-liners in the theater of life were just the murmurings of supporting actors and bit players marking time, waiting in the box-office line to buy their own final, one-way tickets from the cashier.

It was all just whistles and catcalls from the cheap seats, the crowd urging him to get off the stage and whispering Porky Pig's stuttering Looney Tunes benediction—"Th-Th-Th-Th-Th-… That's all, folks."

CHAPTER FOURTEEN

*"Words are less needful to sorrow
than to joy."—Helen Hunt Jackson*

*"What they might lack in intelligence,
they make up for with sheer quantities
of high explosive."—Simon Morden,*
Theories of Flight

When Sheriff Gill Simpson arrived at his home, it looked like a war zone. No birds were singing, and no squirrels were playing in the wooded community. Everything smelled of soot and smoke, and there was a wet stench in the air, like an old dog that had wallowed in muddy waters.

The willows were weeping, the oaks were creaking, the fresh daffodils were drooping, and the dogwood blooms were bleeding red.

Trucks from the fire station in East Tupelo had beaten Gill to the scene. They were still hosing down the house as he pulled up. Neighbors were milling about, gawking at the spectacle, and as the sheriff arrived, a hush fell over the crowd. They watched his every move as he parked, lingered in his car for a moment, and then slowly walked to the house.

He stopped at the crude wooden sign and looked at it for a long time, lost in thought.

It could have been my wife and children in my home...in my home.

Pain rattled around in his heart, and the bitter anger-acid burned a hole in his stomach.

His neighbors began to whisper words of comfort as he passed them. "So sorry, Gill... We are so thankful that your family is safe, Sheriff... Hope you find the people who did this, and that they rot in Hades."

Members of the Tupelo Police Department and the fire marshal's office were taking statements from area residents.

Gill's wife, Elizabeth, had gathered the children from school. When he saw his wife with her chicks snuggled under the comfort of mother-hen's wings, he let out a big, heaving sigh of relief and walked quickly to their side.

Deep, vertical creases were marring the space between her brows, and the stress lines showed around her eyes and in the frown on her face, which sagged from sorrow. Her eyes appeared tired and milky beneath her graying hair, and her skin seemed lifeless and leathery in the harshness of the morning sun's revelations.

He heard a muted or whispered harmony of the restless children hanging onto her. He thought that they sounded something like human mosquitoes, buzzing and singing in unison, just low enough to prompt the question "What did you say?"

But the sheriff didn't need to ask; their little people's eyes said it all. They were confused and scared, but they calmed when they saw their father and heard his deep, comforting voice.

He just looked at his wife and nodded. She nodded back. That's how it was between couples who always had the badge as a constant companion. She was playing the part given her…stoic, steady wife of the sheriff, but on this day, Elizabeth thought that some scriptwriter had not read the fairy tale she had authored in her heart and had rewritten all the lines.

Cathy, the daughter with hazel eyes and light-brown hair, had hung back from the others, patting at her skirt and pulling at her ponytail. She loved Jo-Jo; he was her baby. She moved in front of the others and watched intently as the fire marshal and Tupelo policemen removed the monkey's charred body from the utility room area.

Then she disappeared for a moment and emerged from a small treehouse her father had built for her. It had been a retreat for her and Jo-Jo. Neighbors had remarked that she could climb trees as easily as Jo-Jo. On this day of sorrow, she was holding a bag of pennies.

She walked up to her father, her hurt eyes staring at the ground. She finally looked up through big Coke-bottle eyeglasses that magnified her eyes and said, "Daddy, here's my bag of pennies...pennies from heaven, just like the song I used to sing to Jo-Jo before bedtime every night. It's all I got, but it'll be worth all my pennies, Daddy, if you'll find the men that killed my monkey and blow them up, just like they did poor Jo-Jo."

Gill hugged his daughter, clenched his jaws in an attempt to steel himself, and then he took her bag of pennies.

"Is that enough, Daddy?" asked the tiny child, who had asked for none of the pain of the adult world.

"It's just right, honey. That will help me a lot. Don't you worry," he said, looking at her mother, who was softly crying.

A grim-faced investigator approached the sheriff.

"One of the neighbors saw a man scurrying away from your home this morning. He thought he might be a meter reader, but he said the man was bleeding, blood dripping from his hand," the detective said.

Gill just nodded and looked out over his yard filled with debris. A stray bit of ash came floating by, and a jay returned to his perch high above Gill's home to preach to the neighborhood congregation about all that he had seen.

Gill, hearing the raucous sermon, looked up at the flash of blue and white and wished he could take his statement.

If only I could translate Blue Jay.

Gill turned to the small crowd of officers that had gathered around him.

"I've worked and worked on this old yard and used all the prescribed fertilizer and weed-control agents. Jo-Jo used to ride on my shoulder when I mowed the grass. But it's always a losing battle, isn't it? The more you mow and sow, the more the weeds try to take over. There comes a time when you have to stop trimming things at the surface and get down and dirty," he said.

He bent down and tore a clod of dirt covered in dandelion weeds from the ground.

"You just got to rip up the weeds by the roots, kill 'em dead, and make sure they never grow in your yard again," he said.

He tossed the weeds out of his yard and into the ditch.

"Bimbos, bootlegging, and blackmail buy bullets for the bullies, boys. It's what makes grown men go mad, the pious bend to sin, politicians turn as rancid as sour mash, and widows weep and wail.

"It's past time to put my foot on the devil's throat."

CHAPTER FIFTEEN

"In this kingdom by the sea, a wind blew out of a
cloud, chilling my beautiful Annabel Lee..."
—*Edgar Allan Poe, "Annabel Lee"*

"What was it that you wanted and why
didn't you fight for it?"—*Shannon L. Alder*

Dixie Lee Carter awoke from a bad night at the club. Her
eyes looked like frosted glass. She had a bloody nose and the
mother of all headaches. She felt puffy and bloated, her head
seemed the size of a bowling ball, and her face looked like the
twisted twin sister of a jack-o'-lantern.

She remembered playing her answering machine, but she
didn't know what day or week that was. It was hard to separate the
waking world from the dreamscape. Maybe she listened, maybe
she didn't. She may have erased the messages, or they may have
erased her.

She sat up on the side of the bed, and the room began to
spin around like a carousel. She felt drugged, though she had not
used drugs, and had only drunk that one glass of champagne,
she thought.

Maybe I was drugged. Someone might've slipped something
in my drink. Need to listen to Michael's message again. He
sounded bad, something about death and bombs. Oh no, they're
gone. His voice is dead. Is he dead?

She tore at her hair and began to cry.

That nightmare was awful. I was wandering the streets of
Memphis, asking strangers, begging them to tell me, "Where can I
get rid of me?"

The asphalt was shiny-wet from a storm, and the street-
lights cast an eerie golden hue to a rising fog. An aching emptiness
and aloneness surrounded me in the midst of passersby. I longed

to find Michael. It was all tied up in him, somehow. He knew the way home.

Then that toothless old woman came up to me, skin sagging and wearing rotten, threadbare clothes. She said, "You stop soiling our soil, child. There's only one place to go, honey, when your life is in tatters, when the good days are drifting by the windows of your soul, and you want to dump your second-hand dreams and nightmares—down at the Goodwill store. Do you have any good will left, child?"

Then those phones were ringing, maybe a thousand of them, and I knew it must be Michael calling. I would answer one and say, "Hello, Michael, is that you?" No one was there, and I would answer another one, and no one was there. I would run to the next and the next, but the phones would not stop ringing. I fell to my knees and passed out.

Then I was down by the river, and Mama was hiding me in a basket in the reeds. I was waiting for Michael to find me and take me home. Poison apples were falling from the trees, and a snake asked me if I was shopping for some low-hanging fruit and a prime waterfront lot in the garden.

Brothers were killing their brothers, and the sun was climbing a ladder leaned against the bluest sky I'd ever seen. I thought it was a big, yellow balloon, and I wanted to chase it all the way to heaven. Then a man came by and asked me if I was qualified. I said, "Qualified for what? I don't know. I'm just waiting to be found."

But he just kept asking me if I was qualified. I said, "I don't know. I don't know, but I want to be."

He smiled at me and said, "Don't worry. Someone will be along for you before too long."

I asked him if it would be Michael. He said, "Yes, but he'll be too late."

I remember that I woke up then and sat straight up in bed. I was crying. I don't think I'll be going back to the club any time soon—maybe later, when I learn to be careful and to manage the temptations.

Just when I think I have found the core of my restlessness, it slips away into the dark corners of my mind, and the sands run faster through the hourglass.

I'm scared.

Maybe Michael will call again today.

* * *

After Michael took Sarge to the emergency room in Tupelo for treatment of his bruises and fractures, Sarge insisted that they drive to Nettleton to break the news to Jeanie about Buzzy.

A fine mist had settled over Nettleton when she met them at the door. She was wearing that look of dread when military officers come to inform them that their loved ones won't be coming home.

She wore the garb of sorrow and conflict, the abused simultaneously celebrating and mourning the death of the abuser.

"I knew he was dead," she said. "When I woke up, there was just this void, and I knew he had checked out. I didn't want to turn him in. I wanted to let that sleeping dog lie over there in the corner, but he bit me once too often. He had run up a big debt for his sins, and death was always just half a mile down his backroad runs, around the sharp bends of his fast lanes…waiting to collect. I woke one night last week, and he was sitting by my bedside. He stroked my hair and said, 'Everybody's dying. I'm just dying faster than most.'"

Sarge nodded and said, "He left everything he had to you, Jeanie. As soon as I can, I'll bring it by here, but I'll work with your lawyer on the last will and testament he repeated to me in front of Michael."

She thanked them, but before she closed the door, she said, "As strange as it may seem, when he died, a part of me died, too, and I'll never be whole again. He wasn't always like what he became. The mean man overwhelmed the boy, and I lost him. If you come across that boy one day…on some backroad trying to find his way home, let me know. Time and all that meanness can't erase him from my heart."

As they walked away, they heard a loud shriek of grief from behind her closed door and a sobbing release that made the deputies involuntarily hang their heads.

Sarge was quiet on the drive to his home. When they pulled up in his driveway, he said, "I'll see you at the department when I get cleaned up…to see how we can help the sheriff with the attack on his home. I suspect that's what this meeting is about.

"Our life is like a quilt, a collection of common threads woven by God in a design we can't see or recognize…just one long story—my story, your story, and Jeanie's story. He brought it all home to me in that roaring water today. I was baptized in the spirit today."

After he left Sarge, Michael stopped at a payphone and called Dixie Lee's number repeatedly, until his messages ran out the tape on her answering machine. He was worried about her, but also wanted to talk with her before the meeting with the sheriff, the regular deputies, and the auxiliary officers who had been ordered to report for duty.

When he had met Dixie in Washington, she was searching and would stray off the beaten path now and then after their relationship began. Michael didn't pretend to know the root causes of her unhappiness, but she seemed bent on self-destruction at times, sitting on the front pew of the church of the "new-age religion," worshipping at the altar of confusion.

She was always caught between an urge to leave and one to stay. She wanted to go to a new place to find happiness and scratch that gnawing itch. There was a restlessness within her that made her flee the old place where she thought she didn't want to be, and yet she missed it when she left. It was an endless cycle…a dead-end path to nowhere.

The new place became old, and the old place became new again. All destinations changed names but remained the same, and she always wound up where she had begun. Michael wondered how long she could survive the frantic journeys. After each odyssey, she would have a time of exhaustion, which she mistook for peace, and then it all would begin again.

Dixie Lee was running as hard as she could but never outrunning the face in the mirror. She wanted the quick fixes, the shiny baubles of life. She thought they were on sale with a painless down payment, a personal recognizance bond, and an easy-pay plan, never knowing that the interest was compounding and that her soul had been the collateral.

Michael tried her line again, and it rang and rang... seemingly a thousand times. One time he thought he heard her answer, but she couldn't hear him. The crackle of his walkie-talkie interrupted his thoughts. As the dispatcher asked him his estimated time of arrival at the department, he was watching a bright sun climbing the morning sky.

He thought the daystar looked like a giant yellow balloon that had escaped from the circus, and he had the impulse to lasso it and give it to Dixie Lee to light her life, dry her fresh-cut tears, and chase away the black despair that hid in the shadows across her soul.

CHAPTER SIXTEEN
"It's how you show up at the
showdown that counts."
—Homer H. Norton

"In a gun fight... You need to take
your time in a hurry."—Wyatt Earp

As Michael neared the Lee County sheriff's office, the early decks of puffy clouds had drifted away. The yellow ball was still ascending, and the scattered blue light from the sun had turned the sky a deep, pure, baby blue that reminded him of the dyed eggs of Parker Grove Easter-egg hunts.

A red-tailed hawk circled in the sky over the sheriff's department and the empty field beyond, proclaiming a hoarse, screaming *kee-eeeee-arr*, repeating it with some sense of urgency like a messenger from beyond.

A street preacher in an avocado-green suit and a pencil-thin black tie was walking back and forth between Tupelo Hardware and the sheriff's office. His hair was slicked back, his eyes were on fire, and his face was ruddy red.

Following him were several young men and women, all solemn and stern-faced. Michael recognized one young woman from the investigation of Star's death. He had seen her standing behind Magnolia that day, and here she was. He wondered how she managed to escape the clutches of The Pusher, whom no one had seen lately.

The preacher held his Bible high in the air, and in a classic display of controlled breathing, shouting, and hiccupping, his voice began to rise and then fall in the rhythmic cadence of old-time Southern preachers: "Wells are dry, children are hungry, women cannot prepare meals, no man can warm by the oven, and the flame has dimmed in our souls. The pilot light has been blown away, and only the Pilot can reignite it!

"Repent, you sinners! Repent! Judgment Day is at hand!"

The street was lined with cars—some new, some clunkers. The back lot was overflowing. Grim-faced men milled about out front, smoking cigarettes, spitting tobacco, and whispering in low tones. The hands of a few men were trembling ever so slightly. It had the air of a wake or a gathering of reluctant knights about to embark on a great crusade. It seemed like the calm before the OK Corral.

As Michael passed through the ranks of auxiliary deputies, some nodded, others checked the weapons they had been issued, a few seemed excited, and others appeared indifferent or uncertain. Some had the look of men who wished they were at their regular jobs. Michael caught a whiff of medicinal courage-in-a-bottle on someone's breath.

Earl raised his eyebrows and shook his head as Michael entered the office and slid through the crowd. Big Tom grinned at his first partner as he loaded a 12-gauge pump shotgun with 00 buckshot.

A somber Sheriff Simpson appeared with Jeremiah Owings, the department chaplain and local Baptist pastor, by his side. Gill said, "Gather round, men. Check your weapons. Sarge, make sure all the riot gear is distributed. You handle the surplus hand grenades the National Guard sent and pass out the tear gas canisters."

Michael looked at Tom and mouthed the words "hand grenades?"

"I appreciate everyone coming in today, especially the auxiliary deputies. I know this is a hardship for you and your families," the sheriff said.

"We have always policed according to state law and the Mississippi and US Constitutions. I aim to stay within those parameters that you and I took an oath to support and uphold…but it is time to take it to another level. They've bombed my home. They've threatened my chief deputy with violence. They tried to kill two of my deputies. Two more deputies were roughed up at

Mutt's Place, and the owner of the Rendezvous has said that he is going to shoot my men out of their saddles.

"I can't allow all these things to go unanswered, lest it begets more lawlessness. So we take the first step today. We have a state tax warrant for the arrest of Cal Mattox. He hasn't paid taxes, and we are obliged to serve the warrant. Is it the warrant we want to serve? The one for attempted murder, assault, and the plague of thievery, threats, and death by the moonshine poison he has brought to Lee County? No, but it is a start. We couldn't get a warrant for the threats against the chief deputy, because it was his word against Cal and his witnesses.

"Cal's place is in Pontotoc County, but Sheriff Bill Mullins of Pontotoc County has empowered me to serve warrants there in the past, and he has now renewed that authority, deputizing me and all of you to serve these warrants in his county. They will back us up if we call on them.

"We also have reason to believe that Stanley Still, the suspect in the bombing of my home, will be there today. We have a warrant for him issued by the justice of the peace in Verona," Gill said.

All of the men in the room looked at each other as the gravity of the moment began to sink in. There was a hush over the gathering, and only the soft mutter of passing car tires singing on the hot street outside broke the silence. The usual murmur and banter of inmates from the corridor of cells was muted out of respect for the sheriff.

"I want to maintain radio silence today as we approach the Snake Pit. We don't want them to know that we are coming. So stay off the main S.O. channel. We have National Guard walkie-talkies for every unit, and Mack will pass those out now, along with assignments for each unit," the sheriff said.

"Pastor Jeremiah, would you come forward and say a prayer for us and for this mission we are about to embark on against the grave sin of evil men?" Gill asked.

The tall pastor stepped forward. Michael thought that he had an imposing presence, the strong jaw and prominent features of an older Billy Graham, and the aura of a man accustomed to speaking on behalf of God.

Pastor Owings said, "Let us pray.

"Lord of mercy and might, we pray for victory over the enemies of Your Kingdom, the armies of evil. We pray for Your protection of these officers assembled here today. We pray as David prayed in Psalm 35 and ask, 'Contend, oh Lord, with those who contend with me. Fight against those who fight against me. Take hold of buckler and shield, and rise up for my help.'

"Draw also the spear and the battle-axe to meet those who pursue me; Say to my soul, 'I am your salvation.' Let those be ashamed and dishonored who seek my life; Let those be turned back and humiliated who devise evil against me. Let them be like chaff before the wind, with the angel of the LORD driving them on. Let their way be dark and slippery, with the angel of the LORD pursuing them. Let destruction come upon him unawares, and let the net which he hid catch himself; Into that very destruction let him fall.

"And my soul shall rejoice in the LORD; It shall exult in His salvation. All my bones will say, 'LORD, who is like Thee, Who delivers the afflicted from him who is too strong for him, and the afflicted and the needy from him who robs him?'...I will give Thee thanks in the great congregation; I will praise Thee among a mighty throng...Oh, Lord, do not be far from me. And my tongue shall declare Thy righteousness and Thy praise all day long.

"All these things we pray in the name of Your only begotten Son, Jesus Christ, the perfect Lamb You gave as sacrifice for our sins. Amen and amen!" the pastor concluded.

And all of the men assembled echoed in unison, "Amen!" to the first imprecatory prayer that Michael had ever heard...a petition to God to bring disaster on one's enemies.

Sarge said, "Michael, you are with me."

The small army of deputies began to load up in regular county units and an assortment of private cars and pickup trucks. The long line of warriors snaked out of downtown Tupelo and headed up toward the unincorporated land just beyond Sherman in Pontotoc County.

Sheriff Simpson was in the lead car with Deputy Louis Spigner, a friend from the days when they had played together in Gill's band. People came out of their businesses and on the front porches of their homes to watch what appeared to them to be a long funeral procession led by the sheriff, except that they noticed there was no hearse.

The unforgiving glare of the noonday sun illuminated the tin roof of the Snake Pit and the cars of late-night revelers, sleeping off another nocturnal episode of the attempted great escape...from themselves. The Pit was a destination of distraction for some in the tightknit community of Tupelo-Lee County and a reliable source of moonshine whiskey.

The people who ran the city and county were veterans. They had come home from the war determined to marry, have children, and build a better way of life than they'd had as young men, when many of them had picked cotton or sharecropped. There had been a post-war surge in population as new residents moved in with plant owners looking for cheap labor after the war.

Old Tupelo liked the money that the industries and the Yankee interlopers were bringing to the economy, but the city pulled its collars tight around its born-and-bred lineage. They sneered at the accents and habits of some of the Johnny-come-lately transplants while quietly raising the standard of living and padding old-money pockets with the new money floating around.

When restlessness and war memories burrowed their sharp fangs into the walking wounded, some natural-born Southerners—along with some new arrivals—would roam the nightclubs of the Dixie Mafia and the independent Saturday-night bars and cocktail lounges...before repenting on Sunday.

Moonshine's pale poison, the hammering jukeboxes, pickup bands of the juke joints, the dice tables and poker games, and the female "birds of prey" all served as temporary medicine for a sickness that the underworld could never cure—only exploit.

By day, some of the restless marched along the assembly lines and barked orders in the tire plants, the tool and die factories, and amidst the garment industry looms, but by night, some paced the dance-hall floors and drank white lightning beneath the neon signs of places like the Rendezvous, the Playhouse, and the Snake Pit. They were looking for substitutes for love in the "liquor and lipstick industry," seeking to still the gnawing in their blood.

Cal Mattox awoke to the sound of his dog, Max, barking at the top of his lungs. He staggered into the bar area of his establishment to find numerous men draped over the drinking and gambling tables, sleeping it off. Several of his faithful gang members were curled up on the cots he had provided. The odor of sin permeated the place, but Cal could no longer smell it.

His dog was still yapping and yapping. Cal assumed it was another squirrel the fool dog had treed. The long-tailed rodents sat on their branches and tormented Max, and the mutt bought into the game every time.

Cal grabbed the front door and pushed it open to "shut that mongrel up." He stepped outside his club, momentarily blinded by the bright noon sun. While he blinked and squinted against the light, his eyes focused on the shadow images...and then the line after line of deputies with shotguns and rifles, all pointed at him.

Standing in front of the deputies and near Cal was Sheriff Gill Simpson. Cal knew it was payday.

The sheriff stepped forward and said, "Cal Mattox, I have a warrant for your arrest. You are surrounded, outnumbered, and outgunned. Drop that pistol on your hip to the ground, and put your hands above your head, or we'll shoot you down like the mad dog you are!"

Cal looked left and right. He went into a half-crouch, spread his arms, bowed his shoulders, and his hand instinctively moved toward the gun in his waistband.

"Go ahead then and draw, Cal, and I'll drop you where you stand," Simpson said as he cocked both hammers on the double-barreled shotgun.

Cal's mind was racing. He saw nothing but badges and guns in every direction. Beyond them was escape if he could drop the sheriff and make it to his fast car by feinting and firing. His mind was running a mile a minute.

I got a slim chance of making it to the car. But if I do, they probably got roadblocks up on all the exit roads. They probably even got old Broderick Crawford from TV's Highway Patrol *waiting for me, too. Why not? They seem to have brought everyone else out here. I'd be a fugitive if I made it, but I know I won't survive the dash to the car.*

I wonder which one of my two suits they'd bury me in...the blue one or the shiny, brown-striped one that Ace Connelly bought for me at Lansky's in Memphis? Would anyone mourn my passing? Would any of the pious who drink my liquor say any pretty words over my casket? Would my wife and children even show up after the way I treated them? I can't stand the thought of confinement. I'd wither and die behind bars.

He came back to the moment and the images of so many men with their cheeks lying along their rifle and shotgun sights. He decided to live to fight another day, to call on his financial and political benefactors to bail him out. So Cal, the chief snake at the Snake Pit, gave up his momentary fantasy of going down in a hail of bullets, his own guns blazing.

He put his hands up and said, "All right then. You got me."

The sheriff walked up to him and leaned in to take his gun. Cal spit in his face and tried to kick the sheriff in the groin. Deputies stepped forward and some almost fired, but Gill Simpson was in the line of fire. The sheriff blocked the kick with the barrel of his shotgun, backhanded Cal, and put him flat on his back with an uppercut from the stock of the Remington, just as the deputies rushed in to handcuff him.

The door opened at that moment, and out stepped Stanley Still, his hand still bandaged from his encounter with Jo-Jo. He jumped back into the club and slammed the door behind him.

Michael made a move for the front door with Sarge and Tom, but Sarge grabbed his arm and said, "The sheriff wants you to stand lookout in front of the club. Best you stay here for now."

With that, Sarge and six deputies followed the sheriff into the club, and Michael was left wondering what that was all about. He went over to where two auxiliary deputies were holding Cal, grabbing him by the arm to take him to the cage of his patrol unit.

Mattox sneered at him.

"You boys better quit following and tagging along after Gill Simpson. You deputies better learn that when you stick your hands in the fire, you get burned," Cal said to Michael.

"Jo-Jo's not the one who looks blistered right now," Michael answered as he locked Cal behind the cage of Sarge's car.

After Cal was secured, Michael watched the front door of the club. He heard sounds of struggle and turmoil—men shouting, struggle, glass breaking. A jukebox began to play suddenly and then stopped abruptly, followed by a loud crash.

Everything finally grew eerily quiet, and one deputy asked Michael if they should go in to see if the sheriff needed help. Michael said, "We'd better not. If anyone needs help, I suspect it's not our guys."

The doors flew open, and the deputies emerged with several men in cuffs. The sheriff followed with a battered and bruised Stanley Still in cuffs. "Standstill" was now bleeding from more places than his hand.

Sarge saw the look on Michael's face and asked, "What? He resisted arrest. Do you have any more questions?"

Michael looked inside the club at the wrecked den of iniquity and the shattered jukebox lying on the floor amidst broken 45-rpm records. He pursed his lips, raised his eyebrow, and smiled when he said, "The jukebox must've put up quite a struggle, too!"

CHAPTER SEVENTEEN

*"If you aren't in over your head, how do you
know how tall you are?"—T.S. Eliot*

*"If you can keep your head when all about
you are losing theirs and blaming it on
you...If neither foes nor loving friends can
hurt you..."—Rudyard Kipling, "If"*

The *Tupelo Daily Journal* heralded the news that the grape-vine was already abuzz with...Cal Mattox had been arrested and was being held at the Lee County Jail.

Reporters, neighbors opining across backyard fences, and VFW and Masonic Lodge members all wondered if it would stick this time. Cal was like a cat with nine lives. He always evaded justice—if not by charm, guile, or threats, then through the influence of a small clique of powerful men who invested in and benefited from the moonshine trade and other ancillary markets of organized crime.

One such power broker was businessman and philanthropist Horace Pennington—private benefactor of men like Cal Mattox, Billy Payne, and James Streeter.

Pennington gave generously to his church and local charities—money needed by residents of the poorest state in the nation. Like his good friends and fellows at the Chamber of Commerce, no one questioned where the money came from. Everyone assumed that he was an astute businessman, and he was—both in his public ventures and his private vices.

Pennington was a tall man with vintage 1950s-style black horn-rimmed glasses and a tuft of white hair high on the crown of his head. He paid a visit to Sheriff Gill Simpson to instruct Lee County's chief law enforcement officer on Boat-Rocking 101.

As the sheriff walked through the department on his way to the meeting in his office, he saw Michael and said, "Deputy Parker, would you come to my office and sit with me and my guest for our chat? I think it might be a good lesson for a young officer."

Michael nodded and took a seat in the corner. Pennington looked at him and made Michael feel as welcome as four dead skunks.

"Gill, I thought this was to be a private meeting," Pennington said.

"I have no secrets from my number-one Ole Miss intern, Horace. This is a young man whom we are going to hear great things from in the future. I'm charged with providing him a glimpse of how the world really operates, and that is what I intend to do," the sheriff said.

"Well, it doesn't matter. Maybe you're right. It's time boys like him grow up early and learn the rules of the game," Pennington said with an air of superior condescension.

"I've just come to jawbone a bit, to counsel you on your future, not his. You are up for reelection soon, and some of the things you are doing might have a negative impact on your candidacy," he said coldly.

"Oh? How so?" Gill asked.

"The underground economy is substantial, and it is the oil that lubricates the engines of business and prosperity when times are hard. It's not directly taxed, but the proprietors pay their dues to men who use that money to recruit business and jobs to the area, to make loans to start-up companies, and to help those in need. There are people who would go hungry without it, Gill. There are children who would go to school in rags. There are missionaries in Africa who would have no pennies for the poor. Do you get my drift?" Pennington asked.

"I think so," Gill answered.

"These are turbulent times, and I represent some men who like you and want to see you do well. But there just has to be some tolerance, some live-and-let-live, some discernment to know when to look the other way when you see sinners engaging in harmless vices. I hope you're a man with vision, Gill…a man who we can count on and get behind—else we may have to cast our lot with another nag," Pennington said as he stood to leave.

He pushed the glasses high on the bridge of his nose and looked down at the sheriff and then at Michael. "There are men in law enforcement who have learned how to do some good things within the limitations of an imperfect world. Our judges look the other way when our police plant evidence or leave a drop gun in the hands of some unfortunate criminal who wasn't paying his dues anyway, and when it comes to getting a search warrant to retrieve an old lady's black-and-white TV, stolen by some degenerate junkie to sell to feed his drug habit? Why, just the knowledge that the offender wasn't a team player is all the probable cause our judges need to sign those warrants. After all, the widow lady was buying the TV on time payments from us, at interest rates that service other ventures to further the…common good."

Pennington dropped any last vestige of pretense and became visibly angry for a moment.

"Those good officers can wiretap and take the interlopers into the back rooms, put on the black gloves and administer a good thumping, a good lesson that is heard all the way to Memphis and beyond… You don't come in here and disrupt what has taken so long to build up. They arrest who we say and ignore who we want ignored. They are good lap dogs, and they never turn on their masters nor bite the hands that feed them. Do they go a little too far now and then? Sure, but there will always be what some call 'collateral damage' in any war. The rednecks think we are on their side, that the low wages we pay them are the best they can do. But we keep them awash in their beer, we wave their flags…the US and the Confederate…and we tell them we are the champions of their politics—while we cut their throats. We want better things for Mississippi—a better image for business.

"You are, or can be, a part of that future, Gill, if you just loose that tight halo you're wearing. It's choking off the blood to your brain," Pennington said imperiously with bite in his voice.

"Thanks for coming by, Horace. I think we understand each other," Gill said.

When Pennington left the room, Gill Simpson sighed deeply and looked at a wide-eyed Michael, who sat dazed in his chair, shaking his head.

"I'm sorry to burst your bubble, Michael, but if you learn nothing else during your internship, you must learn that nothing is as it seems. You must keep your guard up, take nothing and no one at face value—particularly those who smile to your face and pick your pocket when your back is turned…those who protect men who bomb your home.

"I don't want you to wind up a sad, old cop who wakes up one day and realizes that he has been a pawn in a cynical game. We do some good if we're lucky—we protect the bystanders in the game, rescue the innocent from the violent—but the minute we go after the wrong people or step on the wrong toes, they come after us. That's when we discover that we've only been enforcers for the status quo," the sheriff said.

Michael thought he sounded like Tim Charles at Ole Miss.

The sheriff stood, patted Michael on the shoulder, and said, "After your shift today, get some rest and come in on the second tour tomorrow. We'll give Mr. Pennington our answer then!

"When all this quiets down, I want to talk to you about maybe helping me with the reelection campaign," he said with a twinkle in his dark eyes.

"It would be my honor, Sheriff," Michael said.

As Michael walked out to his patrol unit, he saw Horace Pennington leaning against his white Cadillac at the curb. He was twisting a gold ring around the little finger on his left hand. The ring contained a large diamond, one that would choke a horse, as locals would say. A kid drove by on a rattling old bicycle that made bumpety-clank sounds against the uneven pavement. He tipped his cap and said, "How do, Mr. Pennington?"

Pennington acknowledged the boy on the bicycle before he looked at Michael and said, "I'm sorry about all of that with Gill, Deputy Parker. He's a stubborn man and refuses to bend with the breeze. He's not young and educated like you. You just call me if you ever need a good job reference. You need to be careful and play it smart. Make sure you aren't hitching your wagon to a dead horse that can't make it 'round the next lap in the track. You get my drift?"

"Yeah, I think so. Thanks for the advice, but I like the underdog, always have," Michael said.

"So be it. You're either in or you're out, and when you refuse the invitation to come in...you're out forever. There is no middle ground. But I suspect you've never walked any middle ground, have you? You're just a cardboard deputy, aren't you, Deputy Parker? Just like those cutouts I used to put in my shoes when I was growing up poor in the '30s. You look like a fancy dress boot, but you got no sole, boy," Pennington said, punctuating his harshness with a coarse laugh.

"I thought it was s-o-u-l-s, not s-o-l-e-s, we were supposed to be worried about, Mr. Pennington," Michael replied.

"Don't lose your head, Deputy. Somebody's liable to pinch it off and spit in the hole. It's just business, son...just business that makes the world go round. No one gets hurt that wouldn't get hurt anyway," Pennington answered as he slid into his Caddy and drove away.

* * *

Michael had no sooner left the station in his patrol unit than Earl called him on the radio.

"Michael, please proceed to 237 Old Collier Road, south of Plantersville. A Mrs. Lucy Barnett called in a report of a breaking and entering and assault," Earl said.

When Michael arrived at the modest brick home nestled in a thicket of pines and red azaleas bushes, a dog lay dead in the front yard from what appeared to be a gunshot wound. There were tire tracks, deep ruts, in the front yard, made by a vehicle that probably slid to a stop in the grass near the front door. Bumblebees buzzed some wild honeysuckle near the house, providing some signs of life to a vision of death.

As Michael stepped up to knock on the door, he noticed that it had sustained some damage, probably from forced entry. The wood was splintered along the frame, and the black scuff mark from a muddy boot marred the light-colored doormat.

Michael knocked and knocked again. He thought he heard movement behind the door, and he called out, "Ma'am, it's Deputy Parker from the Lee County Sheriff's Department."

He heard the door lock click and stood back as the doorknob slowly turned. He rested his hand on his revolver.

The woman who opened the door had been crying. Her eyes were wide, blue, and swollen—windows to a soul in torment. Her lips appeared to be bruised, and the corner of her mouth was cut and had recently been bleeding.

Her yellow hair, the color of fresh corn-on-the-cob, was tangled and needed a brush. Her skin smelled of soap, and she had the look of someone who had been in a long, hot shower.

Underneath those distractions, Michael sensed what was a natural, soft wholesomeness and vulnerability. Her voice was a little-girl's whisper, thin and high. She seemed to be wearing a costume of trauma and shame—something unfamiliar to her... something she was not accustomed to.

"Are you Lucy Barnett?" he asked softly.

"Yes, I am," she replied, her eyes darting to and fro past him, all around her yard.

"Ma'am, did you call us about someone breaking into your home?" he asked.

"Yes, but that was a mistake. I appreciate you coming, but I made a mistake...a big mistake," she said.

"I'll need to get some information to close your file, Mrs. Barnett. Could I come in and talk to you for a moment?" he asked.

"I'm not presentable, but yes, I suppose it will be all right," she answered.

When Michael entered her home, he could see that the chain lock had been ripped from the frame. It lay on the floor with a big piece of her wood door attached.

She sat in a chair and motioned Michael to the couch. She clutched her blouse to her throat and constantly adjusted her dress, attempting to cover herself.

"Could you tell me what happened, Mrs. Barnett?" he asked.

"Nothing…nothing happened. I just got a little carried away with my vivid imagination," she answered as she gnawed on the corner of her cut lip.

Michael saw a dead-end sign ahead and switched gears. "Your dog was very protective of you, wasn't he?" he asked.

The dam of tears burst, and rivulets of water began to seep from her eyes. She dropped her head into her lap as she began to sob and then to rock up-and-down and side-to-side.

"Yes, Tuff Boy was a good dog," she wailed.

"I know, I know," Michael said. "Just tell me what happened, and if you don't want it to go any further, it will remain just between the two of us."

Then it all began to pour out in one gasping, choking release…pain that demanded to be set free.

"My husband, Royce, and I went to that place out in the county, the Rendezvous Club. Royce had…has a gambling problem—it's a sickness. They have these big poker games every week, and they kept upping the stakes and luring Royce back. They extended him credit, and he got in deeper and deeper. I pleaded with him to stop, that we'd find some way to pay them off and get away from those people, but he was sure he would get lucky if he went back just one more time and then one more time…" Her voice trailed off to a whisper before she resumed.

"That man, Payne, who owns the place…he liked me. I could tell. He was always watching me." She swallowed hard and licked her dry lips.

"Anyway, he got his banker friend at Mr. Pennington's bank to give us a second mortgage on our home to pay off the gambling debt and give us some extra cash. But pretty soon it was all gone, and Royce was in deeper than ever," she said, reciting the story as if she were giving a book report in school.

She shuddered all over and began to hyperventilate.

"Payne showed up here today, drunk and shouting for me to come outside, that he wanted a down payment on my husband's debt. I locked the door, and Tuff Boy went after him. I heard the shot, and my dog yelped. He had killed him… And then he put his shoulder against the door and broke in…and then he…" Her voice faded again as she relived the attack.

"He said he would be back to collect on the interest due. I called my husband, and he told me not to tell anyone—to think of how it would damage his reputation if the community learned that he had a gambling addiction and associated with gangsters. When I protested, he told me to think of how people in town and in our church would look at me if they knew that I had been…spoiled. He told me to clean up and forget it, pretend that it was just a bad dream…that we would get a better lock on the door, and he would figure something out. He told me that he had never wanted me tagging along to the club anyway and implied that the assault was my fault…that I had brought it on myself. He said that no one had died—that I shouldn't lose my head over this." She stared out the window at the lifeless body of her only protector and wiped the tears from her eyes.

"I don't know, Deputy Parker. I don't know what I'll do. It does seem like a bad dream…a nightmare…and I wonder how this could happen to people like us. I'm just glad my little boy was in school and not here. But that man told me he knew where my boy went to school, and he told me he knew that I had two younger sisters and that he might have to visit them if I caused trouble," she said with a visible shudder.

Michael was sick and wanted to throw up, but he said, "Let me help you, Mrs. Barnett. Help me put an end to this."

"No, no. You said it could just be between us, and that is how it must stay. I could never testify. Everyone would know everything then, and they would talk about us, and Royce would be embarrassed," she said.

She bounced out of her chair suddenly and said, "Oh, look at the time! Royce will be home soon, and I must fix his meal. He doesn't like it when his meals are late or cold," she said.

Michael knew it was useless. As he left her house, she watched him from the front door and called after him like it had been a polite visit with a neighbor.

"Come back and visit us anytime, Mr. Parker. I know that Royce would love to meet you. He supports our local police. We have a new color TV. We love Mary Tyler Moore. Isn't she the sweetest thing? Bye-bye now. Thanks for stopping by."

Michael thought that Lucy would carry the memory with her for the rest of her life. The scars would not be visible to most, but they would be real, and the scars on her psyche would gnaw at her guts. Michael thought of cases similar to hers that he studied at Ole Miss and suspected that a day would come when she might begin to drink to forget.

She would drink herself into oblivion, trying to erase the horror and to enter the land of sodden forgetting, hoping to awaken from her long alcohol naps numbed and healed from intruding memories—no regrets, no hangovers, and no flaw in the virginal beauty that had drawn Royce to her all those years ago.

But according to Horace Pennington, she was just collateral damage—no real harm done to people he viewed as disposable players, perpetual victims and pawns in a cynical game.

It was life in an artificial world where everyone smiled and said, "I'm okay; You're okay—" where what was important was the Smiths keeping up with the Joneses and purchasing things they couldn't afford.

It all seemed so perfect from a distance—too perfect. But up close, the beauty dimmed, you heard the arguments and weeping behind closed doors, and the ugliness was startling. It was then that you read the fine print on Mr. Pennington's world:

"Don't look too closely…"

* * *

Michael sat in his car a moment before he clicked the mike on his car radio and told Earl that he was back on patrol.

"Michael, residents near Union community called and said that Harold Miller, an ex-con who was in Parchman Prison, is out near Paul Pritchard's old place off Highway 6, and he's digging a big hole in the ground. They're sure that he's burying a body or digging up loot from some old robberies or something. They say that they're afraid of people who've been in prison, because they never change. They want a deputy to confront him and see what he's up to. Do you want me to send another unit to back you?" he asked.

"No, I'll handle it. Thanks!" Michael answered.

When Michael arrived at the location, he could not see Harold Miller, but he did see a big pile of dirt around a giant hole in the ground, and every now and then some more dirt would fly up out of the hole.

Michael walked up to the gaping cavity and looked down to see a man digging away with a shovel and pick, standing ankle-deep in water seeping from the ground about fifteen to eighteen feet below Michael.

The walls of the tunnel above the man had been lined with old bricks, probably to prevent cave-ins and to lower the risk of water contamination, and a crude rope ladder had been tied to a nearby oak tree and thrown into the well so Harold could enter and exit the deep hole.

"Are you Harold Miller?" Michael asked.

A skinny man with decaying, yellowed teeth looked up and said, "Yes, sir. I'm him."

"What're you doing out here, Harold?" Michael asked.

"Well, I just hit this sandy earth, and the water started to flow and looks pretty good. Digging got easier when I hit the sand.

There ain't no sewage lines or septic tanks around, Deputy, and I got permission to dig my well from Mr. Pritchard. Have I broken any laws?" he asked.

"Not that I know of, Harold. I meant, why are you out here digging a well? Is this your well? Are you going to live here?" Michael asked.

"Oh, no, sir, I'm not. These wells aren't for me. They're for anyone who needs to drink at the well of spring-fed living water that runs deep under this earth. I learned in prison about the Philistines who had damned up the wells so that they might drive out Abraham and his descendants, but Isaac kept digging the wells and trusting God. I think there are Philistines out and about now, trying to keep His people from the Promised Land. So I decided that when I came home, I would dig wells that I would never use— just cool water for the weary as they try to find their way home to God's provision," Harold said.

"Harold, if you don't mind me asking, what did a gentle soul like you do to get sent to Parchman?" Michael asked.

"No, sir, I don't mind you asking. I was working for Mr. Pennington's feed store, and one day I changed the number on a paycheck he gave me. My mama was sick and needed some medicine. It was for twenty dollars. I know it wasn't right, and they sent me away for three years. Mama died while I was at the prison farm, and I didn't get to say goodbye," he said. He paused, stifled a sob, and wiped his leaky nose with the back of his muddy hands just as the spring water began to bubble and swirl around his ankles.

"This is kinda my tribute to Mama, too. I know she'd like to know that I had become the man she wanted me to be," he said.

Michael stood for a moment and just stared at Harold. People feared Harold Smith because the state had sent him to prison, a place that should be reserved for the true criminals, like those who ruined Lucy Barnett's life.

"I look forward to stopping by here on a hot day and drinking my fill of your cool water, drinking until I burst," Michael said.

Michael gave him a crisp salute and said, "Carry on, Harold."

* * *

The brilliant sunlight faded, and the sky rushed through peach, pink, and mango before night fell hard over Parker Grove at the end of Michael's long day. When he passed Parker Grove Baptist Church, he pulled over into the parking lot of the small church, rolled down his windows, and listened to the booming voice of the pastor.

"When you sow sparingly, you will reap sparingly. It's not what you say, brothers and sisters; it's what you do in life. Forgive folks, friends. That's when we are most like Jesus, and it's so much easier than trying to drag hate around with you all the time. Man will wipe out fifty years of good over one mistake, but the Lord keeps an account for those who repent. We are like the moon, and He is the sun. We have no light, but we can reflect His. Kindle a fire; love your neighbor. And if you have to ask, 'Who is my neighbor?'…well, you aren't there yet."

Then the pastor stopped for a moment and said, "There's someone listening outside who won't come in, but he wants to. He's cold and wants to warm himself by the fires of the Gospel. I say this to him: You feel like that old car. Your headlights are out…your taillights, too. You don't know if you're coming or going. There's a fault line running under your life, and you think you're alone in the howling wilderness.

"The rocks may melt around you, your seas may catch fire, and the droughts of life may scorch your soul and parch your silver streams. But just because you're stumbling and staggering in the pitch-black night, that doesn't mean that you'll stay there. It means that because you endured and felt your way along in the darkness, crying out and bleating like a lost lamb, you'll recognize the saving beam of the Lighthouse when it splits the long night, and you will fall down on your knees and thank God for the Lighthouse."

As Michael pulled off, the choir began to sing an old song by Flatt and Scruggs:

"Troublesome waters around me do roll. They're rocking my boat and wrecking my soul. Loved ones are drifting and living in sin. The treacherous whirlpools are pulling them in... Troublesome waters are blacker than night, hiding from view the harbor light bright. Out on the ocean I seem as a speck, awful sea monsters are waiting my wreck."

When he walked into his home, Pearl told him that Dixie Lee had called but left no message. Michael tried her number several times but got no answer. He was exhausted, so he finally gave up and fell asleep almost as soon as his head hit the pillow.

He had always dreamed dreams with vivid imagery—strings of vignettes full of symbolism, epics in Technicolor.

He startled awake in the wee hours of the morning, reeling from truncated dreamscapes that wouldn't let him go. He woke momentarily when it became too much to bear, but then fell right back into the thick of the nightmares, where the actors, ghosts, and goblins scolded him for leaving.

He saw an approaching rider galloping toward him on the plains of torment and curses. It was Paul Revere. He was holding a lantern in one hand and the head of Cal Mattox in the other hand. As he rode, he was shouting, "The Dixie Mafia is coming! The Dixie Mafia is coming!"

Following Revere was another rider, a headless horseman. As he drew nearer, Michael could see that it was Ichabod Crane, and his horse was snorting fire and spitting mucus-misery. Crane, holding his head in his lap, stopped at Michael's feet.

The head spoke to Michael and said, "I've lost my head and have this splitting phantom ache. Have you any aspirin you might spare, good Deputy, and have you seen my noggin in the bogging?"

The ghost of Buzzy held onto the horse's tail. He was following Ichabod, looking for his fast car. His own skull was shrunken and leaking, and he looked at Michael with rotting eyes. His slack mouth was open, and his breath was like sulphur.

"They took away all my toys, but there's money and lost souls trapped in them moonshine drums. You can't see 'em, but you can hear the cash registers ringing and the faces of torment spilling out when you pour it," he called out as Ichabod rode away, pulling Buzzy along.

Michael turned to see a headless John the Baptist speaking to Jesus from his platter of doubt. John asked Jesus, "I'm not fit to untie the straps of your sandals, but are you the One?"

John's head then spoke to Michael and asked, "Is this lost world the ditch you want to die in? Sometimes the people you think would take a bullet for you are the ones pulling the trigger. Be careful who you trust. The devil was once an angel."

Michael awoke in a sweat, his heart pounding, trying to beat down the walls of his chest. He was sitting in a chair by Pearl's bed, gasping for breath. He had walked in his sleep, like he had as a child, when the family would find him in Pearl's room, seeking comfort from things that go bump in the night.

Pearl sat up and asked him, "What's the matter, son?"

"Oh, bad dreams, Grandma," he said.

"You just stay right there. I'll be back in a minute," she said.

She turned on the light, grabbed her big tin of King Leo peppermint sticks, as she had so many times in his life, and headed to the kitchen.

Pearl returned with two steaming cups of hot chocolate, peppermint-flavored with the sticks she had crushed.

They sat there with their hot cocoa, the soothing smell of prime peppermint scenting the air. They sipped her concoction as Pearl waited for him to figure out what it was he wanted to say.

"Grandma, all the monsters have escaped from my child-hood nightmares and are out walking around...dressed up like respectable people. So many people can't stop spending what they don't have, can't stop drinking their own poison, and can't stop loving the wrong girl," he said. He paused, thinking of Dixie Lee.

"There is so much pain in the world—so many have crossed the line and don't know how to get back. It's hard to keep your head while so many are losing theirs. Grandma, today I met a well-digger who had his head on straight, and I met a grave-digger who was a tin man—all head and no heart.

"I've decided that I want to be a well-digger."

CHAPTER EIGHTEEN

*"You can run...but sooner or later, you
run out of places to run to."*
—*Nalini Singh,* Play of Passion

*"Ooh, sittin' down in Aberdeen with
New Orlean on my mind...."*—*Bukka White,*
"Aberdeen Mississippi Blues"

The word was out from Tupelo to Memphis to the Gulf Coast...James Streeter was a marked man.

When he slithered out from behind the closed doors of the latest fleabag motel where he'd been hiding, he looked like death warmed over. He was going through five packs of cigarettes a day, washing down pills with vodka, and snorting the nose candy that only intensified his hallucinations and the visits from the accusing dead.

His guts ached, and the pain was so intense that he could barely bend over to tie his shoes. Streeter's hands had a constant tremor, and the fine lines on his face had become as deep as the furrowed rows of Mississippi corn fields.

He couldn't remember when he had slept. His weight was down, maybe thirty pounds lighter, and everything he ate seemed to make him sick. Streeter was paranoid to the extreme, and the bad temper he usually kept on a short leash was now off the chain and out of control.

Brenda, a placid, dreamy little working girl of eighteen with tousled red hair, had a sweetness that mitigated her lack of intelligence. She was as sweet as Southern tea, but her tongue was tied in the middle and wagging at both ends. She was a talker.

With her pixie humor, she playfully teased Streeter about being under the "alfluence of incohol," and he beat her and kicked her with his dirty, scuffed shoes until she passed out. The savage thrashing left her unable to work for over a month. Her fear of the police prohibited any complaint, but the terror that gripped her when she thought of Streeter made her throw up. That alone guaranteed her silence.

She finally became so timid and skittish when meeting new men that she called her mother in Oxford and asked if she could home to stay...and maybe take some classes at Ole Miss. When her mother asked her if some preacher had gotten to her, Brenda said, "No, Mama, I think it was the antichrist himself."

* * *

A man everyone called "Tiny Tim" managed a cheap motel outside of Aberdeen. Tim kept his hogs in a pen behind his single-level inn, the dive where Streeter had been hiding. One day, the diminutive manager told him in passing that some man had been by asking about him. Streeter seized the hapless little man by the throat and began to choke the life out of him, screaming, "What did you tell him? What did you tell him?"

Choking and gasping, the poor motel man said, "Nothing, Mr. Streeter! I didn't tell him nothing about you! I know you! I'm afraid of you! I'd never tell him anything about The Pusher!"

Streeter dropped Tim, who crumpled to the floor in a heap. Coughing and spitting blood, Tim said, "You're not under your real name, Mr. Streeter. I took care to see that no one bothers you, and I told him that I heard that you might be in Corinth. He said if I was lying to him that he would come back, cut me up into little pieces, and feed me to my own hogs."

Tim sat up, still trying to get his breath and cautiously feeling his bruised throat. "He was the weirdest man I ever saw. When I asked him if he ever got out in the sun, the look he gave me sent chills down to my innards and frosted my soul," Tim said.

Streeter's eyes went wild and crazy. "I'll be checking out right away, Tim. Here's some money for your trouble. If he comes back, you better not tell him nothing about me. Better yet, tell him that a man who looked like me came through on his way to Chicago. Pump him full of goose juice and maybe he'll fly away honking.

"If I find out that you ratted me out, I'll come back, burn this place to the ground, kill all them pigs you love so much, and force you to eat 'em raw until you die! I won't say much while I do it, neither. Too many words spoil the magic of watching someone die."

*   *   *

Streeter left Aberdeen under cover of darkness. The moon mocked him, the shadows tickled him with icy fingers that clawed at his soul, and the black cat that crossed his path…died of fright.

He drove through the night, constantly checking his rearview mirror and grabbing his gun every time a creature of the night jumped in front of his headlights. His palms pooled with sweat. He moved carefully and stayed in the shadows, though he feared the things that dwell in dark places. He was back in the jungle, and he could hear the raspy breathing and grumbling of the hungry beasts which crept and slithered through the tangled, wasted wilderness.

Streeter thought about Freddie and the night he found the pale assassin asleep in one of the rooms at the Playhouse. *Right there's where I made my mistake. I should have taken my baseball bat to him, beat him to death, and then drove a spike through his heart so that bloodsucker would never walk this earth no more.*

Thick clouds attempted to choke the moon and vanquish the stars when Streeter rolled into Tupelo at 2 a.m. He drove a nondescript car and had a hat pulled down tight over his ears. Nothing about the car or the driver would suggest to anyone that this could be the flamboyant man known as The Pusher.

He drove past his office on North Green Street, and then came by again and again, driving slower each time. The office and adjoining structures were dark, and the front door to his residence had been padlocked. He ached to stop and cut the lock with bolt-cutters he carried, but he knew that it was too risky.

Underneath the flooring in his home was a safe. It was so well-disguised and hidden that he doubted anyone had found it or the $100,000 in paper currency and coins that he had stashed there. He had other sources of money, but he needed that cash if he was to make a run for it—a sprint that might outrun the reach of the mob's assassin.

He finally gave it up after a Tupelo police cruiser came by. It was hard for him to believe that it was all over…that what he had sold his soul for—this good life—was gone forever. Some part of him still held out hope for reconciliation with Ace…let bygones be bygones and so on. But he knew that couldn't happen. Maybe it could with any other stalking killer…but not Freddie. Once he took a contract, it could not be recalled or revoked. Those were his requirements.

Streeter smiled and then began to laugh uncontrollably, the laugh of a madman. *Have Knife, Will Slice and Dice…Freddie rides again.*

He drove out of Tupelo in the direction of the Playhouse. There were no cars on the road; only the lights on the trailers of the big rigs and the neon signs of the truck stops split the darkness of night.

Streeter left Highway 78 and eased up the blacktop road, winding cautiously through the hillsides and hollows, always watching for an ambush and talking to himself—and occasionally to Star, who had showed up again to taunt him.

"He gonna get you, tough man. You won't be so tough no more when you're dead like me," she said.

"Naw, a hit-and-run ambush ain't Freddie's style. He is the jeeper-creeper who slips up on you and slips his blade in you. He does his work up close," Streeter replied to his friendly ghost.

"No, sir…Freddie told me once that he'd take his time with you if you ever hurt me again. He said he'll do right by you, though. He said the only options he's got for a mark is to make it a quick end or a lingering death, leave a man in a coma for weeks or months. He said, 'Do it right. Respect your victims, your partners in the death dance. Be tidy.' That's what he told me, back when that poor boy loved me. Now I'm dead," she wailed. And then she vanished, giving up her seat as shotgun rider with the man who had killed her.

He was glad to see her go. *The dead ain't got no right coming back to bury the living.*

As Streeter neared the club, he could see that it was pitch-black on the hillside and the surrounding grounds of the compound. Even at this hour, the club would have normally been hopping and sparkling like the jewel he thought it was, an outpost and refuge for confused and careless hearts. The windows that should be filled with light and gaiety were dark and showed no images of revelers shadow-dancing with his girls. No music drifted down to the gates from the giant speakers affixed to the trees.

He passed the gates and drove deeper into the hollows beyond. His springs and shocks were clunking and bouncing against the potholes in the road, and he parked his rattletrap on a side logging road. Slipping out of his car, he stopped and listened, and listened again. There was nothing but a waddling possum that hissed at him and the deafening chorus of bugs—millions of them, he thought

Streeter worked his way up the embankment and through the woods behind the Playhouse, stopping to draw his pistol at the slightest sound, to almost blast a raccoon out on the hunt for food. He finally saw the dim light he was looking for coming from the backroom of the caretaker's shack.

He had hired Tyrone Jackson to take care of the grounds and do odd jobs for him. They had a strange and unique relationship. The Pusher tolerated questions and comments from Tyrone that would have drawn a severe beating or death for other men.

Tyrone's IQ was in the sixties or low seventies. He had no filter between brain and mouth. If he thought it, he said it. But he was totally loyal to Streeter and would die for him, because The Pusher had found him on the streets, alone with no family, and had given him a job and a roof over his head—something no one else had ever done. He was as black as coal, and his eyes were so close set that they almost overlapped. He had a child's mind, yet he could be profound in his own way.

Streeter reached the cabin, peeked in the window, and saw Tyrone sitting in his room all alone, flipping through a comic book about the Incredible Hulk. He tapped on the glass panes—once, then three taps, followed by five...their private signal.

Tyrone hopped to his feet and ran to the front door. Streeter crawled slug-like through the brief, faint light of the open door, keeping a low profile for any sniper with a night scope.

Tyrone was overjoyed to see Streeter. He patted The Pusher's back as he laughed his throaty, braying donkey-laugh. "Boss! What you doing? Where you been? I been so worried about you!" Tyrone exclaimed.

"I'm okay, Tyrone. Thanks for holding down the fort. Where is everyone?" Streeter asked.

"They're all gone, Boss. They run away. Magnolia took off, and then others got scared when you didn't show up for so long. Some said you was dead. Others said you would be soon 'cause Mr. Ace wanted you dead. Some of the girls said that they was going to Memphis to work. Others said they had met some man named Jesus and would never be back," Tyrone said.

"Anyone looking for me?" Streeter asked.

"The constable came by for his payoff and asked about you," Tyrone said.

"Anyone else?" Streeter asked.

"Yes, Bossman, Mr. Freddie was here. He scared me. He told me that he would kill me and leave me in the sun for the buzzards if I was lying about where you were, but I told him that I may not be smart, but that I was smart enough not to lie to a man with a big ole knife like his. He laughed then. I ain't never seen that man laugh before. Boss, you think he is really a white man? He looks more like a marshmallow man to me. What race is that?" Tyrone asked.

Streeter forgot his troubles for a moment and fell over laughing. "Tyrone, you just won't do, boy."

Tyrone jumped and grabbed a tape measure and placed it along Streeter's legs and shoulders.

"What're you doing, Tyrone?" Streeter asked.

"Boss, a man came by selling burial policies and told me that I needed to be laid out in a fine box—that anyone important needed a deep hole and a good box to keep the coyotes and the worms out. I had bad dreams after he left, but I got to thinking, Boss. I hear all these stories about you dying, and I decided my Bossman needs the best box to keep them worms away," he answered.

Tyrone said, "You be thin, Boss, and you be bent over like an old man, but you still the Boss, and the Boss must have the finest box—maybe pecan, like the man said. I got the pictures he gave me. If something happens, Boss, don't you worry. I'll take care of it for you, like always. Won't let no worms eat you!"

Spurred by Tyrone's concern for him, even in death, it all came rushing back—his obsession for control and power…and for Star, the object of his desire. It still stabbed at his drunken heart to recall the low moan of pain she emitted the night when he cut, slashed, and killed her. He heard the old voodoo priestess, GAL, telling him—even when he was a child in New Orleans—that he was born to the occult and had a death wish. So, while his mama was praising God, he was high-fiving the devil.

He smiled and recovered. "You got that sealed box I gave you?" he asked.

"Yes, sir. I got it right back here beneath the place I go potty," he said, lifting up and tilting a shaky, chipped commode in the back room. In a recessed area beneath and in front of his commode was a metal box wedged into the rotting boards that barely sustained the weight of his bathroom fixture.

"Every time I sat here doing my business, I kinda thought that I was sitting on my nest, trying to hatch the golden eggs like that goose laid in my picture book. Mr. Freddie never thought to look under there. He said it smelled bad in here and that I needed some smell-good to kill the odor," Tyrone said with a big, sincere smile.

Streeter took the box and spun the numbers on the combination lock. In the box were two huge wads of money bound by rubber bands. The box also contained a loaded .44 Magnum revolver wrapped in an oiled cloth, and a deed to the property.

He removed a large portion of the bills from one stack and put the Magnum beneath his belt, and slid the 9mm to the small of his back.

"Tyrone, here's $30,000, and I'm signing a quitclaim deed to leave this whole place to you. When I get to where I'm going, I will send in money to pay the taxes on the place so the criminals at the courthouse can never take it from you," he said.

Streeter was uncharacteristically tender with the boy he treated like a son. "I'm leaving, Tyrone, and I won't be back unless I can raise an army. You're a good boy, and I want you to take care of yourself," he said.

Tyrone stared at the money and then at Streeter, trying to process it all. "I ain't never seen so much money, Boss, and I don't know what I'll do without you here telling me what to do," he said.

"You'll be fine," Streeter said as he stepped forward to hug the boy.

"I gotta go now, Tyrone. Got to drive until the wheels fall off—go breathe some air I ain't breathed since I was a boy," he said with a sweep of his arm, his thumb hooked and pointing south.

Streeter turned down Tyrone's oil lamp and moved to the front door to peer into the night.

Tyrone lowered his eyes. "Can I ask you one last thing, Boss?"

"Sure, what's that?" Streeter asked.

"Boss, you were like my comic books. Some days you was like Bruce Banner, and then other days you was the big green Hulk, but you was always the big man—the man people was scared of, the man who hunted other men. You wearing rags tonight and don't seem so loud and proud now. How does it feel to be just like me?" he asked with a child-like honesty.

Streeter's throat tightened into a hard knot. He swallowed hard as he paused at the door and said, "Sometimes, Tyrone, I think you're smarter than me. Don't be afraid of death, Tyrone. It's just like hanging out the 'Do Not Disturb' sign and sleeping in for a long nap. But if you hear the pistols popping, you run on down the hill and hide in the gully. You hear me?"

Then he was gone so quickly that Tyrone wondered if he had really been there.

* * *

Streeter worked his way up the hill to the Playhouse. He wanted one final goodbye look, and if death waited, then so be it. As he drew closer, moving from tree to tree, the club loomed up before him like a ghost town in an old Western movie. He suddenly thought of spooks and spells and wondered if Freddie might be near.

The boards on the front porch creaked as he moved cautiously toward the big front door. He found it unlocked and slightly ajar. He slowly pushed the door open, the .44 always before him, sights aligned with his body and moving left and right, sweeping the interior.

He stepped inside and jumped back when a squealing rat ran across his shoes. His heart was already thumping wildly, and then he stepped into a spider web that covered his face with the sticky gauze—a trap for night bugs. He swatted at the web, bumped his knee on a chair in the lounge, and fell to his knees in a cold sweat.

Streeter paused to wait for whatever might come. Nothing was stirring, but amidst the silence and the stench, the residuals of suffering and sin in his house of ill repute, he could feel the presence of someone. He could almost hear a man breathing, so he raised the big .44 and pointed it in the dark at every perceived phantom noise and ghostly presence, but he didn't panic. His muscles were knotted with fear, and he flinched and ducked at every creak and shudder of the empty building, but he didn't start firing wildly, even though part of him begged his fingers to empty his guns and be done with this madness.

Streeter's breathing was shallow; his body was barely functioning, transferring all energy into survival—his eyes, his reflexes, and the steadying of his hand that had a death grip on the Magnum. The black despair of the cheap motels was gone. The caged lion was now loose and thirsty for the blood of his enemy. Good times might still lie ahead if he could survive this last brush with termination. He could disappear, regroup, start a new scam somewhere...and then come back one day when everyone had forgotten and murder all of his enemies in their sleep.

Even his thoughts were diminished to avoid distractions and a slow response to sudden danger. Only one thought remained lodged in his brain, playing over and over like a stuck record— *I know I'm overdue to check out, but I'm not ready. We're never ready.*

* * *

In the recesses of the abandoned Playhouse, Freddie waited. He knew Streeter well enough to know that he would return to the world where he had been king, to touch it one more time before he fled to someplace to hide. He also knew that Streeter might be ready to end it and take his chances, to come looking for him.

A sliver of moonlight highlighted a cockroach at his feet on the wood floor. To pass the time, amuse himself, and indulge his sadism, he had been breaking the roach's legs, one at time. Just when the roach tried to limp away, Freddie would break one more leg and pinch off another of the bug's antennae.

Freddie could already feel the efficient plunge of his knife as he opened Streeter up a little—just a little—before he disemboweled the man who had killed sweet Star, the only star in the sky above Freddie's oblique world.

He heard the creak of the porch and the squeak of the front door, and he put his nose up to smell the slight breeze coming from the open door. He could smell Streeter, and his heart rate accelerated...his prey was near.

Then he and his adversary heard a new sound, an intruder in their opera of death.

* * *

Michael was restless, unable to stop his racing mind or rest after sleepwalking to Pearl's room...his nightmares, Dixie Lee, the raid on the Snake Pit, and the sheriff's promise that tomorrow would be eventful—it all played in a looping reel in his mind.

Streeter had disappeared, Magnolia had made a run for it, and Michael had seen at least one of the Playhouse girls with the street preacher in Tupelo. So, riding a wave of restlessness, indulging a whim, and on inky instinct, he dressed, picked up his service revolver, and left Parker Grove for the Playhouse.

Michael maneuvered his Mustang through the backroads, and as he approached the Playhouse, a mizzling rain began to fall. The dirty gray rain misted his windshield in fine droplets, just enough to be annoying and require the wipers. The dull rubber of the blades only smeared the remains of a hundred bugs that had chosen the front glass of his car on which to commit suicide.

He saw no lights at the Playhouse. It looked abandoned, like some castle on a hill that had been forsaken and deserted after a plague or a battle had decimated the population.

He parked the Mustang down the slope from the club and walked up the front drive. A nighthawk screeched above him, searching for the rest of the bug population not on Michael's windshield, and a stray calico cat, looking as if it needed a good square meal, scurried across the drive.

Michael saw no signs of life, but in the swirling mist, he could sense something foreboding about the place. There was a smell, something toxic in the air, and an old piece of yellow crime-scene tape from Star's murder investigation blew across his path.

Michael turned on his flashlight intermittently and thought that it looked as if someone had called "Abandon ship!" at the Playhouse. It had fallen into disrepair and gone downhill quickly.

A sign hung sideways, and the front porch was covered in debris from thunderstorms. The flower beds had not been tended, and it looked as if there was a leak in the plumbing that had stained one side of the porch and left a big mud puddle by the steps.

His light fell upon what appeared to be a muddy footprint on the first step, and it looked fresh. He pulled his .38 Police Special from his holster and held it in in his right hand while he kept the light in his left, out and away from his body as his training recommended. In case someone shot at the light, it was always best to keep it away from your body.

The front door was standing wide open, beckoning him to enter, and he thought he heard a faint cracking of wood from somewhere in the club. It was a wet, black night out, but the interior of the club was dusty, musty, dry, and just as black as the night.

He didn't know what he was looking for or what he would do with whatever it was that he might find. His light swept the front parlor. The chairs and couches were covered with dust, and cobwebs adorned the ceilings and corners.

He thought he saw movement to his right…and then to his left. At that moment, his light went out. He shook it and tapped the battery casing, but it was as dead as a hammer.

Michael froze momentarily and then stepped into a corner behind a giant bookcase to his right, good cover and space to defend. He waited for what seemed like an eternity. He could sense the presence of someone or someones. He could almost hear their breathing and wondered if they could hear his.

He slid down into a crouch behind the bookcase, propped his pistol along the bookcase's lower shelf, and shouted, "Deputy Parker, Lee County Sheriff's Department!"

A door banged open to his left, and a dark figure bolted from the room. Michael was tempted to give chase, but he felt someone was still in the building, and so he waited.

He felt a smothering force of evil near him—a predator that stalks victims in the night, a creature that might make St. John's beasts in the book of Revelation seem tame—little more than bunny rabbits and turtledoves.

"Police! Step forward with your hands up!" he shouted.

Then something flew across the room, catching a sliver of silver moonlight just for a moment. It clattered to the floor with a jarring crash.

Michael looked toward the sound for a moment. A door on the right side of the building banged open, and a ghostly figure dressed in mortuary-gray sailed through the opening and melted into the darkness.

Michael's heart was pounding and his hands were shaking. He had felt the icy breath of death, and he felt weak in his knees. He rapped his flashlight against the wall, and it popped back on.

Michael cautiously shined his light on the floor in the direction of the thing that had flown through the air, and the beam fell upon what it must have been.

He walked over to the square object and knelt beside it. His light illuminated a shattered wood frame with a metal signature plate—a painting by Star, signed and dated after she met with the TV preacher and accepted Christ, the day before her death.

It was a rendering of Jesus on the cross and the thief next to him saying, "Remember me, Lord." But scrawled across her painting in angry red letters was a message from the figure in the night...

"He didn't save her."

CHAPTER NINETEEN

*"I know, Ma. I'm a-tryin'. But them
deputies...."—John Steinbeck,*
Grapes of Wrath

*"Come meet my dog." "What's the dog's
name?" "Justice." "Nice touch for a judge.
A dog named Justice."—Allan Dare Pearce,*
Hitler Burns Detroit

The sudden brightness of dawn hurt Michael's eyes as he was leaving the Playhouse, and the puddles of water from the night's rain were rosy from the reflected rays of the sun.

The same light invaded Cal Mattox's cell as he moaned and groaned and called for help. He clutched his chest, claimed his left arm was numb, and said he couldn't breathe. A doctor came to see him, as did his lawyer, who just happened to stop by the jail that day. The attorney filed an emergency petition with the court for an action of compassionate relief for his ailing client.

Judge Davis Fischer, one of Pennington's mutts, took up the petition immediately. He was always barking and woofing about compassion and justice for the connected after getting some tax-free dog biscuits in the mail from the political machine. He ordered Cal released from the Lee County Jail until he could be evaluated by a physician—a Pennington physician, of course.

He also declared Stanley Still's arrest warrant invalid for lack of evidence after the sheriff's neighbors failed to positively identify him as the man running from the sheriff's home, bleeding all over the lawn, hammering the sign in the ground, and driving away just as the bomb went...*Boom!* Some of them received calls suggesting they should come down with a sudden case of amnesia if they loved their families. To punctuate the message, one resident found the family cat hanging from the dogwood tree in their front yard.

The judge said, "The case against Mr. Still was a flimsy one at best, but I'll give the sheriff the benefit of the doubt, since neighbors originally identified Mr. Still as the man running from the scene of the crime. And the sheriff certainly has the court's sympathy after this scurrilous attack on his home. It is of some concern to see the condition of Mr. Still after his arrest, but if he was indeed the bomber, one might suspect that he has already been given a lesson in deterrence that he won't soon forget."

When the judge's order came down, Cal was taken out of the jail in a wheelchair by a somber group of friends. As he was helped into the car, he appeared to be in great agony...until the car rounded the bend of the road. He crinkled a face already pinched with sin stains around the corners of his eyes and smiled a sly, wicked grin.

Cal said, "Yahoo! Let's go get a drink at the Pit, boys! First round's on me!"

After Michael had showered and changed into his uniform, he picked up his mail and showed up early for the second shift. Earl broke the news of Cal's great performance and said, "He's a faker. Ought to give him the Academy Award!"

Michael walked down the hall and tapped on the door to the sheriff's office.

"I was out late last night. I just heard the news," he said.

"It's just a temporary setback. If anyone believes he had a real heart attack, I have some swampland to sell them...cheap!" the sheriff exclaimed.

Then he sighed and said, "No matter... We have warrants to execute tonight."

Michael said, "If the Playhouse was one of our targets, you should know that it is deserted and defunct. Everyone's gone."

"What? When?" the sheriff asked.

"Not sure exactly, but I was there last night. I think that Streeter was there, and somebody else, too...but I couldn't identify them. It was so dark, and then they took off," Michael said. He sensed the sheriff's dark mood and decided to try to lighten the moment.

Michael smiled and said, "Yep, they're all gone. One of them told me that the sole ambition for many of them, before they grew too old and lost their charm, was to get out of the business by marrying one of the old men who visited them. She said that those girls wanted to marry a rich old man with one foot in the grave and the other on a banana peel!"

The sheriff laughed until his sides hurt. "I needed something to relieve the pressure before tonight. Get ready, Michael. The rest of the deputies will be in soon. We're going to hit everyone tonight—every club and backdoor bootlegger in the county. We are going to load up the jail with the low and the high of the syndicate on charges large and small. My special undercover deputy from Louisiana, Fats Arcenaux, has been buying all over the county, and we're going to put the hurt on them tonight.

"I've only called in the men I know I can trust. I haven't called the constables who work for the bootleggers. I haven't told the local town marshals or chiefs of police. No one is to know anything until we're riding to hit everyone simultaneously.

"You and Sarge won't be on the main team. I have a special assignment for you to kick off...one that will be an ongoing operation. I want you to blockade the Rendezvous Club and squeeze Billy Payne and bleed him dry...let no one in, no one out but his band. Let him pay them to play to nobody. He can't threaten to shoot deputies and go scot-free. There must be consequences," the sheriff said.

As Michael walked down the hall, he could hear the sheriff laughing and saying something about banana peels. Laughter is the best medicine, and joy is something that you can't let the world steal or buy on the cheap.

Michael needed it, too. A letter from Dixie Lee had arrived, and he went to a backroom in the department and closed the door to read it again.

Dear Michael:

We keep missing each other. I miss you. When you are near, I'm okay. When you're not...not so much.

I don't know why we ever agreed to date other people, or why I resisted your offer to transfer to Memphis State when we moved home from Washington. Commitment issues? Washington seems so long ago, doesn't it?

Remember the time we had split up, but you showed up at my door after the street thugs jumped you and broke your nose? I held the ice pack to your nose and rocked you all night, stroking your hair. Remember listening to Elvis in the night? I saw him on Lamar Boulevard the other day. He was in a car with the Shelby County sheriff. They were headed south.

What happened to us? What happened to me? I was once a square, but now I seem to be without any fine lines, just sharp angles.

I've met some people that you wouldn't approve of. I just want to have fun, to stop the noise and the memories from my past...the things I told you about. Life is full of abrasions, little ones and big ones, but I think it's the little ones, the death by a thousand nicks, that undo us.

Some days I think about babies who look like you, about gardens and tending soil under hot suns that brown us and cool rains that refresh us and grow our plantings and children. Other days, I want to party until I drop, until the well runs dry, I guess.

I can't tell if the curtain is rising or falling, if the walls are crumbling or getting too high to climb. Do walls ever fall, and if they do, do they crush us?

Maybe your inn has no more vacancies, and you'll leave me at the altar. Maybe you should.

I wish you would come to see me soon...even if it's just one last time. I hope you will remember me as something more than a mistake, like a bad dinner you once had that you found too spicy and just indigestible.

Maybe you'll remember the girl who was thrown in the pool in Washington and wandered in, dripping wet, to watch you shoot eight ball...the girl with the trembly mouth and soft kisses, a fragile package stamped "Open with care!"

I'm cold, so cold. Would you set yourself on fire to warm my world? Would it be wrong for me to ask you to when I am freezing?

Feel my head, Michael. Do I have a fever?

Forever Yours,

Dixie Lee

The days with her seemed suddenly all too brief and time-endangered. He folded the letter, opened it again. His eyes flickered across the words once more, and a lone tear escaped his eyes and slowly trickled down his cheek. He wiped it away quickly with the back of his hand when Sarge called, "Michael, the sheriff is ready for us now."

* * *

Sheriff Simpson called another meeting of deputies and lawmen whom he trusted. They were all there, the men Michael had come to respect and admire for their dogged pursuit of what they thought was right.

"No one will expect us to hit the county again, not so soon after the Snake Pit, but Fats has done a good job undercover, and it's time to serve up the fruits of his illegal whiskey purchases," Gill said.

"Fats came to Mississippi to enforce justice and the law. Stand up and take a bow, Fats!" he said.

The big man stood and bowed, and everyone applauded.

"The weekend is about to kick off, so Tom and Matt will back Sarge and Michael to cover the two main roads into the Rendezvous. We are going to shut…them…down. Nothing moves. We are going to starve the beast.

"Check every car for tags, licenses, and registration. Look for DUI and DWI drivers, people with outstanding warrants, open containers of beer, weapons, items on our stolen lists from burglaries, anything to make players and revelers avoid that road like death and put the stink of poison on the Rendezvous when the word gets around," Simpson said.

"I have also asked the health department to put a temporary quarantine on the club until we can investigate reports we've received of possible infectious diseases and toxic waste out there," the sheriff said with a slight chuckle.

Sarge and Michael loaded the long guns into their car and headed out to the northwest intersection of roads above the Rendezvous Club. Matt and Tom headed to the southeast approach.

The deputies had just set up at their posts when the first car, a Caddy bearing Tennessee plates, came down the rural road. The driver was a rough-looking man who might have been the bodyguard for the man he was driving, a man who had an air of authority and wore an emblem of a playing card—an ace of diamonds—on his shirt. The man was not happy to be turned away.

Caravans of cars—filled with people the deputies suspected to be high-stakes poker players and pool sharks—were stopped, questioned, and denied entrance to the Rendezvous after whiskey bottles in plain sight were seized and destroyed. A few of the drivers who couldn't pass the sobriety test were carted off to the drunk tank.

Coca-Cola trucks, snack vendors, and gasoline trucks for the tanks behind the club were also denied passage. Some of Payne's low-level employees with outstanding warrants were jailed.

Others heard of the blockade and stopped coming for fear of getting pinched for their old warrants. More DWI and DUI arrests were made, drivers with expired or no licenses at all were arrested, and numerous weapons were seized as sheriff's units came and went to transport prisoners and contraband.

Sarge and Michael worked twelve-hour shifts from noon to midnight, with other units relieving them. The runners, revelers, and ramblers were slowly but surely shut down. Only the band was allowed through, and they ceased to come when the paychecks stopped.

Rumors began to fly on the grapevine.

Billy Payne was desperate. He couldn't get any shine, so he was trying to make his own in washtubs behind the Rendezvous. Some who had tried it became deathly ill, like Billy himself, who had been drinking his homebrew. He turned junkyard-dog mean and ran off all of his remaining loyalists holed up with him in the club. When the last car came out, Michael saw that they had Stanley Still unconscious in the backseat. The driver claimed Stanley was sick from bad food, but deputies later learned that he had been severely beaten by Payne for a grievance against Cal Mattox.

With no customers to drink, dance, and gamble at cards, no one was there to hit the slot machines in the back either, the machines owned by Ace Connelly. Word had it that Ace was not a happy man after coming to the club and being turned away by Sarge and Michael. Payne worried when Ace was unhappy and feared the worst.

One day in the second week of the blockade, Constable Robbie Hawkins showed up. He roared up to Sarge's car, churned up a cloud of yellow dust and gravel, and jumped out before he got the lurching car in gear. He was hopping mad, foaming at the mouth, and drunk.

Even when he was a kid in grammar school, Robbie had majored in the cheap and meaningless, minored in ways to fudge the line between right and wrong, and was absent the day they taught about conscience. Robbie taking on Sarge was like someone charging the defenders of the Alamo with a broken toothpick.

"What can we do for you, Robbie?" Sarge said as the deputies stepped out to meet him.

"You can stop this madness, this harassment of an innocent businessman. That's what you can do for me," Robbie demanded.

"What's the matter, Robbie? Your tribe ain't got the bribe no more?" Sarge asked.

Before he could answer, Sarge continued, "You and your boss ain't got no more sway or the money to try to sell a little girl into prostitution?"

Robbie shot a look at Michael, whose jaw was clenched, his eyes boring into Robbie's soul.

"You better get your sorry carcass out of here before you make my high-minded young deputy go bad, and he does something his professors at Ole Miss wouldn't approve of. You better get in that car while you can, before I march over to you, you coward, and pistol whip you all upside your head," Sarge said as he stepped toward Robbie.

Robbie froze and sputtered, "Now, you just wait a minute!"

Sarge walked up to him, nose-to-nose, with Michael right behind him holding the cruiser's shotgun.

"I'll be relieving you of your pistol. Smith and Wesson are both ashamed of you. They told me so, you low-voltage hood," Sarge said as he pulled Robbie's revolver from his holster.

Sarge flung the gun down the hillside, where it bounced and landed in a deep mud puddle.

"And that badge there, Robbie... You ain't worthy to wear it. I'll just be taking it until we can get the word out on you and tell the voters of your district who you really are," Sarge said.

"Sarge, don't you push me too far! I...I'm warning you," Robbie said, his hands shaking and his voice quavering with nervous emotion.

"Push you? Like this?" Sarge asked as he slapped him hard across his face, leaving the imprint of Sarge's open right hand on his cheek.

"How about this...and this?" Sarge asked as he slapped him again and again with both hands until Robbie, his face red with welts and his eyes leaking tears, bent double, covered up, and cried, "Stop! Please stop!"

Sarge then slowly and gently unpinned the badge from his shirt and ripped the constable patch from his shoulder.

"Get out of here, Robbie! Don't let me see you again. And don't come to the department with any of the saps you arrest for the syndicate. We won't take them," Sarge said.

Robbie slunk back to his car and hugged the steering wheel, crying uncontrollably. He finally cranked the car, spun his tires on the loose rock, and disappeared down the road, his car fishtailing as he went.

* * *

The Lee County Jail was full for a week or so with the bootleggers and solicitors the other deputies had arrested in raids across the county. The justice-of-the-peace courts were handing out fines left and right. Normal underground activity had been disrupted, and Sheriff Simpson's message was heard loud and clear.

Traffic in and out of the Rendezvous had virtually ended after three weeks. No one attempted to enter the road to the club, and Sarge had just asked the sheriff how long the blockade was to continue when the saddle-shooting loudmouth arrived.

Just as the setting pink sun kissed the treetops and the evening birds began to sing, a disheveled Billy Payne staggered, zombie-like and spaghetti-legged, up the road toward Sarge and Michael's post.

Michael wouldn't have known Payne. His skin was yellow, as yellow as the goldenrod along the road. He appeared intoxicated or drowsy and confused, and in the grip of delirium or dementia. His eyes were glassy and as jaundiced as his skin. What looked to be dried vomit clung to his chin and the side of his mouth. The fists he had once used to settle disputes and clear the dance floor at the club were now just masses of knobbed knuckles, and the backs of his hands were speckled and spotted.

His weight had crashed. Billy was emaciated but had a puffy, swollen look. He was thirty-eight, but appeared more like sixty-eight. The rugged face had sagged into a permanent basset-faced droop. He looked weary and out of shape, and he wheezed when he spoke or exerted himself in the slightest. Michael thought he might be in the grips of cirrhosis of the liver and hepatitis.

"Murder is all I've got left, Sarge," Payne said, his voice husky, like he'd been kicked in the throat. "My pistol told me that I'm going to kill you, Sarge!"

"Your gun lied, Billy. Your brain is fried and your heart is hard-boiled," Sarge replied.

"You're dying. I'm dying. We are all dying. Let's not hurry it along, Billy," Sarge said.

Billy fidgeted and rubbed his belly near his gun. His shirt was open and his gut had large, blue-green bruises.

Then Sarge began to carve him up like a Thanksgiving turkey.

"I can already see the wisp of smoke when my gun fires and the look of your skull, Billy...without its brain and blood, that look when it explodes like a rotten watermelon in the hot sun, all collapsed, sunken in, and putrid. Your body functions give up and the stench of urine and fecal matter are just your final protest and plea to a world that won't miss you.

"Strangers will come to get your body and paw over it and cut you up for the autopsy. They shoot you full of morticians' juice, and then they have your funeral. But no one comes because you were such a rotten excuse for a human being who lived mean all your life. In the eulogy, the preacher-for-hire will say what everyone knows—you were a weakling who got his jollies by brutalizing the helpless and hapless, because you were impotent and power was your drug.

"The day you join the six-feet-under society, the shovels will cover you with that suffocating dirt, your club will be boarded up, and your girlfriend will move in with a younger man. No one will remember you, Billy. The few who do will try their best to forget they ever knew you, the man who lost his music when he drowned in a pity-pool of tears and beers," Sarge taunted him.

Michael had begun to watch Sarge out of the corner of his eye.

Payne was shaking like a loose wheel on a '58 Ford as he turned to walk away. He suddenly and clumsily reached for the pistol under his belt, screaming in frustration, "I'm gonna kill both of you!"

As he fumbled with the revolver, it discharged with a loud *Bang!*

Sarge and Michael's guns were fixed on him, but Payne turned around slowly with a look of disbelief on his face as his pistol fell to the ground. They saw the hole near Billy's beltline and the sudden spreading of red on his shirt and pants. Billy staggered toward them and then fell at their feet. He rolled over onto his back, clutching his gut and moaning.

"Help me, Sarge. I don't want to die! I want to make music again. I want to find my way back to what I lost. I'm sorry for all that I've done. I'll never do no more wrong if I live. I'll make amends. I swear I will! Tell God, Sarge! Tell Him, please!" Big Billy Payne sobbed and lamented.

Sarge said, "Radio for an ambulance, Michael."

Sarge knelt by Billy and applied pressure to the wound, ripping the shirt to look at the injury.

"You aren't going to die, Billy. It's in-and-out through your fat gut. Just lie still," he said.

"I'm not? Thank you, Sarge! Thank you!" he said.

"The ambulance is on the way. You're a sick man, Billy. Your hands are dirty, and you have much to answer for, but this may be a blessing in disguise," Sarge said.

Michael came back from the car and said, "The ambulance should be here in a minute. They were on their way back from an aborted run to Corinth, and the radio operator diverted them to us."

Matt and Tom arrived, and all of the deputies watched as the ambulance attendants drove up and began to work on Billy.

The bleeding man on the ground had changed. Moments before, he was someone to be feared, but as he lay leaking red and staining the ground and then the gurney, he looked pathetic—an object of pity.

His clear eyes had clouded and obscured his criminal way of life from those who didn't know. The party people, the smell of stale perfume, the taste of bad whiskey, and sounds of clinking glasses and honky-tonk melodies, were all fading away, no more than ghosts in a Lee County graveyard.

As they loaded him into the ambulance, Billy began to shout, "We gotta hurry. Time is short. Got to get a move on."

The attendant said, "He looks like he's going to be all right, but people near the end get this way. They get anxious and think they have an appointment to keep, that they got to get on down the road."

The ambulance roared away, lights flashing and siren blazing.

The deputies leaned against the hoods of their cars, and Sarge asked Michael, "Well, what do you think, partner?"

Michael said, "I think the party's over. I'm tired. Let's go home."

* * *

Payne was assigned to the intensive care unit at the North Mississippi Medical Center in Tupelo. The infection around his gunshot wound healed nicely. He gained some weight and was put on the waiting list for a liver transplant. All agreed that he had made a remarkable recovery—so much so that his momentary guilt and remorse, driven by fear of dying, had evaporated. He cursed the pastors who came by to offer a better way of life, and he rejected and mocked Jesus.

The old Billy reemerged, and he was planning his come-back. A new Rendezvous, bigger and better, financed by Horace Pennington and backed by Ace Connelly.

Pennington came by to see him and made a donation to the hospital to ensure that volunteers, like the candy-stripers and the Red Cross Gray Ladies, tended to Billy's every want and whim. Ace sent word that all was forgiven.

That's why Billy's sudden death in the carefully monitored ICU came as such a surprise to everyone.

When the nurse found Billy dead, he had been gone for some time from what was ruled as asphyxiation. A crumpled pillow was by his side. All of his monitors had been disconnected, and his mouth was open, his eyes fixed in a stare of horror and recognition.

The investigation revealed that he had ingested a sedative, though none had been prescribed. Detectives on the case believed that it was murder, what they called *burking*, simultaneous compression of the torso and smothering. They believed that someone had sat on Billy's chest and held the pillow over his nose and mouth.

The last person on record to see Billy alive was one of the Gray Lady volunteers, a respected and genteel lady married to a prominent Tupelo businessman. There was certainly no motive for murder that could be found in *her* angelic face.

There were whispers once upon a time about her husband's weakness for poker games, but most agreed that it was unsub-stantiated. Horace Pennington told the detectives that his bank held the mortgage on the couple's home and that any rumors of her husband's gambling problems were just scurrilous, idle gossip by people jealous of his position in the community. Pennington assured them that the woman wouldn't hurt a fly.

When the detectives interviewed the Gray Lady, Lucy Barnett, she told them, "It's just terrible, that poor man dying. It just upset me so. I don't know if I can ever forget this, but as my husband, Royce, always says, you just have to clean up and move on, just pretend that it was all a bad dream. I know it may sound strange, but I haven't been this upset since my precious dog, Tuff Boy, died suddenly."

No one claimed the body, and due to the manner of death, it was a perfect candidate for medical schools where young surgeons needed bodies to practice on. Cadavers were in high demand.

Billy's girlfriend sold his body to a medical school just before she moved in with a young guitar player whom she'd met at the Rendezvous. She had no funeral or burial-site expenses, no funeral-home hassles, and the medical school promised to bury the body after they were done with it. She agreed with Lucy that it was time to move on, just pretend it was all a bad dream.

In Billy Payne's more lucid days, when he was a writer, singer, and self-styled philosopher, he'd once said, "Breathing is to life what a gun is to death. Breathing is not all of life, and a gun is not all of death, but a gun *will* take your breath away." In the end, it was not a gun, but a Gray Lady with a pillow who took Billy's breath away.

Sarge's predictions had come true.

CHAPTER TWENTY

*"He had steam in his soul for the one he
loved so. He had death on his mind...He
gonna run through the world 'til we
understand his pain...He took this morning
for a drive yesterday...That cat was mad."*
—Jalacy J. Hawkins, "Little Demon"

*"Hard is trying to rebuild yourself, piece by
piece...no clue as to where all the
important bits are supposed to go."*
—Nick Hornby, A Long Way Down

Ever since The Pusher left town, Tyrone had been restless.
He filed the deed Streeter had given him, and he buried most of the
money in a hole beneath the Playhouse to keep it away from the
crooks at the courthouse and the treasure hunters who came out
with their metal detectors at night to sweep the hillside around
the Playhouse.

The rumors were rife that Streeter was dead or on the run
and had left a fortune in silver and gold coins with Tyrone, but all
that Tyrone buried was paper money, which he had sealed and
double-sealed in heavy-duty plastic baggies to keep out moisture.

He was sweaty and chilled, even in the formidable September
heat that clung to Lee County like a visiting relative who wouldn't
leave. He'd seen his share of danger and hard times, and there
wasn't much that scared him, but lately, he was always looking
over his shoulder. Tyrone had the longing for something or someone. He wasn't sure who or what. It gnawed at his innards like
hungry rats.

He hadn't felt this way since that day long ago at the
orphanage when the social worker had told him of his mother's
death while giving birth to Tyrone and his stillborn twin. He heard

the staff in their starched uniforms whispering about him...
something about lack of oxygen to his brain during the difficult
birth accounted for his diminished mental capacity.

He was working in his shack one evening as the sun settled
on the horizon and made the sky over the ridges and trees a soft
orange color. Then the sun disappeared and dusk blued up the sky
just before the stars began to pop out.

Tyrone noticed that the birds had stopped singing and the
bugs had stopped clicking, and everything was deathly quiet and
still. He suddenly had the feeling that he was not alone. He felt a
presence, heard the slight creak of the floor boards, and smelled
the nearness of danger.

He turned to find himself staring into the red eyes of
Fredrick, who looked at him like a predator looks at a meal. He
wasn't a bug-eyed alien monster or a giant, radioactive spider,
like the ones Tyrone had seen on the late-night horror movies
on channel 13 out of Memphis. He hadn't crawled up out of the
sloughs like that Swamp Thing in the comics.

Tyrone knew it would be futile to try to run, and he was
smart enough to know that this was probably not going to end
well...just when he had come into the windfall from Streeter and
finally had something to entice Charlene, one of the girls who had
left the Playhouse for that man called Jesus. She was working for a
local church, and Tyrone attended services just to look at her.

He thought that he could look at Charlene all day long and
never find a flaw in her beauty. But with his new prosperity, he
thought a woman like that might give someone like him a second
look, a chance at a future together, so he had given generously to
the offering plate when it came to his pew. All of the "what-ifs"
and "might-have-beens" ran through Tyrone's mind and began to
melt away like snow in May.

*I watched Freddie down at the pond in the spring, when he
was there with Star. He would catch something and reel it in just to
play with it and make it bleed. He'd put it in the water and watch
the blood spread across the water. Star told him that he shouldn't*

like to hurt things and people, so he wouldn't do it so much—just to please her. But after she died, we heard that he went crazy, hurting and killing full-time.

When we played touch football, he tackled me one time and rolled over on top of me. His eyes changed like the eyes of a snake. His tongue flicked in and out, and he hissed like he was going to strike me. His eyes were burning out of his sockets, but Miss Star shouted at him that day and said, "No, Freddie! No!"

He gave me nightmares, and to watch him watch me made me sick at my stomach, like I am right now. No, I don't think I'll ever see the bossman again, and Charlene won't be my wife, and we won't have no smart babies, neither.

Tyrone's chubby brown cheeks were shaking and jiggling, his jaw was slack, his mouth was open and drooling, and his lips and tongue were in the grips of a full-blown spasm, causing him to stammer and stutter.

"Hi, Fre...Fre...Freddie. You come for my mon...mon... money?" Tyrone asked.

"No, Tyrone, it's not your money I want. It's Streeter. I need to know where he is, and I know you'll know. You're the only living thing in this world that he cares about, and I know he was here with you the other night when the deputy showed up," Freddie said.

"I don't know where the bossman is, Mr. Freddie. Honest I don't. He just gone. That's all I know," Tyrone said.

"You're going to tell me, Tyrone. We can do it easy and quick, or we can do it the hard way, but you're going to tell me. They all do," Freddie said.

At that moment, a big logging truck thundered by on the darkened road down the hill, and Tyrone ran to the open window and screamed, "Help me! Help me!"

"It's too late for that, Tyrone," Freddie said as he pulled his hand from his front pocket. That was when Tyrone saw the switch-blade that Freddie favored.

Freddie tortured poor Tyrone for two days and three nights, carving him up piece by piece, but he wouldn't give up his old bossman.

Like a hog on the assembly lines of the packing houses in Tupelo, Freddie strung him up and gutted him slowly.

It was only when Tyrone gave up the ghost and died that his shoe fell off. That's when Freddie saw the folded scrap of paper tucked into a crevice near the heel.

He opened it and saw the name and address: *Lizzie Boudreaux, Faubourg Maringy, 1449 E Streeter Avenue, New Orleans, Louisiana.*

Freddie smiled, looked at Tyrone, saluted, and said, "You were the toughest of them all."

He gathered up all of the pieces of Tyrone, dragged the spare parts and Tyrone's body up to the Playhouse, doused it and all of the building with kerosene, and set them ablaze in one giant funeral pyre.

The thick black smoke was billowing over the canopy of the dense forest as Freddie made his way down the hillside for the last time. He stopped on the last high ridge, where he could still see the feathery plumes wafting upward as the boiling flames burned away the grit, grime, and sin of the place that had been the ruin of many lost souls. He sat there for a long time without making a sound, watching in fascination as the blackened frame of the building collapsed in on itself—the final cremation of what might have been.

Finally, he cranked his car and said, "Goodbye, Star. I think I'll go on down to the city of New Orleans, buy a voodoo doll that looks like your murderer, dig the pins in a little deeper, and have some beignets and blood just for you."

CHAPTER TWENTY-ONE

"When one with honeyed words but evil
mind persuades the mob, great woes
befall the state."—Euripides, Orestes

"Elections belong to the people. It's their
decision. If they decide to turn their backs
on the fire and burn their behinds, then they
will just have to sit on their blisters."
—Abraham Lincoln

Election Day rolled around at last.

The campaign for sheriff had commanded unusual attention, and an extraordinary amount of money was spent on ads. For the first time in memory, a plane flew over Tupelo with a banner streaming behind the tail. The aerial ad read, "Vote for Gill, the Real Deal."

It wasn't the sheriff's idea. His loyal supporter had seen one advertising some bar when he was relaxing on the white sands of Ft. Billings Beach, Florida, and thought, "Why not?" So he had the banner made and hitched it to the back of his crop duster, and up, up, and away he went. Old-timers thought that it was pretty strange and not the way things were done in Mississippi. They also thought that it may have hurt Gill more than it helped.

Big ads ran in the *Daily Journal* with Michael's picture next to Gill's...the new centurion college boy endorses the country sheriff in his first venture into political races. Michael told Sarge, "I don't know if it will win the sheriff one vote, but I don't think it will hurt him like that airplane banner, either."

Whispering campaigns were in full gear, fueled by Pennington's agents.

"Did you hear that they wrecked county cars chasing some man with some bootleg whiskey? Reckon how much that cost the taxpayers?"

"Well, Margie, my husband told me that the sheriff let the crime rate run wild just because he was obsessed with a few harmless bootleggers. Honey, would you please tell Betty the beauty operator to turn down my hairdryer? It's frying my brain."

"Would you take a little off the top today, Douglas? Not as much as was burnt off the top of that monkey. You know, word is that Gill never liked that monkey. Some folks think he mighta done it himself. Please splash on a little of that Old Spice when you shave my face. Mama thinks it makes me smell rugged, like I just come in from the sea...like that man in the commercial."

"Our preacher said the collection plates have been mighty shallow since the sheriff shut down the bootleggers. All it did was run good money across the county line. What kind of sense does that make? I heard Mr. Pennington himself say that county church support of foreign missions may be hurt, and my sister's boy may have to come home from his post in the Philippines."

"Mr. Pennington told me that he knew the crops weren't so good this year, and if I needed some time on the house payments to his bank and some discounts on the supplies at the feed-and-seed store, he might help me. He said he would hate to see our kids go without Christmas this year through no fault of my own.

"Then he said, 'That Sheriff Simpson hasn't done a very good job, has he?' I said, 'No, sir. Now that I think about it, he's about the worst sheriff I've ever seen. Who's running against him?' Mr. Pennington smiled and asked, 'Does it matter?'"

Pints of whiskey were passed out in record numbers at the polling places. It wasn't exactly the blind leading the blind, but more like the drunks leading the drunk-as-skunks.

Flyers were all over the county, some nailed to trees near the voting sites. They were anonymous, of course, and implied that Sheriff Simpson had neglected his duty to protect and serve—that the crime rate was up, response time was down, expenses were up, and taxes might have to be raised if he were reelected.

Petty crimes were going unsolved, they said. Citizens were endangered by all the high-speed chases...all because Sheriff Simpson had abandoned his broader duties to indulge his obsessions, chasing and harassing a few marginal men who just sold a little white whiskey now and then. And that only drove some of Lee County's tax base to other counties that focused on the greater good and building a lasting "You scratch my back, I'll scratch yours" community of practical neighbors who knew when to be deaf, when to be blind, and when to be mute.

When the returns came in, the news was not good. All the areas around the clubs were lost, but some boxes dominated by good church folks who didn't understand the game (or pretended not to understand) were also lost.

The celebration was on early at the Pennington "eat-all-you-want, drink-until-you-pass-out" campaign parties. It wasn't that the syndicate thought the new sheriff would be any better or that he was their guy. They just knew that he couldn't be any more hostile to their business than the incumbent.

The Simpson campaign office was deserted by nine. Some of Gill's supporters had gone for the free food and frolicking festivities to pretend they were with his challenger all along. No one liked to be with a loser.

But Michael didn't think Gill was a loser.

He walked into the darkened front room of the building. The signs were up, the balloons were blowing to and fro in the gentle breeze of a rattling window air-conditioning unit, and the TV sets were all silent. Some had dropped their campaign buttons and signs on the floor, which was littered with might-have-been, shoulda-coulda dreams.

Michael heard the distant sound of the lonely, solitary fiddle playing from behind closed doors. He followed the sound of the steel strings and short rhythmical bowing, and then the sound of the smooth bow. Gill was much more than a "stick it under your chin and scrape away" fiddler. He could play the sweet sound or the crunchy. Tonight he was playing the music, caressing the instrument as therapy, and the keen and wiry fiddle sounded mellow and supple like a violin at times.

Michael stopped outside the door and listened. Gill was playing and softly singing an old Bill Monroe classic, "Our Little Cabin Home on a Hill."

"Now when you have come to the end of the way and find there's no more happiness for you, just let your thoughts turn back once more if you will, to our little cabin home on a hill."

Michael tapped lightly on the door, and Gill stopped playing and said, "Come on in if you're going to."

"Hi, Sheriff, just checking in," Michael said.

"Well, hello, Michael. Pull up a chair if you'd like."

They sat quietly for a moment before Gill spoke. "It didn't turn out like we hoped it would, but it did end up like I suspected it would after our fight with our cheap little gangster-monkeys and their circus masters," Gill said.

"No, it didn't. I hope my pitiful endorsement didn't hurt you," Michael said.

"No, that was one of the highlights of the campaign for me. Now, the banner behind the plane…that might be another matter," he said with a chuckle.

He ran his fingers through his hair, scratched his head, and heaved a big sigh of release. "All's not lost, Michael," he said. "When I took office, the syndicate had free rein, the run of the county to provide what some might call 'harmless vice.' They offered girls, games, grog, and graft.

"People came to their card games, stopped at their stores, and discovered, after a cool beer or lunch, that their cars wouldn't start. The mob mechanics showed up, fixed it in five minutes with the 'worn-out parts' that the mob had disconnected while the pigeons were distracted. They just spray-painted, reinstalled, and charged them for their own parts. Then the marks would have to pay on the spot or else they got hurt, or one of the cooperative constables would show up and threaten them with jail.

"Then there was the moonshine, the drugs, the thefts, the prostitution, the shootings at their clubs, the payoffs to officials at all levels, the broken homes, the threats, and the games—all kinds of games that folks like Pennington run. Regular folks just didn't understand all of that. I guess they still don't, because today, they turned out...to turn me out," he said with a catch in his voice.

"But we fought the good fight, didn't we? It will take them a long time to recover...if they ever do. And here's some more good news that I think you may not know. The medical reports showed that Cal Mattox didn't have a heart attack. He is as healthy as a horse. The judge ordered him back to jail to serve the remainder of his six months in jail. I think maybe the powers that be weren't so interested in him after I was defeated, and they just let that loose end dangle. Cal was getting to be too high-maintenance for them, I think. He was brought in by the Pontotoc sheriff tonight. I gave him the best room in the jailhouse!" the sheriff said.

Michael didn't say much. He just listened and nodded.

"How're you going to write all of this up in your final papers on your internship? I hope the time with us was worthwhile. Be sure and say that we tried to do it all legal and such, within the laws we had. We didn't burn the clubs to the ground like one of my predecessors was fond of doing. And we weren't sheet-wearing vigilantes, either," the sheriff said.

"I'm just going to tell it like it is, like it was, and save the best for when I'm older and become a writer," Michael said with a big smile.

"A writer, huh? Well, son, you'd make a good one. Those *routine incident reports* of yours were anything but routine. When you wrote up the case summaries, it was enough to make a grown man cry!" he said.

They both laughed, and then a long, uncomfortable sadness hung in the air.

"What will you do when your term ends?" Michael asked.

"Oh, I have an offer to work for the Motor Vehicle Department, checking gas stations and so on, and I might run for office again. I have been sheriff and tax collector, and they are splitting those offices. So I might decide to run for the new, stand-alone position of tax collector, though they were despised in the Bible—in our day, too," he said.

"Go on and get some sleep, or maybe surprise your girl-friend in Memphis. You know…the fair is coming. Maybe she'd like that, if you'd buy her some cotton candy or win her a teddy bear. Go get her, ride the Mad Mouse with her, and scream at the top of your lungs. Be a kid again, Michael. Sail through the Tunnel of Love on those tiny boats, hold her hand, and forget all of this for a while," the sheriff said.

He smiled and rose to shake Michael's hand. "I'll see you on your next shift. I may be a poor, lame duck, but we've still got a few quacks left in us before we have to lay down our badges and give up our county pistols," he said.

"If you can't make it tomorrow, just let Earl know. You're going to make a fine lawman," he said as he patted Michael on the back and picked up his fiddle and bow.

"Oh…Michael…if you do write about it one day, be sure and tell them that it was a cancerous canker of corruption, and we just tried to cut out the rotten core the parasites were feeding off of…without killing the patient," the sheriff said as he cradled the fiddle across the bridge of his shoulder and tucked it beneath his chin.

"Add, too, that along the way, we also played some good music at our campaign rallies and at the end of some long, hard shifts. There were times when we just needed to crawl out of the muck and mire with a tune or two. Then there were the nights when the poor inmates back there in the jail needed a bit of joy and a gospel tune or two, just to let them know that life was not over for them until the Almighty said it was. It's not over for us either, Michael," the fiddling sheriff added.

When Michael left him and closed the door, Gill resumed his playing and singing, and Michael lingered a bit to listen.

"Tonight I'm alone without you, my dear. It seems there's a longing for you still. All I have to do is sit alone and cry in our little cabin home on the hill. Oh someone has taken you from me, and left me here all alone. Just listen to the rain beat on our window pane, in our little cabin on the hill."

It was then that Michael knew he had to go to Memphis right then to see Dixie Lee, and he had to go unannounced.

* * *

The lights of Memphis formed an arch of white over the horizon as Michael neared the city. His mind was racing, and he wasn't sure what it was he hoped to accomplish. Maybe he wanted just to look at her, maybe he wanted to speak of old times and faded flowers of memory that she had pressed between the pages of his mind.

Just as he crossed the bridge over the Mississippi to West Memphis, the rains blew in, obscuring the lighted barges pushing loads down the river. The storm's moist breath seemed to envelop his car as the storm within closed in on him, cloaking his heart with the sudden, dampening pallor of despair.

As he neared her apartment, someone opened the heavenly faucets, and the rain began to pour from the sky in "forty-days-and-forty-nights" torrents. He neared her place and could dimly see car lights through his water-blurred windshield. Then he saw her, running through the rain to the cover of the stairwell above her unit.

It was wonderful to see her. His heart was racing. He longed to surprise her, to hold her, to speak of the future, their future. She stood near a security light, and it bathed her in soft, golden hues as she shook the water out of her hair, fluffed a wilderness of tangled blonde curls, and closed her umbrella. He could already feel her against him, the perfumed texture of her hands and throat, the taste and warmth of her lips. He imagined the surprise and the familiar mischief in her eyes and the sudden huskiness in her voice.

Michael quickly maneuvered into an open parking place and was just opening his door to run to her…then he saw him.

A sudden flash of lightning illuminated a man who came out of the shadows near the car she had emerged from. The flashes of lightning gave him a stutter-like movement as he moved toward Dixie Lee.

The man had strong features, a prominent, square jaw—and he moved with confidence, a quick, cat-like gait. His broad smile was captured in the security light as he neared her. He shook himself like a wet dog when he came to her out of the rain, and they both laughed in a perfect rhythm and symmetry. He grabbed her and she melted into his arms with familiar murmurs of love and laughter.

Dixie's hair was shimmering under the nightlight, her head was tilted to one side, and her eyes were closed as they had once closed for Michael. He knew that under those lids, her blue eyes were clouding with emotion. A weight began to press on his chest, and he couldn't catch his breath.

Michael couldn't see much after that—but it wasn't because of the water outside. He sat in his car long after the happy couple disappeared from sight. He heard a sound like glass breaking, and he realized that it was the shattering of his heart.

He came to see her one more time at her invitation, and she confessed what he already knew. She asked if he would fight for her. But he looked into her blue eyes of stormy confusion and saw no chance there for him…no path to tomorrow. All of the uncomfortable things had been seen and said, and the knight-errant could not fix it. It was over and beyond repair.

He would never tell her that he had seen her in the rain that night as she found a new port in her storms. He wouldn't confess that he had never felt more irrelevant standing on the periphery of her life, realizing it was too late. How could he explain to Dixie

Lee the pain of being on the outside looking in, watching as someone assumed his role as leading man in the story of her life?

There would be no towering wedding cake, no diapers, no
children, no percale sheets, no books of S&H Green Stamps, no
color TV bought on time payments, no newspapers in the drive of
the modest brick home, no punching time clocks, no Timex
watches with twistable bands, no sparklers and firecrackers, no
Fourth of July bar-b-ques, no rocking around the Christmas tree...

There was just the soft mutter of the Mustang's tires on the
long, lonely highway to Tupelo, and the memory of how she had
closed her last letter to him.

"I'll be your woman and you be my man, my everything...
forever yours."

CHAPTER TWENTY-TWO

*"Don't go to bed with no price on your
head. Don't do it. Don't roll the dice if you
can't pay the price."—Grusin-Ames,
"Keep Your Eye on the Sparrow"*

*"Hang down your head, now what have you
done? Hang down your head and cry...
it's time to say goodbye. It's time for
you to die."—Farrant-Rawson,
"Hang Down Your Head"*

Lizzie "GAL" Boudreaux lived in New Orleans all of her seventy-two years, residing in a shotgun house near the French Quarter for the last twenty-five.

The style of the house took its name from its size and design: if all of the interior doors were open, someone could shoot their shotgun and have the pellets go clean through the house, even though there was no hallway—and that had happened more than once over the years she had been there.

There were always dissatisfied customers with her black magic—those who felt she hadn't sufficiently ruined their enemies, and the jealous lovers who thought she might have possessed their men's bodies for physical intimacy, not for spiritual control on behalf of her clients.

Lizzie had been a singer and dancer when she was young, a bone rattler, a poultice doctor, a charm maker, and the self-described Voodoo Queen of the French Quarter. Some said she was the reincarnation of Marie Laveau, and Lizzie never discouraged those stories. She even began to dress like the old pictures of Marie and go down at midnight to sit on Marie's tomb and talk with her.

Some called her a witch. In Lizzie's heyday, she had doled out curses, spells, magic potions, and charms, and attracted large crowds to her rituals in old Algiers, especially after her trip to Haiti to learn more about that brand of voodoo.

But for her own peace, she would sneak down to the French Quarter at night and listen to the mournful clarinet of Pete Fountain and the horns of Al Hirt, a young Louis Armstrong, and Louis Prima.

She had always been a free spirit who embraced the unconventional lifestyles of the musicians, artists, beatniks, and hippies who were like moths to a flame to New Orleans and its dark spiritualism.

She hadn't seen her family since they moved to Tupelo after the tornado of 1936. Her sister, Vera, had written—mostly about her son, James, his brushes with the law, and his prison time. But money for travel was tight. The last time she heard from her nephew, James Streeter, was the occasion of her sister's death. Vera and her daughter, Tamara, had been killed in a car wreck.

Streeter's dry telegram said, "Car wreck near Memphis. Mama died. Tamara died. Enemies all around me."

So Great-Aunt Lizzie made an Ouanga, a charm to poison his enemies, made from the roots of the figuier maudit tree, which was native to Africa. The charm contained the powder of the toxic tree roots, bones, nails, other roots, holy water, bread, incense, and candles, and sometimes even crucifixes, as voodoo had adopted some tenets of Roman Catholicism.

She didn't hear back from her nephew, so she didn't know if her charm was effective or not. It didn't matter, though, for Lizzie had grown dissatisfied and disenchanted with voodoo. Her business had declined, and now drug dealers came to her for spells to protect their drug smuggling, demanding that she bite the head off of live chickens and drink their blood, as some high priests of voodoo were offering in their acts of voodoo show biz.

Most of her clientele of African descent had fallen away. Many had come to believe that voodoo was superstitious and silly, and they had turned their backs on Lizzie's services. One of the last gatherings of the faithful had heard Lizzie try to save her community and drive out the gangs, streetwalkers, burglars, and thieves...and drug dealers like her nephew. Her sister had told Lizzie that they called him The Pusher.

Then one hot afternoon, she had a revelation. As she sat and listened to the fifteenth consecutive customer who wanted a better love life, to be rendered irresistible to women, and to make his lover always faithful, she had a revelation...it was time to move on.

She broke with voodoo completely in favor of fundamental Christianity. She became a faithful member and singer in the choir at the Holiness Church of the Quarter. This woman, whose name had once been shouted for good luck by gamblers when they rolled their dice, became a volunteer to help the homeless and a sought-after hairdresser whose services were requested by the ladies of some of the more affluent households of New Orleans. Sister Lizzie Angel, as she was known, made no more potions and cast no more spells, for she had fallen under the spell of Christ. Her life was peaceful and serene.

And then one day, she opened the door to her shotgun house, and there was her nephew, suitcase in hand.

"GAL, it's me, James. I've come home!" he said.

"Boy, I can't believe it!" said a stunned Lizzie as she grabbed hold of her last living kin and squeezed him until he couldn't breathe.

They talked for hours, through a big orange sunset and through the rise of a giant midnight moon. Streeter laid it all out in a rushing release of the poison that festered within him. He didn't sugarcoat it, and Lizzie wept, wailed, and called on God. She had left darkness behind, and now darkness had come to live with her.

"GAL, I need to tell you that someone is on my trail—someone hired to kill me. He's a vicious killer, worse than me if there is such a man. I read the *Jackson Clarion-Ledger* newspaper when I stopped there on the way here. My club was burned to the ground near Tupelo, and my man there was murdered. He was just a simple boy, and now he's dead because of me," Streeter said.

"I fled like a coward and holed up in a dirty hovel near McComb. I couldn't sleep. I sweated. I cried. I'd get up and look out the window to see if the killer had found me. When I did sleep, I fell into a nightmare, and I was walking down the streets of a strange place. It was like that movie...*The Night of the Living Dead*," he said as the fear poured out of him like the buckets of sweat drenching his brow and upper lip.

"There was fire and smoke and heat and misery everywhere. The killer had followed me to the gates of that place. I was looking back at him, and he was smiling...like he had driven me to his master. When I turned around, there was the devil. He grabbed me by the throat, and I was gagging, twisting, and struggling, trying to break free.

"Aunt Lizzie, he just looked at me, laughed, and said, 'Welcome to Hell, James. What did you expect...a sauna? Some hot stones to ease your aching muscles and soul? Some heat to sweat out your guilt and still the voices of your victims? This is Hell, your home for all time. You won't be selling autographed pictures of Jesus here, James. Your game is ended. Your road has run out, and no one gets out alive. It's just over, that's all. Just think of me as the bill collector. You are behind on your payments, and I've come to repossess all the sin that you bought on my generous time payments.'

"I woke up screaming, jumped in my car, and drove here as fast as I could," Streeter said.

He had run out of words and began to weep uncontrollably. His body was wracked by deep, halting, hiccupping sobs. He gagged and vomited on her rug.

Lizzie put her arms around him and began to rock him to and fro, patting him on the back just as she had when he was a baby. "There, there, James. There, there, my boy. Jesus loves you," she said.

"No one could love me, and they shouldn't. I've done so many bad things, Aunt Lizzie. I'm behind the eight ball and can't see around it," he said.

He looked up at his aunt and noticed for the first time that there was a change in her. She didn't seem to be the same woman he had known as a child. There was something about her face and her smile. There was a strange light, where there had once been darkness. He looked at her in wonder, and she smiled his fear away.

When the sun came up, they were still on the couch, and he was sleeping deeply and soundly...the first such sleep in a long time for Streeter. The killer's head was in his aunt's lap, seeking comfort and forgiveness, even though he'd had none to dispense to others during his life of crime.

Lizzie took him to her church the following Sunday, though he was afraid to enter. "I'm afraid the big Hit Man up there might strike me dead if I enter His place, Aunt Lizzie," he said.

She tutored him. She loved him. She prayed for him. Slowly but surely, the child she remembered began to emerge from somewhere inside the monster that her sister's little boy had become.

He offered her money, but she told him that she didn't need nor want money that he had made serving the devil. Then one day he began to quietly donate money to the shelters where she ministered to the homeless and hopelessly addicted.

Her church members welcomed Lizzie's nephew to their Holiness congregation near the French Quarter, and then one night, when Bishop Augustin Dupart was preaching at a revival meeting, the unthinkable happened—something people in Tupelo could not have imagined.

The pastor was preaching, and he was on fire with the Holy Spirit. He was riding the Gospel Express and calling "all aboard" for the last train to the pearly gates. The church was packed, and after two hours, people were fainting from the heat and the pastor's message.

"There is the presence of the Lord in this house. I can feel Him here right now. He's breaking every shackle. He's mending the broken. I thank Him. I thank Him. Oh, someone is here, someone who has traveled the hard road home to New Orleans. This is your night. This is your night! God has brought you here to be healed. God made an appointment with you. It is no accident that your path led to the front door of His house. Don't be ashamed.

"He designated this night long ago. Walk away from darkness. Walk into the Light. He is here right now. Come forward and see your chains fall to the floor. You think He won't forgive you, but He is waiting. Why do you delay? Run to Him now! Deliverance is at hand," the bishop preached, hanging on to the pulpit with one hand, waving his Bible with the other.

"Somebody can rebuke the grip of the enemy. Somebody can break free of the prison of sin they've lived in since they were a child. Satan, take your filthy hand off this child of God. He's not yours any longer. The Holy Spirit is working on him, purging you from his mind and heart...the blood he has spilt is like the waters of the Red Sea, but he can see those waters being parted and his sins swallowed up. He is hearing the Sermon on the Mount pouring through him, and he is almost ready...almost ready to bow before the Savior of the world, who stoops to serve the lowly...almost ready to pick up his cross and follow Jesus. He is being prepared for communion with his new family...the Father, the Son, and the Holy Ghost. Come down! Come down here tonight and break the yoke of sin," the bishop shouted.

The organist began to make the keys weep, and the choir began to sing and sway, "All to Jesus, I surrender. All to Him I freely give...I surrender all. I surrender all..."

James Streeter was in the church, sitting on the back bench, hiding from God. But he knew that the pastor was speaking right to him. He felt the tug like a giant magnet pulling him, willing him to come forward.

He stood, against his will. He tried to run out of the church, but he couldn't. He was sweating, and his heart was pounding louder than the drummer beating the snare drums behind the organist. He began to take baby steps toward the aisle.

Lizzie was watching him. She was transfixed, crying, and echoing the bishop's call. "Yes, Lord…Yes, Lord. Set him free!" she shouted.

Her nephew stumbled and fell to his knees. The congregation felt a mighty anointing fall on the church, and they urged him on. The bishop was smiling and encouraging him. "Come, brother, come. He's been waiting so long for you to surrender all."

James Streeter couldn't stand. He couldn't walk. But he began to crawl to the altar, inch-by-inch.

The bishop came to him and lifted him up, and the man known as The Pusher fell into the pastor's arms and said, "Everything I feared in life, all the monsters under my bed and in the closet…I became all those things, Pastor, and now the end is rushing toward me. There is a curse on me that no voodoo priest can cure," Streeter said.

The bishop held him in a gospel grip and pulled his head down on his shoulder.

"James Streeter, this is your Damascus Road encounter. Jesus is calling you—not to whitewash, but to blood-wash. Do you repent of all of your sins and wicked ways?"

"Yes, yes, I do!" Streeter cried.

"Do you renounce the devil and all of his agents?" the bishop asked.

"Yes, turn me loose, Satan. I renounce you and all your demons!" Streeter cried.

"James Streeter, do you accept Jesus Christ as your Lord and Savior? Will you be covered by His tender mercies? Will you follow Him and only Him for as long as you may walk upon this lost world?" the bishop asked.

"Yes, yes…Thank you, Jesus!" Streeter cried.

The bishop was still holding Streeter up. The sweat was pouring from both men, and he began to pray for James and to encourage the congregation to come forward and lay hands on James.

The crowd surged toward the two men, hundreds of hands outstretched, and voices in unison pleading the blood of Christ over James Streeter. Lizzie Boudreaux saw all of her prayers answered, and the shouts of the parishioners were heard throughout the Quarter—"Signs and wonders…signs and wonders!"

Shortly after he was saved, James Streeter was baptized, and everyone began to call him Brother James. Everyone who met him in the church, on the street, or in the shelters would testify that the Author of second chances had done a mighty work in him, that the old man had been torn down to make way for the new man. All the members of GAL's church said they didn't know a nicer, kinder man.

* * *

Freddie waited in the alley that ran down the side of Holiness Church of the Quarter. He had watched GAL's house for days and had Streeter's habits and daily schedules down to a science.

After the meeting for the church homeless ministry, Streeter stepped out of the church and began his walk back to his aunt's house. He was on top of the world. He felt as if a giant weight had been lifted from him, and he wondered at the wonder of Christ, Who could save someone as wretched as him. He spoke to everyone he met, and they greeted him without the fear and fake cordiality that he had been accustomed to in Tupelo.

I been caged all my life. There was bound to be a wild animal in that pen. How could there not be? But no more, no more, I got a second chance. I dried up as a boy, then I blew up as a man, but now I've grown up in Christ.

He bounced along, singing a Joe Tex tune. "I believe that I'm going to make it. I'll be home before you can say Jackie Robinson…"

There was one alleyway on his walk home, where he noticed that the streetlight was out. That block was bathed in darkness. He could barely see the path in front of him. As he passed the alley, Freddie stepped silently out of the black night and hit Streeter in the head with a sock full of steel ball bearings. Streeter dropped to the pavement like a sack of potatoes, his Bible still in his hand.

Freddie rolled Streeter into his Ford Fairlane hidden in the alley and bound his hands and feet. He drove him to a carefully chosen place of torture where no one could hear his screams, a squalid shack surrounded by cypress trees in a swamp outside of New Orleans. Streeter was still unconscious when Freddie dragged him into the backwater hovel. The night bugs were chirping, buzzing, and whining. A giant moth fluttered against the dirty window panes as Freddie used duct tape and baling wire to strap Streeter to an old wooden table.

Freddie stood over his unconscious victim for hours, the light from a lone candle illuminating his vigil. He was impatient and eager to begin the satanic torture rituals which he reserved for special victims. "Wake up, James. Wake up!" Freddie demanded. When there was no response, he slapped Streeter hard…again and again, snapping his head left and then right.

Freddie's pulse was racing, and his breathing was erratic as he bent over Streeter to shout in his ears. "I want you awake for this. Ace could have sent anyone to this bayou to dispatch you, but he chose me," Fredrick said.

Streeter began to come out of the haze of the sucker blow to his head and saw the blurry, monstrous visage of the albino looming above him. Streeter moaned and tried to speak.

"Um, oh…Freddie, is that you?" he asked.

"Yes, Brother James, it's me. You are my brother in death, and my face is the last you will see before you join all the others you have killed, the wicked and the innocent, like Star…*my Star*. I had a chance at happiness, but you took her from me. Now you must go to the holding bin. I got this giant waste basket in the dark corner of my mind. That's where the scraps of my victims are—my chosen ones—all crumpled and wadded, waiting for the day I join my master…waiting for my death to shred their images and set them free," Freddie said.

Streeter squirmed against his restraints but realized he was bound and helpless.

"I'm not scared, Freddie. I've been waiting for you. I knew you'd come. I knew that you'd be the one he sent. I didn't dread today; I longed for it. I wanted to tell you that I'm a new man, and you can be, too," Streeter said.

"Men like us don't change, James. You know *that*. You're just scared and trying to talk yourself out of death," Freddie said.

"No, no, Freddie…that's not true. I came here running. My soles were so worn that they flapped, and I thought it was the ghosts of the dead following me…but it wasn't. It was the sandals of my Savior. I know that no one who knew the old me will believe it, but the old man is gone. God tore him down and built the new man who was running from himself…not you, Freddie, and not Ace. God's mercy is a mystery," Streeter said, trying to catch his breath against the tight bands across his chest.

"Why would you expect me to believe a cold-blooded killer like you would follow the enemy of my master?" Freddie asked, tilting his head left and then right.

"Because, Freddie, I killed so many men—so many died by my hand—but Jesus was the only one who *chose* to die for me. I put Him on the cross to die for my sins and wickedness. He was pierced for my transgressions, and He died for me…for someone like me. His stripes have healed me," Streeter said.

"Don't say that name!" Freddie said, recoiling at the sound of the name—Jesus.

"Jesus, Jesus, Jesus, sweetest name I know," Streeter cried loudly and reverently.

Freddie put his hands over his ears, bent double in pain, and shouted, "Stop, stop, stop!"

"Jesus, remember me when you come into your Kingdom," Streeter cried, echoing the thief on the Cross and the painting by Star, the very woman he had murdered.

"No more ghosts, Freddie. No more voices, no more hounds from Parchman after me, barking in my dreams. God's heart is revealed in His Son. Jesus told me that I will be with Him today in Paradise. I'm set free, and you can be, too, Freddie. Come join me and find the peace that only Jesus can offer. You can't kill The Pusher; he's already dead," Streeter said.

Freddie was bent double in pain, his arms were spasming, and his feet were stomping the floor. "Stop saying his name! Stop saying that word that stabs my heart!" Freddie demanded.

"Amazing grace, how sweet the sound that saved a wretch like me. Thank you, Jesus, thank you, Lord Jesus!" Streeter shouted.

Freddie was reeling to and fro. Water was leaking down his ghostly pale face, and his red eyes were rolled back up into his head. "Stop, stop, stop!" he cried.

"Not my blood, not the blood we've shed, Freddie. Nothing but the blood of Jesus!" Streeter shouted.

Then Freddie shrieked and started stabbing wildly...the air, the walls, the table...swinging and slashing. He stabbed until he could no longer hear the name that cut him to his core, and then he fell to the floor covered by the blood of his enemy but robbed of his revenge. Freddie knew that Streeter was right. The man that he had longed to kill was beyond his reach by the time he found him. Freddie had failed Star, and his anger and self-loathing became unbearable...endless fuel for murderous rampages to come.

And James Streeter—who had been addicted to the smell, taste, and texture of death since he was a boy, when he had slept on the graves in Tupelo—now experienced it in the first person...and found that it had no sting.

* * *

Two weeks later, a Boy Scout troop was on a field trip documenting wildlife around the brackish waters of the giant estuary outside of New Orleans. Just as the first gray light of morning broke across the water, they found Streeter's bloated and mutilated body washed up on the northern shore of Lake Pontchartrain.

The St. Tammany Parish deputy sheriff who was called to the scene interviewed Chip Benoit, the Eagle Scout who had led the field trip and the first scout to find the body.

"Chip, I know it's hard to see a dead man—especially one who's been murdered—and it's going to be difficult to forget this day...but is there anything you remember seeing that might help us?" the deputy asked.

"Not really. But besides the stab wounds, there's an image I can't get out of my mind. Something I'll never forget was that his right hand was extended—frozen in death. It was straining and reaching up. Isn't that strange?" Chip asked.

"He could've been trying to block the attack of his assailant," the deputy said.

"No, sir, I don't think that was it. He had this smile on his face, too—a look of peace. Peace...when someone was hacking him to death? It was like he was reaching up to someone, someone he recognized, and he was smiling. Who was the last person he saw? It couldn't have been his murderer," Chip said. "Who did he see, Deputy? Who did he see who could have given him such peace in the midst of such horror?"

* * *

When the good people of the Holiness Church of the French Quarter heard of Brother James's death—of his smile and the raised hand frozen into his body's death throes—they had no doubt who he'd seen.

The deacons of the church bore his casket from the funeral home down through the Quarter to the church. It was a reversal of the usual jazz funeral that takes the body to the graveyard. Somber dirges and hymns were played right up to the door of the church where Bishop Augustin Dupart waited.

The choir swayed in unison and sang "Just a Closer Walk with Thee" and then went into "Oh come, angel band, come and around me stand. Oh, bear me away on your snow-white wings to my immortal home..."

Bishop stepped to the pulpit with tears in his eyes. "Brother James Streeter has been fighting the devil for a long time. The devil thought he had him, and he almost did, but Brother James finally said, 'Devil, this is not my battle, and you're a schoolyard bully. I'm going to step back and introduce you to my Big Brother, my Heavenly Father...Jesus Christ, and I'm going to just stand back and watch the fight. You ain't got a chance, devil!'"

"Amen, Pastor, preach it!" the congregation said.

"Brother James Streeter was reading the Twenty-Third Psalm with us the night he was attacked. He was certain that goodness and mercy were following him all the days of his life, however many days or how few hours he had left, and that the Lord was preparing a table for him in the presence of his enemies.

"But he was full of remorse and asked me, 'Pastor, what will I say when I see Star in heaven?'

"I told James that for him, just as it was for her, Jesus said that there would be more rejoicing in heaven over one sinner who repents than ninety-nine of the righteous who do not need to repent. I asked James if he knew the parable that Jesus told of the lost coin. He knew of it but wasn't sure he understood it.

"Jesus said, 'What woman who had ten coins and lost one, would not light a lamp, sweep her house, and look until she finds it. And when she finds it, calls her friends and neighbors to say, Rejoice with me for I have found my lost coin,'" Bishop Dupart said, his voice rising and falling, punctuating each line of redemption's song.

Lizzie Boudreaux was crying, and the congregation had entered into a low, whispering harmony of heavenly praise. The rafters of the old church creaked and sighed.

"I told him, 'James, you and Star were His lost coins. You were lost, but now you are found.' No devil...no enemy...can understand God's kind of love, mercy, and grace, or His desire to redeem all sinners, including Brother James Streeter.

"You are defeated, Satan! You lost him. You lost him... Oh, Mary don't you weep. Tell Martha not to moan. The enemies of God have all drowned in the Red Sea. Every saint has a past, and every sinner has a future in Christ," the bishop said as he closed his Bible.

That was a signal. The final goodbyes had been said, and in New Orleans tradition, they had "cut the body loose." The deacons bore him out to the hearse, and as it began to pull away from the church, the jazz procession ceased to mourn and instead began to celebrate with upbeat songs.

People danced, swayed, twirled parasols, and celebrated the life of a killer-turned-believer who was headed home…

The horns came up like Gabriel's trumpet, and everyone in the first and second lines began to high-step, smiling big at the opening of the Pearly Gates. They reached their hands up to the sky, just like Brother James, as they sang…

"Oh, when the saints go marching in… Oh, Lord, I want to be in that number, when the saints go marching in."

CHAPTER TWENTY-THREE

"I'm gonna to lay down my sword and
shield, down by the riverside."
—Terry Rendall, "Down By the Riverside"

"You're searching...for things that don't
exist...Ends and beginnings—there are no
such things. There are only middles."
—Robert Frost, "In the Home Stretch"

Michael wandered down the midway of the Mississippi-Alabama Fair and Dairy Show, an annual event in Tupelo that was like Christmas, New Year's Day, the Fourth of July, and Happy Birthday all rolled into one.

Bands from near and far marched in the big parade opening the fair on "school day," just as they had when Michael was in the band. People came to show off their livestock and hope for a blue ribbon, to display their homemade jams, jellies, and cakes, to sell hamburgers and Cokes to raise money for schools. They came in droves to clutch their tickets and hold their breath as drawings were held for a new car every night of the fair. Some lucky ticket-holders would drive home a new Ford or Chevrolet—the stuff of dreams in a poor state like Mississippi.

People also came to taste the cotton candy, corn dogs, and caramel apples, and to win stuffed animals for girlfriends. Everyone knew the games were rigged, but they still lined up to shoot rifles with twisted barrels, to throw baseballs at bottles that would not fall from a direct hit, and to shoot basketballs at small goals that were not regulation size.

Others just wanted to ride the gentle Ferris wheel, the thrilling roller coasters, or to ride the Bullet, with its g-forces guaranteed to make the participants leave their corn dogs and cotton candy on the sawdust walkways.

So many memories lingered around every turn of the tents...happy times with friends and girlfriends in the haunted house, the house of mirrors, and the fun house. And there were also the sideshows with men and women the promoters swore were descended from the survivors of Atlantis, kings and queens from the jungles of Africa, or shamans from the remote rain forests of the Amazon. There were also some exotic dancers like "Little Egypt," whom wives made sure their husbands did not patronize.

Over the years, Michael had seen some famous people at the fair. One year, he saw Lash Larue, the western serial star clad in black with his trademark bull whip. And in 1956, when he was eight, Michael got to see Tupelo's favorite son in his home-coming concert. Elvis Presley had been twenty-one years old at that historical event—long before he became Lee County's newest deputy.

Michael looked up to see Horace Pennington approaching, strolling slowly and stepping lightly on the sticky sawdust spread over the midway after the heavy rain. He was plucking at the red suspenders beneath his blue seersucker suit and eating a corn dog.

"Well, Deputy Parker, word around town is that you're leaving our fair little city," Pennington said.

"Only temporarily. Tupelo will always be home," Michael answered.

"The voters rained on your parade, didn't they, son?" Pennington asked.

"Seems so, but the day may come when not a single drop of that rain will accept responsibility or blame for the flood," Michael said.

"Well, I told you that you should be careful about trying to catch a falling star. It's always the rising star you want to ride with," Pennington said with a contrived air of parental concern.

"Thanks for the advice, but you opened my eyes," Michael said.

"Coming 'round to reality, are you? Seen the light finally?" Pennington asked.

"No, but I thank you for being an example of all I never want to be…all I want to oppose in life…and for reminding me of the cost of selling out," Michael said.

Pennington's eyes narrowed, but then he smiled.

"Smile, boy… Smile and accept life as it was, as it is, and as it will always be. It ain't like the movies. You aren't Superman— bullets won't bounce off of you, and you can't leap tall buildings in a single bound. And truth, justice, and the American way is just public relations—a trap for the gullible dreamers like you who stomp around the landscape looking to champion the maimed, save the lost, and rescue damsels in distress.

"There's a reason that they're lost lambs, Parker. They're weak and needy, and they will pull you right down into the hole they live in. So, you just toss a few coins their way, chair the local fund drive, and have your photo made with the mayor. If things ever get out of hand and there's a demand to find and punish the guilty, you just serve up one of the innocent sheep to take the fall. But you never, ever get emotionally attached or involved with losers. You just feel the weight and comfort of the money that is cooing to you from your fat billfold and forget the rest," Pennington snapped, all the collegial façade fading away.

"This is heaven right here on earth if you know how to play the game. This is the golden age for men with the Midas touch. Every word you utter just proves old P.T. Barnum right: there is a sucker born every minute. So smile and just roll with the flow. You're no better than the rest of us, and you're gonna have to learn to keep your hands out of other folks' cookie jars," he added.

"I can't smile," Michael said.

"And why is that, Deputy? You still all broke up over Gill's defeat?" Pennington asked.

"Defeat? The Playhouse is burned to the ground. Buzzy is no more. Cal's in jail. The St. Tammany Parrish sheriff in Louisiana told us that Streeter is dead. Billy Payne survived a gut-shot from a self-inflicted wound, cirrhosis of the liver, and hepatitis, only to wind up a practice body for medical students…probably the only good thing he ever did. That might cause some to smile, but I can't. The foul smell is still in the air, and if I go along to get along with you—to smile the smile of the servile, as you suggest—some of the stench from your world might settle on my teeth," Michael said with his best boyish grin.

Pennington's crocodile smile disappeared completely, his face flushed red with anger, and his eyes narrowed to thin slits. Michael knew that he had gotten to the political boss and hit him where he lived.

"People don't want you to tell them the truth. They want you to make them feel good and lie to them, even when they know you're lying. You're going to lose and lose big in life, Parker. You're not only a rebel without a cause. You're a rebel without a clue!" Pennington snapped.

"Maybe so, but I will lie down at night with a clear conscience. Do you even remember what that's like, or did you bully and shake down all of the other babies in the nursery? I bet you cornered the market on Pablum, didn't you?" Michael asked.

Pennington dropped his corn dog and ground it into the sawdust with the heel of his right shoe.

"When you come back to my town, no matter what badge you're wearing or what crusade you're on, tin soldier, you'd better bow low, go with the flow, and tippy-toe when you see me coming," he said with a sharp-edged bite in his voice.

The two men were in a staring contest when a familiar voice shouted Michael's name from behind them.

"Mr. Michael!" the petite girl shouted as she ran to him and bear-hugged him in a rib-cracking embrace.

"It's me, Mary, Mr. Michael! Remember me?" she exclaimed as she looked up at him with sparkling eyes. The words just burst out of her like the fireworks that exploded in starbursts over the fairgrounds every night.

"How could I forget you, Mary?" Michael asked.

"How're you doing? I'm so glad to see you. The paper said that Sheriff Simpson lost and you'd be leaving for Ole Miss. I just wanted to tell you thanks for everything," she said.

"Oh, this is Bobby Joe Senter from Fulton. We're going steady. He just gave me his ring," she said, wiggling her ring finger at Michael.

"Hi, Bobby," Michael said, shaking the hand of the freckle-faced teenager.

"Mary, I see that you're keeping your chin up. Your crown is still riding high atop your curls," Michael said.

"Yes, sir, just like you told me," she said, grinning from ear to ear.

"Well, I just wanted to say hello and...goodbye," she said as her dark, wet eyes drilled into Michael's heart. She hugged him one last time and pressed her cheek against his chest.

As the couple walked away, Bobby Joe asked her, "Who's that old guy? I don't know if I like the way you look at him. Should I be jealous?" He looked at her like he had never believed in magic until the day he laid eyes on her.

"No, silly. He's the reason I'm here with you tonight. He's someone who loved me enough to say no to me," Mary said.

She took the boy's hand and looked back at Michael over her shoulder, showing him one last smile of innocence reborn. The two kids marched down the midway, fingers interlocked, arms swinging by their sides, not a care in the world...dreaming of parades, picnics, proms, and pennies they'd toss into a wishing well.

She'd grown up hard, seeing things time couldn't erase. She was aging way too fast, losing things money couldn't replace. But the Referee had called "Time-out!"

Just then, the carnival barker shouted through his megaphone, "Step right up, ladies and gentlemen, and see the greatest show on earth!"

Michael turned to look at Pennington, and the long look that passed between them after the testimony of Mary's new life needed no more words and no translation.

"Bull…" Pennington said, his mouth already forming the expletive, teeth bared into a mad-dog snarl, his face beet-red with anger and pinched into a scowl by the ugliness of pure hate.

At that moment, a boy on a small tractor drove by pulling a trailer housing his blue-ribbon-winning black Angus bull. As the tractor passed Michael and Pennington, it ran through a mud puddle and splashed wet, black mud all over Pennington's saddle oxfords and right up to the seat of his seersucker suit.

"Now *that's* funny, Mr. Pennington. See, I'm smiling! That money isn't whispering sweet nothings to you—it's swearing at you," Michael said.

* * *

Michael's walkie-talkie squawked at him.

"Michael, the sheriff asked if you could run by the station as soon as possible," Earl said.

"Everything's possible for Possible," Michael answered mischievously.

"What?" Earl asked.

"Never mind…a family joke. On my way," Michael said.

When Michael entered the sheriff's department, he saw Sheriff Simpson giving a tour to two tall men. One was in his late twenties, and the other was an older man, who looked to be nearly six-and-a-half feet tall. He had an eerie resemblance to the coach Michael had once seen sitting atop his tower on a football field in Tuscaloosa.

"Michael, I want you to meet two men you need to know. This is John Edward Collins, future director of the Mississippi Bureau of Narcotics, and Major Clay Strickland, just back from Vietnam," the sheriff said.

"Pleased to meet y'all," Michael said as he shook hands with the men.

"Sheriff Simpson tells us that you are about to exit the sanctuary of Ole Miss and stick your toes into the turbulent waters of real policing," Collins said.

"It appears so," Michael said, "but Sheriff Simpson has prepared me, I think."

"Well, son, I'm not offering a toe in the water to test the temperature to see if you can stand the heat. I'm going to give young men and women a chance to be baptized through the fire of service to their state and their country. Clay here has just come from the jungles of Southeast Asia, where he was an intelligence officer. He's been on the front lines. It's not abstract to him, and he's come home to help me build this agency and fight this fight," Collins said gruffly.

Clay Strickland chuckled and said, "What Mr. Collins is trying to say in his diplomatic way is that he wants to create something special and unique in Mississippi with a few good men and women coming out of college, untainted by the good-ole-boy system in Mississippi and unafraid of long hours and hard work... dangerous work, too. That's why I've signed up to be his chief of intelligence. This is going to be special, Michael...something to write about when you're old, I think. The sheriff told us that you like to write."

Collins laughed then. "That's why I wanted Clay by my side. He used to go into those US Army camps and call out the generals on lax security and things that endangered the troops. He's fearless and focused," he said with a smile that quickly faded.

"We are going to infiltrate the organizations. We are going to take the fight to them in Mississippi, and we are going to enforce the laws given to us by the legislature without favor or exception. If you want to be a part of history, you better get on down to Jackson. We start testing next week...written tests, psychological tests, physical endurance, and interviews by Clay and me. It will be rigorous and not for the faint of heart, but you can get in on the ground floor with only one way to go...up!" Collins said.

Strickland smiled and winked behind Collins' back.

"Sounds good to me. I'll see y'all in Jackson," Michael said.

"Good deal. We'll see you in Jackson, then," Strickland said.

"Thanks, Major Strickland," Michael said.

"Call me Clay," he said with an infectious grin as he shook Michael's hand. Michael felt a kinship with him—as if he had known him forever. Michael felt a rising tide of excitement at the prospect of working with men such as these.

Everyone shook hands, and Collins thanked the sheriff.

As the two lawmen headed toward the front door, Collins turned and looked at Michael.

"Tim Charles at Ole Miss is my friend. He has already had a long talk with me about some of his students. He talked a lot about you and what kind of agent you'd make. He said you ask lots of questions and think you can do things that haven't been done before. He said that you are idealistic and hardheaded, too.

"Nevertheless, you come on down and take the tests. If you do well, I think we can grind off your rough edges…but not so much that we break the vessel. We'll just polish you and your fellow agents enough so you stand out and shine in a dirty world. Everything the sheriff shared with me about your grit as a deputy suggests you might be up to the challenge. Oh, and good work on those boys from St. Louis, by the way. I like risk-takers, as long as you remember not to leave me hanging out too far on any of those thin limbs," Collins said.

As the sheriff followed them outside to say goodbye, Sarge walked up behind Michael.

"So, you think you might go to work for those guys?" he asked.

"I'm not sure, but they seem like the real deal…folks you could count on when the going got rough… And what about you? Where will you go?" Michael asked.

"I've been offered a job as a deputy sheriff in Hattiesburg, and I think I'm going to take it. The life of a deputy is all I know, but I think there are some good things I can do down there to make a difference.

"There are bold deputies and there are old deputies, Michael, but there are not many bold, old deputies. I hope to hang around long enough to become one of them—a bold, old deputy!

"They say that God chooses the foolish to confuse the wise, and ever since Buzzy tried to kill me and his gun misfired, I think God has been calling me. If He's looking for the foolish to serve Him, He sure found the right man," Sarge said.

"God bless you, Michael. Something tells me that you've only just begun, and that triumphs, trials, and tribulations await you," he said.

He shook Michael's hand, gorilla-hugged him, wiped his leaking eyes, and honked his nose with his handkerchief. He disappeared out the back door before Michael had time to tell him that he had learned more from him than all the textbooks at Ole Miss.

* * *

Michael knocked on the door and knocked again. A robin was worming in the front yard, a mockingbird was singing from his perch on a spindly limb of a giant oak tree, and a pink sun reflected against low clouds on the horizon, painting the evening sky a peachy-purple.

He was lost in the moment until the doorknob rattled and the front door opened.

"Hello, Michael. How're you?" Clara asked.

"I'm good, ma'am. How're you?" he asked.

"We're fine, just quilting and canning for the winter. It'll be here before we know it. The seasons come and go, like old friends and new friends," she said.

"I hear you're leaving Tupelo," Clara said.

"Yes. I only have one semester left at Ole Miss, plus two correspondence classes. I'm going to Jackson to take some tests and maybe work for the narcotics bureau, if they offer me a job. Grandma's worried about me, but it'll be all right," he said.

"Wouldn't that be something? You be sure and come by to see us if you're up this way," she said.

She reached into her apron pocket and said, "I have something for you. This came for you today."

She handed him a pale-blue envelope postmarked *Birmingham*. Then she said, "Please feel free to sit in the porch swing if you'd like. I'm going to give you some privacy and leave you with it." As she turned to walk inside, she hesitated.

"I had a dream, Michael. I saw Star, and it was so real. An angel was holding her hand and leading her to the very doorsteps of heaven. Star wasn't limping anymore. Those lustrous gates were shining as they swung open. She stopped at the edge of the shining city and looked back at me. She said, 'Thank God, Mama. Thank God, it wasn't too late for me!' Michael, those were the sweetest words I have ever heard," Clara said with tears tracking down her face.

"God bless and keep you from all harm, and may His face shine upon you," the kindly old lady said as she hugged him and then closed the door. It was then that he realized she had been holding his hand the entire time.

He sat in Clara's weathered, wooden swing, swaying back and forth, slowly at first, and then moving the wooden seat higher and faster with his feet, just as he had done as a child in Parker Grove.

He opened the envelope. Inside he found a folded picture and a note written on blue, scented stationery to match the envelope. He opened the note first and began to read it as the voice of the writer spoke in his mind.

Dear Michael,

I hear that while the cat was away, the mice were playing and are long gone from the Playhouse, so I expect you will take your mousetraps and move on.

All things come to an end, and I'm glad that my days of not knowing enough to go out and come back in again are no more.

So we suffer pain patiently, and we endure, don't we? We continue, we exist, and we endure.

You will hold up a mirror, and many will not like what they see. But you will keep your will to resist. You won't quit, even though you will be judged harshly, and many will feast upon your tears. But your tears will not drown you. God has His alarm set to wake you one day, when it's wake-up time. It's already beginning to ring, but you just can't hear it yet. You are not alone, Michael.

You and me, we're like them old snapping turtles. We got a mouthful of the world's tail, and we won't let go until we hear the thunder of the drum-rolls in heaven, signaling the coming of the Lord.

You will always live in my memory book, and when I'm in my mind's darkroom developing pictures, I will think fondly of you.

Tell Miss Pearl thank you for her buttercups. They'll still be blooming the day He comes.

"When you give a feast, invite the poor, the crippled, the lame, the blind, and you will be blessed for they cannot repay you. For you will be repaid at the resurrection of the just." (Luke 14:13-14)

Graveyard Girl

He opened the folded picture. It was a giant magnolia tree in full bloom; huge white flowers, which looked like orchids, contrasted against the brilliant green of the waxy leaves. The earthly ornamental was so tall that it seemed to reach up to the gates of the Celestial City.

Standing beneath the tree was a girl with an angelic smile, the caged bird set free and born again.

It was signed…

"I am blooming where God planted me."

A sudden zephyr swept across the porch and rustled the wrinkled paper of Magnolia's letter. The leaves of the giant cottonwood above the house reflected the light from the sun, fluttering and glimmering like silver confetti in a ticker-tape parade.

Michael looked up, squinted into the bright light, and cocked his ear toward the heavens. He could have sworn that he heard the distant ringing of an alarm…

EPILOGUE

Gill Simpson went on to work for the Mississippi Tax Commission and was later elected as Lee County Tax Collector.

Cal Mattox rolled his car trying to outrun the police south of Memphis; he was paralyzed from the waist down. He ran a country store from his wheelchair and had one last run-in with Gill Simpson when he tried to cheat his son's widow and children out of their inheritance. He died of old age, a mere shadow of the man who had terrorized Lee County.

Buford Pusser died in a car wreck that some suspected was no accident. People came from far and wide for his funeral. Rumors circulated that a somber Elvis Presley was seen at the Pusser home the day of the funeral.

Sarge moved to Hattiesburg after Gill Simpson's defeat and retired there as a deputy. He led many men to Christ in jail and baptized hundreds in a big washtub.

Magnolia married, had a little girl she named Star, and became a well-known evangelist.

James Streeter was buried in one of the ancient cemeteries in New Orleans. His tombstone bore a simple cross and these words: "Whosoever will, let him come. A sinner saved by grace."

Pennington suffered a massive stroke and could only remember Bible verses he had learned as a child. No one came to see the kingmaker in the nursing home. The U-Haul trailer full of his gold and silver, which he had joked would be behind his hearse, was nowhere in sight. His born-again granddaughter donated it all to a foundation to evangelize the world...a foundation she named Pennington's Penitence.

Reggie Morris, the lawyer for the KKK, became the top mob attorney for the Mid-South and reaped what he had sown in life.

Buzzy's girlfriend drove "White Lightning" for the rest of her life. She volunteered at an abused women's shelter with a woman named Lucy Barnett, who was there day and night, leaving her husband home alone to fix his own meals.

The St. Louis mobsters escorted out of Mississippi for defrauding homeowners gave up the siding racket and were arrested by the FBI in a new scam involving a 105 Howitzer during the Vietnam War.

Dixie Lee Carter, often confused with the actress, was destined to meet Michael again. Ace Connelly and Fredrick would crash their reunion.

Young Mary Allison married, had children, and is a great-grandmother living near Fulton, Mississippi.

Michael Parker left for Jackson and became one of John Edwards Collins' agents in the initial "drug wars," sidekick and best friend of Clay Strickland, and the first captain in the Mississippi Bureau of Narcotics.

* * *

**Follow Michael in *A Ghostly Shade of Pale,*
A Rented World, and *The Redeemed,*
available in print books and eBooks.**